Invitation to Anthropology,
Fourth Edition

INVITATION TO ANTHROPOLOGY, Fourth Edition

Luke Eric Lassiter

ROWMAN & LITTLEFIELD
Lanham • Boulder • New York • Toronto • Plymouth, UK

Published by Rowman & Littlefield
4501 Forbes Boulevard, Suite 200, Lanham, Maryland 20706
www.rowman.com

10 Thornbury Road, Plymouth PL6 7PP, United Kingdom

British Library Cataloguing in Publication Information Available

Library of Congress Cataloging-in-Publication Data

Lassiter, Luke E.
  Invitation to anthropology / Luke Eric Lassiter. — Fourth edition.
    pages cm
  Includes bibliographical references and index.
  ISBN 978-0-7591-2253-6 (cloth : alk. paper) — ISBN 978-0-7591-2254-3 (pbk. : alk. paper) — ISBN 978-0-7591-2255-0 (electronic) 1. Anthropology. I. Title.
  GN25.L37 2014
  301—dc23   2013039826

Printed in the United States of America

For my parents,

Max and Laura

Contents

Preface to the Fourth Edition   ix

PART I: ANTHROPOLOGY, CULTURE, AND ETHNOGRAPHY

Chapter 1: Evolution and the Critique of Race: A Short Story   3

Chapter 2: Anthropology and Culture   35

Chapter 3: Ethnography   71

PART II: ETHNOLOGY: SOME HUMAN ISSUES

Chapter 4: History, Change, and Adaptation: On the Roots of
Our World System   109

Chapter 5: Sex, Power, and Inequality: On Gender   135

Chapter 6: Work, Success, and Kids: On Marriage, Family, and Kinship   161

Chapter 7: Knowledge, Belief, and Disbelief: On Religion   187

Afterword   205

Glossary   209

Suggested Readings   219

Index   231

About the Author   239

Preface to the Fourth Edition

As in previous editions, this new edition of *Invitation to Anthropology* in-cludes updates, corrections, and clarifications throughout the text. I have, for example, briefly expanded or clarified descriptions of evolution, language, histories of ethnography, fieldwork, population statistics, gender identities, family, and belief systems, as well as updated the suggested readings list. I have also added several new examples of current anthropology via textboxes that are new to this edition. These are titled "Anthropology Here and Now: Check It Out!" and feature brief descriptions of research, work of individual anthropologists, or references to further information about a particular topic. Each of these includes links to a Web source. My hope is that these brief sidebars may encourage further exploration about particular topics, as well as provide links to current and ongoing conversations of anthropology's rel-evance to contemporary human problems. As this is somewhat experimental for this edition, I would greatly appreciate readers' feedback on these addi-tions, as well as hear about examples of anthropology "here and now" that you think I should include in future editions.

Along these lines, I have greatly appreciated the correspondence I have received from faculty, students, and others who have read this book. In many cases, I have tried to incorporate suggested changes as space allows and to clarify terms and concepts that seem confusing. I realize, of course, that this text in several places embraces an unconventional discussion of anthropol-ogy, and chapters like the last (on religion) continue to strike many as a bit too unconventional for an introductory text. As I have noted before, I have never intended this work to replace more exhaustive surveys of anthropology. My goal was, and remains, more modest: this relatively short manuscript is meant to raise a selected set of issues that will hopefully inspire readers to explore beyond these pages and engage the much wider discipline of anthropology in its many and varied forms. I understand that this text has been used accordingly in many classrooms, and I hope that it will continue to serve this purpose in some way or another.

Even still, though, I realize that many have hoped for broader contextualizations or the incorporation of additional viewpoints in some parts of the book. With this in mind, the plans for this fourth edition actually began several years ago with the intention of incorporating individual reading selections by anthropologists and other scholars dispersed throughout the chapters. This would have changed the text markedly, of course, and after much discussion with the staff at AltaMira Press (now Rowman & Littlefield), I decided to expand the reading selections and instead compile these as a separate reader meant to accompany this book. My former Ball State University colleague Colleen Boyd, who has used *Invitation to Anthropology* in several of her classes and who helped further develop the project considerably, coedited and published with me *Explorations in Cultural Anthropology* (2011). *Invitation* can certainly be read without this reader or, indeed, with other readers or case studies (as many instructors have done). But I should note that Boyd and I selected several of the readings in *Explorations* with the intention that these would either subsidize or provide additional viewpoints to what is offered herein.

The overall framework of this text has stayed the same. It is written in two parts. Part I ("Anthropology, Culture, and Ethnography") focuses on the underlying assumptions and concepts that have driven anthropological theory and practice since its modern inception (particularly in, but not entirely limited to, the United States). Narrowing my focus to culture (and, more specifically, sociocultural anthropology), I explore a few of the driving stories, metaphors, and analyses from which contemporary anthropologists draw their inspiration, their theories, and their methodologies. In part II ("Ethnology: Some Human Issues"), I explore three cross-cultural human issues—namely, gender, marriage/family/kinship, and religion. In the first chapter of part II, I anchor this exploration by offering a brief discussion of the larger world context in which these human issues currently reside—

a discussion to which I return many times. As in part I, each chapter in part II considers the ways that looking at cross-cultural issues through an anthropological lens offers us both relevant insight into human beings and relevant models for thinking and acting. How can we, for example, use anthropological knowledge to address pressing human issues about culture and society? About gender and its relationship to universal human rights? About the dwindling role of the family in human societies around the world? Or about how strong beliefs (and disbeliefs) prevent us from forging more lasting human relationships across religious divides? These are among the questions that anthropology has a unique ability to address, questions that have defined the discipline's trajectory since the early twentieth century.

Several people deserve thanks for helping me develop this text over time. Thanks most of all to my wife and partner, Elizabeth Campbell, who, as always, has done so much to help me say what I want to say. Thanks also to the many folks who helped shape this material either through early discussions that framed the first edition or through their direct responses to the text at one time or another: Tim Arnold, Lee D. Baker, Thomas Biolsi, Liz Burke-Scovill, Karstin "Kari" Carmany, Alys Caviness, Samuel R. Cook, Clyde Ellis, Amy Keeney Hale, Trish and Jim Hatfield, Michelle Natasya Johnson, Jonathan Marks, Joe Miller, Larry Nesper, Celeste Ray, John Rhoades, Erica Stepler, Christopher Thompson, Monica Udvardy, and Christopher Wendt. Thanks, as well, to Danny Gawlowski for his ongoing photographic contributions that help to illustrate this text.

In addition, I want to take this opportunity to extend my gratitude to all those at Rowman & Littlefield who make writing and publishing such a pleasurable experience. They have treated me and this text with the utmost professionalism and have always been more than eager to explore my many and varied ideas—even those that haven't panned out as I originally thought they might. Such experimentation in a text's actual publication is rare these days, and I deeply appreciate having the opportunity to work with Rowman & Littlefield.

I

ANTHROPOLOGY, CULTURE, AND ETHNOGRAPHY

1

Evolution and the Critique of Race

A Short Story

Simply put, **anthropology** is the study of human beings in all of their biological and cultural complexities, both past and present. But what exactly does this mean? What do anthropologists actually know, and what do they do? Who are anthropologists, what is their philosophy or outlook, and why do they choose this particular (some might say *peculiar*) area of study? I plan to address all of these things in this book, but I think it is best to begin with a story, a narrative about why anthropology emerged in the first place. The story is rather involved—in fact, one that I split into several sections, but one that has a lot to tell us about the scope and trajectory of the discipline.

I begin like this because story is such a powerful way to get our attention. Story helps us get to know someone or something. Think about it. We all tell stories about ourselves—whether about our childhood, our families, our unique experience last year or yesterday. In fact, all human beings tell stories about themselves, translating their raw experience into a formed narrative. Once we begin to tell a story, the actual experience, of course, is over: here, story translates experience into language. Through the language of story we can gain understanding of one another. Experience, story, language—this is the stuff of human life.[1]

Like any individual human being or human society, anthropology has had a unique experience, has a unique story to tell, and tells it through a unique language (a *vocabulary*, if you will), a language that I hope to impart in this and the coming chapters. But I'm getting a little ahead of myself. I need to set the stage for the story.

THE SETTING: CHANGE AND EVOLUTION

The story of events that set modern anthropology into motion begins in the recent past, the eighteenth and nineteenth centuries. This story has its roots in a heated debate about the concept of change—that is, the process of being one thing, then becoming something different. Today, we take change for granted: we assume that our lives will change when we take a new job, that this year's new cars will be different from last year's, that winter will come after fall, and that summer will come after spring. Even so, many of us do not appreciate the constancy of change. Did you know, for example, that the earth's magnetic field has reversed hundreds of times in the past several million years? Did you know that Mount Everest—young mountain that it is—actually grows vertically by about one centimeter each year? Did you know that the small islands that make up the Outer Banks of North Carolina, like many "barrier island systems" along North America's Atlantic coast, are slowly shifting westward toward the state's coast? Did you know that, since the 1940s, when insecticides were first widely used in the United States, insects have adapted and changed in such effective ways that they now account for some 13 percent of crop losses, whereas in the 1940s they accounted for only 7 percent? Did you know that each year the influenza virus travels all over the world, adapting and changing as it moves from body to body? Did you know that certain bacterial infections are now entirely resistant to the antibiotics once meant to eradicate them? Did you know that the human body continues to change and adapt— that it is different now from what it was a hundred thousand years ago, or fifty thousand years ago, or even a hundred years ago? Did you know that, despite what you may have seen on television, there have actually never been any static societies, "lost in time"—that every human society ever in existence has always been in a constant state of flux and change?[2]

All of this is to say that anyone who observes the natural or cultural environment—both its past and its present—can easily recognize one thing: that the earth, and everything that lives on it (including human beings), is always in a state of transformation. Everything is always changing. Nothing is in stasis; everything is in motion. Indeed, as the Greek philosopher Heraclitus once said, "There is nothing permanent except change." This idea, this concept, is important for us to consider because of its bearing on almost every discipline in the physical and social sciences today—from medicine to physics, from chemistry to mathematics, from geography to anthropology. And this is where my story comes in.

The process of change is all around us. The small islands that make up the Outer Banks of North Carolina, for example, are slowly shifting westward, like many so-called barrier island systems along North America's Atlantic coast. Although North Carolina's famed Cape Hatteras Lighthouse (the tallest lighthouse in the United States) was originally built over a quarter of a mile away from the ocean in 1870, by the late twentieth century the ocean had reached and begun to erode the building's foundation. It faced imminent destruction. In 1999, the lighthouse was moved on a large platform (center) one-half mile inland. It will need to be moved still farther inland in about a hundred years. Photo courtesy of the North Carolina Department of Transportation.

While we may take the idea of change for granted today, people have not always understood it so well. Well into the eighteenth and nineteenth centuries, people in the Western world (Europe and North America) generally tended to see the earth as unchanged since creation. They understood their world through a fixed order created by God, a fixed order called the **Great Chain of Being**.[3]

The Great Chain of Being was an assumption about stasis rather than change. It assumed that the world was only a few thousand years old, that its fundamental design had always existed as God had created it, and that it had changed little since creation. Furthermore, God had created everything on the planet within an eternal hierarchy. Thus, all things abided somewhere on

a scale of perfection, from minerals and plants on the bottom to insects, rep-
tiles, and lower mammals, respectively, to human beings, who were just below
the angels, who were, in turn, under God—who was, of course, at the very top.
In the Western world, many early scientists sought to elaborate God's plan as
they collected plants and animals from around the world.

Although the Great Chain of Being obviously left little room for change,
early scientists wondered about the fossil forms they collected that had no living representatives. Most scientists in the seventeenth and eighteenth centuries explained these extinct forms through the Christian-based framework of
catastrophism, a theory, at the time, that the earth had changed only through
major catastrophes set in motion by God, like the Great Flood detailed in the
Bible. This earliest form of catastrophism thus helped to explain "modifica-
tions" within the Great Chain of Being and allowed the hierarchy of living
things to remain intact and static.

Not everyone accepted the Great Chain of Being and its bedfellow,
catastrophism. Indeed, many thinkers advanced theories that were in direct
conflict with it. One of the most prominent was a Scottish geologist by the
name of Sir Charles Lyell, who wrote *Principles of Geology* (which he revised
eleven times between 1830 and 1872). He challenged catastrophism by advancing a geological theory positing that the earth's physical features result
from steady, gradual processes (a theory called **uniformitarianism**). Basing
his conclusions on close observation of geological forms, he argued that the
earth was much older than Europeans had previously thought: not thousands but millions of years old. Slow, steady change was a constant process
on planet earth; geological forms (say, for example, the Grand Canyon) had
not existed unchanged for thousands of years just as God had created them.
Geological forms (like the Grand Canyon) were created by years and years
of natural wear and tear. One geological form, Lyell suggested, is constantly
giving way to another.

Although he may not have meant to, Lyell really rocked his world. It may
not seem like much today, but at the midpoint of the nineteenth century the
debate about stasis and change was among the hottest going (among Western
intellectuals, that is). And for good reason. Among Lyell's most important
ideas was that geological change, although continuous, is nondirectional and
nonprogressive. Lyell's close observations revealed that there seemed neither
rhyme nor reason to the changes in geological forms. Remember that, before

this time, scientists generally accepted that change was brought on by cata-strophism, which, of course, was directed by God. To suggest that change was random and directionless and that perhaps God had little interest in it was serious indeed.

In challenging the assumptions behind catastrophism and the Great Chain of Being, Lyell helped to set into motion a deeper and more complicated de-bate about change among the scientists of the day. A whole new set of ques-tions emerged: If geological forms have gradually changed from one state into another, do other living things partake in this process? If change is a dominant part of the natural world, are human beings and other living things a part of this ongoing process? If so, how? Are there natural laws that dictate change? For example, if we have found fossils that do not represent any liv-ing creatures, why are the ancient creatures they do represent not around anymore? Are they, perhaps, ancestors of living organisms? If so, what *causes* an organism to change into a new organism or to become extinct altogether? How did we end up with such a diversity of living organisms on the planet?

These questions bring me to a very important part of my story. Charles Ly-ell's work had a major influence on Charles Darwin and his own theory about *biological* change. Long before Darwin, many philosophers, writers, and sci-entists (including Charles Darwin's grandfather, Erasmus Darwin) had begun to think about what made biological change—or **evolution**—work. But it was not until Charles Darwin wrote *The Origin of Species* in 1859 that a theory of evolution gained acceptance—that is, Darwin's observations did more than anyone else's to explain what made change work for living organisms.

Darwin observed how farmers and animal breeders selected certain traits to create new breeds of plants and animals. He wondered, could, or *did*, na-ture do a similar thing? Was there a natural force that caused a living thing to change that was comparable to the breeder's changing the form of, say, a domesticated animal? If so, could this force explain the changes observed be-tween living organisms and the extinct organisms found in the fossil records? With these kinds of questions in mind, Darwin suggested that changes in the environment wielded a pressure on all living things to change so that they might survive through time. Much like a breeder who wields pressure on farm or domestic animals to change, a changing environment wields a pressure on the organisms living in that environment to change. To live in the changing environment, organisms must be able to reproduce or face extinction.

Darwin observed how farmers and animal breeders selected certain traits to create new breeds of plants and animals. The Holstein, for example, is a breed of cattle selected for dairy production, originating in Europe about two thousand years ago. Photo by Danny Gawlowski.

Darwin called this pressure to reproduce and survive **natural selection**. "As many more individuals of each species are born than can possibly survive," wrote Darwin, "and as, consequently, there is a frequently recurring struggle for existence, it follows that any being, if it vary however slightly in any manner profitable to itself, under the complex and sometimes varying conditions of life, will have a better chance of surviving, and thus be *naturally selected*. From the strong principle of inheritance, any selected variety will tend to propagate its new and modified form" [emphasis in original].[4]

Thus for Darwin, among the keys to natural selection were variability (or biological diversity in a population) and differential reproduction. Because this is a pretty tall order, I need to explain briefly just what this means.

Here is a relatively recent example, and a classic case, of how natural selection works. In Manchester, England, the lives of peppered moths have been heavily documented. Prior to 1900, within the population of peppered moths the vast majority were lightly peppered, but a very few were heavily peppered in their pigmentation. After 1900, however, the population changed. The more heavily peppered moths—that is, the darker-shaded ones—were now in the majority, and a very few lightly peppered moths occurred in the population (only about 5 percent). In the 1960s, the peppered moth population began to change back to the pigmentation ratio seen prior to 1900.

Now what is going on? Obviously, the population's makeup is changing. But what is *causing* the population to change? Well, natural selection is what is going on here: a change in the environment wielded a pressure that forced a change. Here's the big picture. Prior to 1900, all peppered moths produced both lightly and heavily peppered moths as offspring, but the lightly peppered moths were in the majority—in other words, "parent peppered moths" could expect to have several lightly peppered "baby moths" develop from their larvae but only a few heavily peppered moths. And here's why: The heavily peppered moths (after emerging as adults) usually did not live very long. Because of their heavily peppered bodies, birds could easily detect them and pick them off as food. The lighter-shaded moths, in contrast, could easily escape detection, especially against lichen-covered trees that resembled their body color. And, because these lightly peppered moths could escape detection, they could mature and produce the next generation of moths with greater success than the heavily peppered moths.

After 1900, something happened in the cities of Britain. Industrialization was going full speed ahead. With no antipollution or clean air laws, Manchester was a dirty place indeed. Within a very short period of time the trees turned gray and black. This was a change in the environment, and it reversed the situation for peppered moths. Now birds could easily detect lightly peppered moths. The heavily peppered moths were more concealed, especially against the now-dirty, lichen-covered trees that resembled their body color. As a result, very few light-colored moths reached maturity to produce the next generation of larvae.[5] After the 1960s, however, clean air and antipollution laws led to a cleaner Manchester, and once again, the population changed back to the form observed prior to 1900.[6]

My peppered moth story is a terribly oversimplified description of the process of natural selection, but suffice it to say that this phenotypical change in the population of peppered moths was driven by, first, a shift in the surrounding environment and, second, the ability of some individuals to reproduce and pass their adaptive success to the next generation. The process of reproduction, however, must have something with which to work if it is to promote survival and change. In the case of the peppered moths, without their genetic diversity—that is, if they had had no heavily peppered moths in the population in the first place—they probably wouldn't have been able to survive after 1900 when the environment changed. This is important. The *need* for heavily peppered moths did not drive the change in the population; natural selection could work only with the available variability. This is what Darwin had in mind when he wrote that "unless profitable variations do occur, natural selection can do nothing."[7] For Darwin, then, variability and reproductive success (the ability to produce the next generation) is what ultimately made natural selection work in environments where survivability of all individuals is always limited. Indeed, without the ability to adapt to changing environments through reproductive success, every living organism faces extinction. Considering that 98–99 percent of all the species that have ever lived on the planet are now extinct, all living things must struggle to keep changing. Without that ability, we will quite literally cease to be.

Darwin's overarching question concerned the origin or divergence of species—how and why one species would develop into another over time. Although Darwin understood that the agent for variability and reproduction was heredity, he did not fully understand how the actual interaction of heredity with the local environment worked through the process of reproduction to create biological change. Especially since the emergence of modern genetics, the complexities of biological change are today known to be much more complicated than Darwin could have imagined. Yet at the base of our current understanding of biological change is Darwin's original idea of adaptation through natural selection. It is among the mechanisms that allow insects, for example, to adapt so successfully to insecticides—like some fruit flies that have developed over a thousandfold resistance to insecticides, some mosquitoes that have adapted insecticides as food, or the diamondback moth (a pest that threatens cotton crops), which has developed an adaptation whereby its legs actually detach when it lands on crops that have been treated with insecticides (untainted, the moth flies safely away and new legs replace the old). It is among the mechanisms that permit the flu virus to adapt and change as it moves through human bodies around the world. It is among the mechanisms that explain why changes in the human body continue to unfold. To be sure, this is the stuff of biological change, or, in Darwin's terms, evolution, and it has been demonstrated in the laboratory as well as observed in the natural world innumerable times.[8] For example, while Darwin proposed that evolutionary change occurred slowly and gradually over generations and could be described only in retrospect because of the millions of years it took, scientists have actually *observed* the evolutionary process. In some animals, especially those that reproduce quickly, like insects or birds, they have watched the evolutionary changes take place in just a few years (or even faster).[9] Such overwhelming evidence has compelled some scholars of biological change to refer to evolution itself as a law rather than a theory.[10] To be sure, we know beyond a shadow of a doubt that biological change itself is an indisputable fact (we know of absolutely no biological organism that does not change). But *how* evolution works—this continues to be the central question of evolutionary theory. Among human

---

ANTHROPOLOGY HERE AND NOW

You can learn more about the complexities of evolution and how anthropologists and other scientists are continually expanding our understanding of life on planet earth at the website "Evolution: A Journey into Where We're From and Where We're Going" at www.pbs.org/wgbh/evolution. The site includes numerous resources and links to original source materials, videos, articles, and interactive pages.

CHECK IT OUT!

---

beings, for instance, we are just beginning to understand how fast viruses and bacteria change and how our bodies are continuing to evolve as a result.[11]

This may strike you as a lot of talk about evolution, but it is central to the anthropological story. With the stage set, I now turn to the story's opening.

THE OPENING SCENE: EVOLUTION, MISINTERPRETATION, AND RACE

Ever since Darwin first proposed natural selection as the mechanism of change in living things, people have misunderstood it. For most English speakers, in everyday speech, the word *evolution* often implies progress, the purposeful movement from something worse to something better or from a state of imperfection to one of perfection. But for Darwin and many of the more astute scientists since, evolution has not been about "progress" in this sense; in reality, this is a value that we place on the process of evolution.

Like Lyell, Darwin's *Origin of Species* would eventually set into motion the idea that change was nondirectional, that it was not necessarily going anywhere in particular. In the case of the peppered moth, for example, the moths are not progressing toward some "more advanced" or "perfect" form; they are merely changing from one form into another. While such changes may produce complexity, evolution does not necessarily "dictate" or "command" it. And while evolutionary adaptations such as these may be useful in the short run, they may turn out to be detrimental in the long run (i.e., highly specialized adaptations can lead to an organism's extinction). Is this progress? Did I miss something? Why, yes, you did miss something: biological change inter-acts with the changing environment—however that process may unfold—not with some omnipresent idea of "progress."

If progress is not what is meant by evolution today, where do we get the idea that evolution necessarily *implies* progress? Darwin's theory of natural selection had an enormous effect on both scientific and popular musings about how and why human beings, in particular, change over time. But, not surprisingly, Darwin's theory of natural selection has been continually re-cast through the lens of progress.[12] In nineteenth-century anthropology, for example, a body of theory known as **social evolution** (also called *evolution-ism* or *unilineal evolution*) held that all human ways of life passed through similar sequences or stages of development. Social evolutionists such as Lewis Henry Morgan argued that all human beings could be categorized within this sequence of development, with so-called savages on the bottom, "barbar-ians" in the middle, and the "civilized" at the top. Contemporary "savages" represented earlier stages of evolution through which civilized Europeans or Americans had once passed.[13]

Evolutionism was very similar to another, more popular and more extreme misuse of Darwin's theory of natural selection, which came with one Herbert Spencer, a social philosopher who advanced an idea that he called "survival of the fittest." That's right—Darwin did not invent the term *survival of the fit-test.*[14] Although Darwin would eventually use the phrase to describe an indi-vidual's biological ability to reproduce within a breeding population, Spencer coined "survival of the fittest" to advance his own ideas about the so-called favored races of humanity. Significantly, Spencer used Darwin's natural selec-tion to advance his own ideas about human social progress, which he argued resulted from "more fit" or favored human societies and groups prevailing over less fit and less favored societies.[15]

This is where my story takes a rather ominous turn. Spencer's vulgarization of survival of the fittest as the mechanism for human progress played promi-nently into what has been called **social Darwinism**, a form of social evolution holding that so-called savages were not just technologically or materially infe-rior (as was the argument of evolutionism) but also mentally and biologically inferior. Contemporary "savages," the argument went, had failed to reach a civilized state because of their "stunted" biological development. Although social Darwinism was prevalent primarily among intellectuals like Spencer and

When social evolutionists encountered the ruins of ancient civilizations, they often presumed that they must have been built by early European explorers and traders. That they had been built by the ancestors of local groups of so-called savages was unthinkable. Pictured here is the exterior wall and an interior passage (insert) of Great Zimbabwe, the ruins of an ancient city built in southern Africa (in the modern-day country of Zimbabwe) by Shona-speaking peoples between a thousand and seven hundred years ago. Photos by the author.

his contemporaries in the United States and Europe, this thinking spilled over into the public mind. It had an enormous effect on how people thought about race—a reverberating effect that is in many ways still with us today.[16]

Before the eighteenth century, the term **race** was used infrequently to describe differences among human groups, but by the early 1800s the word became a regular part of English speech to denote presumed biologically inferior and superior groups of people. While Europeans and Americans (and many other societies, for that matter) had indeed differentiated people based on observable phenotypical characteristics like skin color, never before had the word *race* been linked with survival of the fittest and carried such powerful social meanings: because Europeans (and, by extension, Euro-Americans) believed that they were more advanced than their neighbors, the law of nature, they reasoned, dictated that they should dominate other groups—in theory and in practice.[17]

Such was the "logic" of social Darwinism. But it was a logic that helped to set into motion the consequences of racial thinking for the next century. By the early 1900s, many people—scientists and laypersons alike—accepted that biology, behavior, mental capacity, and individual ability could be explained by a person's race. In the United States, for example, it was widely believed that white Americans who had ancestry in northern or western Europe (except for peasant, Catholic Ireland) inherently had better genes for intellect and for disciplined, civilized behavior. They were *naturally* civilized. By contrast, African or Native Americans were inherently inferior and were *naturally* predisposed to undisciplined, uncivilized behavior. Black men and women, for instance, were widely believed to harbor in their biology an irresistible sexual urge, common—social Darwinists argued—to the "lower, inferior races." Such thinking helped to justify a growing conviction that such sexual "impulses" could be curtailed only by public torture and lynchings, which reached an all-time high in the United States before and after the turn of the twentieth century. For example, in the eight-year period between 1888 and 1896 alone, there were well over fifteen hundred documented lynchings.[18]

What is perhaps the oddest thing about these lynchings was how public they were—testimony to how widely Americans believed in the racial inferiority of African Americans.

For example, in 1916, thousands came out to see the lynching of a young boy, Jesse Washington, in Waco, Texas. W. E. B. DuBois, a pioneering African American sociologist, wrote of the event,

> While a fire was being prepared of boxes, the naked boy was stabbed and the chain put over the tree. He tried to get away, but could not. He reached up to grab the chain and they cut off his fingers. The big man struck the boy on the back of the neck with a knife just as they were pulling him up on the tree. . . . He was [then] lowered into the fire several times by means of the chain around his neck.[19]

While such events may appall us today, they were not at all unusual in the decades prior to and after the turn of the twentieth century. This was a time when newspapers, popular magazines, and movies like *Birth of a Nation* fueled growing and popular ideas about the superiority and inferiority of the so-called races. And "science," under the guise of social Darwinism, explained, rationalized, and justified these ideas.[20]

There was more. If superior and inferior races existed as biological facts, it followed that the races should not mix. If they did, the inferior races would taint the superior ones. The United States had already implemented miscegenation laws prohibiting the marriage of whites and blacks, for example, laws that dated back to the early nineteenth century. But after 1900 many white Americans became increasingly worried that the "lower races" and immigrant groups from eastern and southern Europe were contaminating American society. Was there a way, they wondered, that America could weed out "unfit" people from the gene pool? The answer was called **eugenics**, a popular movement that focused on the selective breeding of the "fittest" people and the weeding out of "unfit" people.[21]

In the United States, several state governments implemented policies to forcibly sterilize those deemed "unfit" or of "inferior stock." The state of

Lynchings were very public events in America before and after the turn of the twentieth century. This famous 1930 photograph of a lynching in Marion, Indiana— witnessed by thousands—was sold and distributed as a souvenir, even finding its way onto postcards. Courtesy of Archives and Special Collections, Ball State University.

Virginia, for example, sterilized thousands completely arbitrarily with neither rhyme nor reason.[22] They did so in accordance with the popular science of the day in both the United States and Europe. In 1929, for example, Indiana University professor Thurman Rice wrote,

> We formerly received practically all our immigrants from northern Europe. They were for the most part of an excellent type and would blend well together. . . . The situation is very different to-day; most of the recent immigrants who are coming to-day . . . have come from eastern and southern Europe, and from other lands even less closely related; they do not mix with our stock in the "melting pot," and if they do cross with us their dominant traits submerge our native recessive traits; they are often radicals and anarchists causing no end to trouble; they have very low standards of living; they disturb the labor problems of the day; they are tremendously prolific.[23]

In Europe, a popular biology textbook written in the 1920s read,

> If we continue to squander [our] biological mental heritage as we have been squandering it during the last few decades, it will not be many generations before we cease to be the superiors of the Mongols. Our ethnological studies must lead us, not to arrogance, but to action—to eugenics.[24]

Adolf Hitler apparently read these very words in German. While in prison, he used this biology textbook and others like it to support the ideas he set forth in *Mein Kampf*. Indeed, they formed the basis for his emerging racist ideology. Hitler did not just dream up the idea of producing a superior Aryan race through selective breeding, nor did he dream up the idea of eliminating other groups from the gene pool.[25] Unlike other eugenicists of the day, however, Hitler and the Nazis took these ideas to an unprecedented extreme. So disturbing was Hitler's use of eugenics that in the wake of murdering six million Jews and millions of other "unfit" undesirables such as the handicapped, Catholics, Gypsies, and homosexuals, many prominent eugenicists began to question the very ideological foundations of eugenics and social Darwinism.[26]

But they were not the only ones who were questioning social Darwinism and eugenics. Indeed, another critique had been in the making years before the dawn of World War II.

THE STORY OF FRANZ BOAS, THE CRITIQUE OF RACE, AND THE EMERGENCE OF MODERN ANTHROPOLOGY

Recall for a moment the setting and the opening scene of my story: a debate concerning the idea of change in eighteenth- and nineteenth-century science sets into motion a chain of events linking Lyell's *Principles of Geology* with the emergence of Darwin's *Origin of Species*, which, in turn, becomes the raw material for misinterpretations of evolution ranging from evolutionism to Spencer's survival of the fittest, social Darwinism, and eugenics.

Now we come to the point in the story when modern anthropology comes into play. I say *modern anthropology* because, in actuality, *anthropology* was the label often given to studies of human beings in the eighteenth and nineteenth centuries; the label was frequently applied to contemplations of so-called primitives and, by extension, to musings about social evolution. But *anthropology* was a generally ambiguous label. It did not begin to emerge as a distinct discipline until the mid-nineteenth century. And the ideas and concepts that set the foundation for *modern* anthropology (at least in the United States) did not begin until after the turn of the twentieth century, being set into motion mainly by Franz Boas—among the most important and influential figures in the founding of American anthropology.[27] Ultimately, Boas would establish the modern form of the discipline on a critique of both race and social evolution in its various forms.

Boas was a German-trained physicist and geographer. Of Jewish descent, he left Germany at the age of twenty-eight, immigrating to the United States in 1886—partly because of the anti-Semitism he had experienced in his young life. In the United States, he became among the foremost critics of evolutionism, social Darwinism, eugenics, race, and racism. Modern anthropology—particularly American anthropology—emerged most strongly around the teachings of Boas and his students. It is with Boas that American anthropologists like myself place the dawn of the discipline that would become the anthropology we know and love today. So here is the rest of my story.

In the midst of the debate about social evolution in the late nineteenth and early twentieth centuries, Boas began to espouse a radical idea: that **society** or **culture** was a complex of meaning, not things or technology, and that any one culture or society could not be understood solely in comparison to European or American society. In a couple of words, he espoused the idea of

Franz Boas. Courtesy of the
American Philosophical Society.

cultural relativity—the idea that each society or culture must be understood on its own terms, not on those of outsiders. He argued that words like *savage, barbarian,* or *civilized* were relative terms, terms that were used to judge other peoples from the outside. He argued that, in order to understand others unlike yourself, you must understand their world from their point of view. To do so, he said, scientists must live with other people and experience other societies firsthand.

Franz Boas came to this conclusion not through conjecture but by living and studying geography with the Eskimo, or Inuit, in the Arctic in the 1880s. Many social evolutionists (social Darwinists, for example) assumed that people like the Inuit—that is, "savages" on the sequence of development toward civilization—had simpler minds than Europeans. But Boas found that the Inuit had incredibly complex ways of organizing the landscape, much more detailed than the maps made of the Arctic region by his own contemporaries in Europe. Boas thus reasoned that different environments created different kinds of needs, which led different groups of people to create different technologies in response. Simply put, different environments created different needs, and societies or cultures created different technologies to meet these needs.

Boas also recognized that the Inuit people faced many of the same problems as "civilized man"—the food quest, marriage and family, birth and death, conflict—but they went about solving these problems in very different ways. For Boas, this could be explained by differences in culture rather than differences in biology. For example, complex knowledge of the landscape had little to do with the biology of the Inuit but more to do with how culture had created, over the generations, a practical guide to living in the harsh physical environment of the Arctic. Boas realized that, although the harsh physical environment created certain needs, many Inuit cultural practices had little to do with their surroundings. In fact, language, economics, politics, religion, marriage, family composition, and conflict resolution had more complex foundations. The most important thing to understand about why a particular society is different from another, Boas said, rested in a particular people's history.

Boas's approach to understanding a particular society eventually would be called **historical particularism**, which postulated that each society or culture was the outgrowth of its past. Boas argued that a particular society or culture was much like an individual: if you want to get to know someone, it helps to know where they come from. An individual, like a society, is essentially the collision of unique experiences that have transpired in that individual's past. Simply put, for Boas you are the outgrowth of your unique past; by extension, Boas suggests, a society is an outgrowth of its unique past.

Boas thus maintained that any culture or society, like any individual, is too complex in its uniqueness to be compared to another. He argued that comparing individual societies to each other (as the social evolutionists did in their sequence of development from savage to barbarian to civilized) was more an exercise in value judgment than an exercise in science. Comparison is relative to those doing the comparing, he said. Indeed, from an Inuit point of view, Europeans—who, unlike the Inuit, had standing armies, warfare, widespread poverty, and dirty cities—were the "savages."

Seen in this light, perhaps it is easier to understand the flaws of social evolution. Social Darwinists, for example, presumed the consequences of successful war exploits, imperialism, and colonialism to be a fact of nature— a product of the more fit (read, "the civilized") surpassing the less fit (read, "the savage"). They did not consider that "exploitation" or "domination" or "colonialism" were social and historical constructions of their own making. Social Darwinists, in turn, assumed that those who "have" do so because of their inherent or biological constitution. But, as you and I both know, having a degree from Harvard has as much to do with family history and socioeconomic status as it does with inherited intelligence. A Harvard degree and its payoffs are social constructions, not biological ones.

At any rate, Boas spent a large part of his career advancing modern anthropological theory along these lines. In arguing that differences could be explained by culture and not biology, he played a significant role in the critique of race in the United States. Boas certainly was not alone. Many other critics (like W. E. B. DuBois) railed against the racially oriented perspectives of social Darwinism and eugenics in the years before and after the turn of the twentieth century and up to World War II. But Boas was surely one of the most vocal.

After years and years of studying data collected from diverse populations all over the world, Boas could find absolutely no evidence supporting the idea that one race was superior to another or that one race was inherently more intelligent than another. It was not that the idea was politically correct or socially sanctioned—at that time it was definitely against the grain—it was just that Boas could find no evidence for it. In 1928, Boas wrote that "[a]natomists cannot with certainty differentiate between the brains of a Swede and of a Negro. The brains of individuals of each group vary so much in form that it is often difficult to say . . . whether a certain brain belongs to a Swede or to a Negro."[28] Boas's critique went much deeper than this, however. The idea of superior and inferior races was ultimately flawed because the very *concept* of race was flawed. With this in mind, consider the following.[29]

The concept of race presumes that there are more biological similarities *within* a particular race than between them. In this logic, European Americans, for instance, have more in common with each other than with African Americans and vice versa; it follows, therefore, that clear differences demarcate these racial categories, making them separate from one another. But what Boas and subsequent anthropologists found was that there were, first, more *differences* between those within a so-called race and, second, more *similarities* between those individuals of supposed different so-called racial categories. So, contrary to the logic of race, people are just as likely to share similarities across racial lines as they are within them depending on what traits we examine. "From a purely biological point of view," wrote Boas, "the concept of race unity breaks down. The multitude of genealogical lines, the diversity of individual and family types contained in each race is so great that no race can be considered as a unit. Furthermore, similarities between neighboring races and, in regard to function, even between distinct races are so great that individuals cannot be assigned with certainty to one group or another."[30]

Let's take a look at this, focusing solely on the categories of "white" and "black." Boas is saying essentially that the differences *within* a so-called race are much more profound than the differences *between* the so-called races. What exactly does this mean? Well, let's look at skin pigmentation.

Among human beings, skin tone varies from very light to very dark. Among Europeans, for example, skin color varies from very light in the northern latitudes to medium in the Mediterranean region. Many Americans might decide to place these Europeans in the racial category of "white" if they lived in the United States, based on the fact that they have ancestry in Europe. Among Africans, skin color varies from medium in the north to very dark in parts of central and southern Africa. People in parts of northern Africa have skin tones very similar to their European neighbors in the Mediterranean, and in some cases they are lighter; yet many Americans might decide to place some of these northern Africans in the racial category of "black" and others in the racial category of "white" despite the fact that there may be little to no difference in color between these Europeans and Africans, these so-called whites and blacks. Conversely, many Africans might decide to place these individuals in completely different categories of white and black. Herein lies the problem.

In skin pigmentation alone, there are more observable similarities between a so-called white woman living in the Mediterranean and a so-called black woman living in northern Africa, *and* there are more observable differences in skin pigmentation between a so-called white woman living in the Mediterranean region and a so-called white woman living in northern Europe. Conversely, there are more observable differences in skin pigmentation between a "black" woman living in northern Africa and another "black" woman living in southern Africa. Where one draws the line and where one falls within a racial category is completely subjective and ambiguous. Simply put, if you were to line up all the people in the world based solely on skin pigmentation from light to dark, the place where you would draw the line between "white" and "black" or between "white" and "yellow" or between "yellow" and "red" is completely arbitrary—that is, any given individual might place the line anywhere. This was Boas's point. Race, he demonstrated, was not based on empirically sound evidence; it was an arbitrary, human-made creation, a social construction. Furthermore, Boas argued, when speaking of biology, human beings as a whole had more similarities than differences, mainly because we have all been interbreeding since the emergence of *Homo sapiens.* "The history of the human races . . . ," wrote Boas, "shows us a mankind constantly on the move; people from eastern Asia migrating to Europe; those of western and central Asia invading southern Asia; North Europeans sweeping over Mediterranean countries; Central Africans extending their territories over almost the whole of South Africa; people from Alaska spreading to northern Mexico or vice versa; South Americans settling almost over the whole eastern part of the continent here and there; the Malay extending their migrations westward to Madagascar and eastward far over the Pacific Ocean—in short, from earliest times on we have a picture of continued movements, and with it of mixtures of diverse peoples."[31]

Archaeological and genetic evidence has only reinforced Boas's point: no one group of human beings has ever stayed put or been isolated long enough to create a separate breeding population that would buttress a separate biological subspecies, or "race." Contemporary human biology concurs: when examining human DNA, the racial divisions of humans break down. Indeed, we are generally the same on a biological level.

Given this, though, Boas was *not* arguing that biological differences are illusionary, for they are very real. Things like skin pigmentation, body stature, hair type, or eye color obviously exist and are reproduced over and over again within populations. But the problem with the concept of race, Boas argued, had to do with the presumed *relationship* between observable characteristics like skin pigmentation, body stature, hair type, or eye color. Boas found quite the opposite, actually. For example, while many East Africans have dark skin, they are generally tall, like many Native Americans from the northern plains. While many Native Americans from the northern plains are tall, they generally have dark eyes, like many southeastern Europeans. While many southeastern Europeans have dark eyes, they generally have wavy hair, like

Although many might think of country and folk music singer Willie Nelson as "white," he also claims Native American ancestry. He has, for example, been chosen as "Outstanding Indian of the Year" twice. Many Americans, in fact, have in their ancestry a mixture of several different populations from around the globe, including those of Europe, Africa, Asia, and the Americas. Indeed, all humans, not just Americans, represent a biological mixture of diverse peoples—hence, as Boas pointed out, our common biological heritage. Photo by Danny Gawlowski.

some Australian aborigines. While some Native Australians have wavy hair, they generally have dark skin, just like many East Africans—and so on, and so on, and so on.

Once again, Boas argued that the problem concerns the category of race. Depending on which observable biological characteristic we focus on, we end up with different racial categories. If we decided to focus solely on populations that generally have tall body stature—in the same way that we often focus solely on skin color—our race of people would include East Africans, Native Americans from the northern plains, and even Scandinavians.

Once again, contemporary human biology concurs with Boas. Take blood types. The distribution of A, B, O gene frequencies does not correspond with our concept of race. In East Africa, some populations have an A, B, O gene frequency distribution that is almost identical to some European populations. But, in this regard, these Europeans and East Africans are very different from West Africans, many of whom tend to have a much higher distribution of the B blood type in their population (which is similar, by the way, to some Asian populations). Simply put, when considering A, B, O blood distribution alone, some Europeans and East Africans can have more in common than East Africans have with West Africans.[32] This kind of overlap is not the exception; in fact, it is often the rule. As anthropologist Jonathan Marks writes, "A large sample of Germans, for example, turns out to have virtually the same [A, B, O blood distribution] as a large sample of New Guineans. . . . A study of Estonians in eastern Europe . . . finds them nearly identical to Japanese in eastern Asia."[33]

With blood-type distributions in mind, let's take another example: sickle-cell anemia, a disease of the blood cells that ultimately affects blood circulation. Sickle-cell anemia is a condition often associated with African Americans in the United States. That is because many have ancestry in particular African populations who also have the condition, even today. But sickle-cell anemia is not limited to Africa. It also materializes in the Mediterranean region and in parts of southern Asia and the Middle East.

This raises an important point in understanding how human biology works. From a biological point of view, biological variations like sickle-cell anemia are associated with **populations**, not races. The recurring presence of sickle-cell anemia in Africa, the Mediterranean, southern Asia, and the Middle East corresponds closely with the presence of malaria in these regions. People in these populations who are born heterozygous for sickle-cell anemia (i.e., they have inherited a sickle-cell allele from one parent, not both) have an adaptive advantage over those who are homozygous for sickle-cell anemia (i.e., they have inherited a sickle-cell allele from both parents, which can be deadly if left untreated). Because the heterozygous genetic arrangement protects against malaria, these individuals can and often do live to reproduce within a population plagued by both sickle-cell anemia and malaria. (It is, of course, an imperfect evolutionary trade-off, but as you now know, natural selection does not work toward perfection; it works with what it has to advance survivability in a changing environment.)[34]

All of this is to say that biological characteristics like sickle-cell anemia— or the distribution of blood types, skin pigmentation, body stature, hair type, or eye color—work in concert with natural selection (and several other mechanisms like sexual, directional, or stabilizing selection) to produce and reproduce a range of biological characteristics that advance the survival of a particular population within a particular region. Native southern Africans, for example, conventionally have dark skin, may be tall, have a near absence of sickle-cell anemia, have dark-colored eyes, have a high distribution of the O blood type, and so on because of where they live and with whom they marry and have children, not because they fall within a racial category that many would call "black."

I am, of course, glossing what's called **cultural selection**: the impact of society or culture on biology. More Americans, for instance, will marry within their so-called race, reproducing over and over again certain observable characteristics that they can see, like skin color. But this brings me back to Boas. Boas, his students, and succeeding generations of anthropologists argued that race is created by society or culture, not biology. Indeed, they said, it is a social construction: the modern concept of race that collapses biology, behavior, and intelligence, instead of being an empirical fact, had emerged in European and American history as a folk concept that has since had enormous power to shape how people think about human similarities and differences and consequently how people live and experience their own lives and interpret those of others.[35]

To illustrate this point, let's backtrack a bit to Carolus Linnaeus, who developed the classification system we today call **taxonomy**, or **Linnaean hierarchy** (kingdom, phylum, class, order, family, genus, and species). Linnaeus was among the first to define race for the scientific community. In the 1758 edition of *System of Nature*, Linnaeus defined four races and their characteristics:

Homo sapiens europaeus (a.k.a., "white Europeans")
"White, serious, strong. Hair blond, flowing. Eyes blue. Active, very smart, inventive. Covered by tight clothing. Ruled by laws."

Homo sapiens asiaticus (a.k.a., "yellow Asians")
"Yellow, melancholy, greedy. Hair black. Eyes dark. Severe, haughty, desirous. Covered by loose garments. Ruled by opinion."

Homo sapiens americanus (a.k.a., "red Americans")
"Red, ill-tempered, subjugated. Hair black, straight, thick; Nostrils wide; Face harsh, beard scanty. Obstinate, contented, free. Paints himself with red lines. Ruled by custom."

Homo sapiens afer (a.k.a., "black Africans")
"Black, impassive, lazy. Hair kinked. Skin silky. Nose flat. Lips thick. Women with genital flap; breasts large. Crafty, slow, foolish. Anoints himself with grease. Ruled by caprice."[36]

Now, it doesn't take a rocket scientist to realize how biased Linnaeus's categories were and how he, like the social evolutionists, was judging others based not on knowledge, but on perception, a perception firmly entrenched in Europe at the time.

The kind of assumptions expressed by Linnaeus, in which white Europeans were "serious and strong" and all other races were "melancholy and greedy" or "ill-tempered and subjugated" or "impassive and lazy," persisted among both scientists and the public right up until the time that Boas came onto the scene. "This explains," Boas wrote, "why numberless books and essays have been and are being written based on the assumption that each race has its own mental character determining its cultural or social behavior."[37] Once again, Boas found ample evidence to establish with certainty that there was absolutely no basis for these assumptions. Differences in *behavior* were passed from generation to generation through the mechanism of society and culture, not biology.

The concept of race itself especially illustrates this point. The ideas set forth by Linnaeus and others have had, as I said, enormous power in directing how people define themselves and others from generation to generation. To be sure, race as a social category is very, very real (recall the widespread practice of lynching in turn-of-the-century America). Such ideas linking biology and behavior continue to inform our convictions of how "whites" or "blacks" or "Indians" or any other so-called racial group should act and behave—regardless of which group or groups we may belong to. Not only do we reproduce certain biological characteristics by selecting our mates based on the presumptions of biological race, but we also reproduce our behaviors within and around the racial categories we ourselves have created and maintained. Race is a powerful matrix within which we live—regardless of whether we are conscious of it.

Having said this, I should recast something I said earlier. I said that in the world of biology there are no clear boundaries between racial categories.

This only applies to biology. Culturally and socially, strong similarities within groups and boundaries between groups do indeed exist.

Boas thus set forth what appears at first glance to be a contradiction: race does not exist. But it does. To suggest that race does not exist *biologically* is not to suggest that it doesn't exist in people's minds and in their everyday experience. Boas, and many anthropologists since, argued as contemporary anthropologist Audrey Smedley does: "Race has no intrinsic relationship to human biological diversity. . . . [S]uch diversity is a natural product of primarily evolutionary forces, whereas race is a social invention."[38]

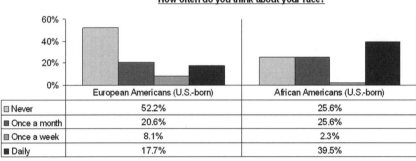

How often do you think about your race?

	European Americans (U.S.-born)	African Americans (U.S.-born)
☐ Never	52.2%	25.6%
■ Once a month	20.6%	25.6%
☐ Once a week	8.1%	2.3%
■ Daily	17.7%	39.5%

Just because race does not exist biologically does not mean that race somehow does not exist in people's everyday experience. Its legacy is still very much with us. Current polls suggest that nearly half of all African Americans, for example, have experienced racial discrimination in one form or another and, as a result, are forced to think about their racial identity more often than white Americans. One two-year study of college students thus reports that as many as 52 percent of white students never think about their racial identity, while 39.5 percent of black students think about their racial identity every day.

Source: Figure adapted from table 2.2 in Melanie E. L. Bush's *Breaking the Code of Good Intentions: Everyday Forms of Whiteness* (Lanham, MD: Rowman & Littlefield, 2004), 65.

But, of course, the social invention of the racial groups in which we live today was not created in a vacuum. It arose from the very beginning, when scientists made linkages between biology and behavior—to justify and rationalize inequality, plain and simple. Through the lens of history, it becomes absolutely clear that the concept of race emerged to give credence to institutions like slavery and to ideas such as social Darwinism and eugenics. Slaves,

primitives, or barbarians were called slaves, primitives, and barbarians because of a racial category to which they were assigned. And so-called slaves
and primitives and barbarians *had* to be dominated, as the logic went, because
of their presumed inferior status; they were, as social Darwinists argued, like
children. To be sure, the concept of race emerged among people who, within
the context of power relations between and among groups, thought themselves to be superior. And science had as much to do with constructing this
folk idea as deconstructing it. Today, we still live with the remnants of this
social invention. Whether we realize it or not, race continues to be, as Audrey
Smedley writes, "about who should have access to privilege, power, status and
wealth, and who should not."[39]

So it was through Boas that modern American anthropology began to solidify around the critique of race and a more rigorous study of human biology
and human culture. In addition to framing American anthropology within
systematic methodologies and theoretical structures, Boas was very active
in the public arena. His anthropological work provoked him to extend his
critique of race and racist policies into the public realm. He practiced what he
preached. A close friend of W. E. B. DuBois, Boas publicly supported the for-
mation of the National Association for the Advancement of Colored People
and spoke at its first organizational meeting.[40] Taking such public stands, of
course, led to a number of criticisms both within and outside anthropology.
But it did not seem to faze Boas.

Teaching at Columbia University, Boas took as students people whom other
emerging anthropology programs often denied—namely, women and so-called
people of color.[41] His students included Zora Neale Hurston, whose works in
African American literature and folklore were way ahead of their time; Ella
Deloria, whose works on Native Americans are still used in American Indian
studies programs; and Margaret Mead, whose pioneering work on women and
children changed the way America thought about gender and adolescence.
Importantly, these and a number of other students would carry on Boas's tradition of establishing behavior in culture and not biology, critiquing race, and
engaging the wider public in this knowledge—a tradition that continues in
much of anthropology to this day. (I'll return to this in the next chapter.)

ANTHROPOLOGY HERE AND NOW

Anthropologists are still actively involved in educating the public on the problems of race. The American Anthropological Association recently developed a traveling exhibit called "Race: Are We So Different?" as part of this larger project. You can take a virtual tour of the exhibit, see where it's traveling next, access resources, and explore current research at www.understandingrace.org.

CHECK IT OUT!

THE STORY'S LESSON: A METAPHOR FOR ENGAGEMENT

Every story has a purpose for its telling, whether that purpose is explicitly or implicitly expressed. In the realm of our everyday experience, we choose among a multitude of encounters to evoke as memory and, in turn, to shape as story. The discipline of anthropology is the same way.

The experience and history of the discipline is complicated, polyphonic, and diverse. And so are its stories. Lots of others besides Boas helped to set American anthropology's central tenets, including Anténor Firmin, Lewis Henry Morgan, James Mooney, and W. E. B. DuBois.[42] As anthropologist Lee D. Baker writes, "Boas's contributions were significant, but he did not work alone."[43]

Thus, I could have chosen to tell a number of stories. In the field of anthropology, stories like Boas's are told many times over because of what they mean to us today. Although the story I have told is about anthropology in particular, it has something to offer us all. One of the most profound lessons it teaches concerns the problems of race. Unfortunately, we still live in a society that continues dangerously to equate biology with behavior. Although you and I are living at a time when attitudes about race are in the midst of significant flux, as recently as the 1990s, marginal social scientists—legitimized by extensive media coverage—were claiming in widely read books like *The Bell Curve* that blacks are intellectually inferior to whites. These so-called scientific studies carried authority and power because they were passed off as "science" and legitimized as reasonable voices in a discussion about race. As such, they are still, even today, being used to justify racist thinking and practices in much the same way that social Darwinism was used to justify Euro-American domination of non-Western peoples. To paraphrase Cornell West, "Race still matters."[44]

As an anthropologist, I feel deeply compelled to speak out against the continuing reverberations of such studies and their implications. But I think we should all feel compelled to speak out. The story about Boas, in particular, is not just a story about the maturation of a discipline. It presents us with a powerful metaphor for engagement—it is about challenging the status quo, speaking out against inequality, and putting knowledge into action. Not limited to Boas or anthropology, it is a story that has been enacted in our own nation's history many, many times. Importantly, it should illustrate to us that knowledge is a powerful tool having powerful consequences that affect people's lives. Both social Darwinists and Boas used knowledge to change how people thought about race and difference. But in the end, I would like to believe, the rigorous search for Truth and Wisdom will prevail. And *this* is what Boas's story is all about.

NOTES

1. See Edward M. Bruner, "Experience and Its Expressions," in *The Anthropology of Experience*, ed. Victor W. Turner and Edward M. Bruner (Chicago: University of Illinois Press, 1986), 3–30.

2. See, for example, Ronald T. Merrill, "Geophysics: A Magnetic Reversal Record," *Nature* 389 (1997): 678–89; Trimble Navigation Limited, "Measuring Mount Everest," *Trimble News* (1996–2000); Outer Banks Lighthouse Society, "Saving Cape Hatteras Lighthouse from the Sea: Options and Policy Implications," *Lighthouse Society News* (1988); Jonathan Weiner, *The Beak of the Finch* (New York: Vintage Books, 1995), 265; World Health Organization, "Influenza," *FS* 211 (1999); Harold Neu, "The Crisis in Antibiotic Resistance, *Science* 257 (1992): 1064–73; Christopher Wills, *Children of Prometheus: The Accelerating Pace of Human Evolution* (New York: Perseus Books, 1998); and Stephen Shennan, "Population, Culture History, and the Dynamics of Culture Change," *Current Anthropology* 41, no. 5 (2000): 811–35, respectively.

3. For deeper coverage of the following discussion, see Peter J. Bowler, *Evolution: The History of an Idea*, 3rd ed. (Berkeley: University of California Press, 2003).

4. Charles Darwin, *The Origin of Species* (New York: Avenel Books, 1979 [1859]), 68.

5. For a much more thorough and nuanced discussion, see H. B. D. Kettlewell, "Selection Experiments on Industrial Melanism in the Lepidoptera," *Heredity* 9 (1955): 323–49, "A Survey of the Frequencies of *Bison betularia* (L.) (Lep.) and Its Melanic Forms in Great Britain," *Heredity* 12 (1958): 51–72, and *The Evolution of Melanism* (Oxford: Clarendon Press, 1973).

6. See, for example, J. A. Bishop and Laurence M. Cook, "Moths, Melanism and Clean Air," *Scientific American* 232 (January 1975): 90–99.

7. Darwin, *Origin of Species*, 132.

8. See Weiner, *Beak of the Finch*, for numerous detailed descriptions of this evidence.

9. See, for example, Peter R. Grant, *Ecology and Evolution of Darwin's Finches* (Princeton, NJ: Princeton University Press, 1986).

10. See, for example, Abe Gruber, "Evolution: More Than Just a 'Theory,'" *Anthropology Newsletter* 38 (September 1997): 7.

11. See, for example, Randolph M. Nesse and George C. Williams, "Evolution and the Origins of Disease," *Scientific American* 279, no. 5 (1998): 86–93.

12. Even Darwin, in fact, recast many of his original ideas through the lens of progress, such as in *The Descent of Man* and in later editions of *Origin of Species*.

13. The following discussion relies heavily on Lee D. Baker, *From Savage to Negro: Anthropology and the Construction of Race, 1896–1954* (Berkeley: University of California Press, 1998); Jonathan Marks, *Human Biodiversity: Genes, Race, and History* (New York: Aldine de Gruyter, 1995); Audrey Smedley, *Race in North America: Origin and Evolution of a Worldview* (Boulder, CO: Westview Press, 1993); and Alden T. Vaughan, *Roots of American Racism: Essays on the Colonial Encounter* (Oxford: Oxford University Press, 1995).

14. Spencer, however, convinced Darwin to use "survival of the fittest" as a synonym for natural selection, which Darwin did in later editions of *Origin of Species* (Jonathan Marks, personal communication).

15. See Baker, *From Savage to Negro*, 26–53.

16. Ibid.

17. Smedley, *Race in North America*, 36ff.; Vaughan, *Roots of American Racism*.

18. Baker, *From Savage to Negro*, 26–53, 248.

19. Excerpted from ibid., 131.

20. Ibid., 54–80, 127–42.

21. Marks, *Human Biodiversity*, 77–97.

22. See Samuel R. Cook, *Monacans and Miners: Native American and Coal Mining Communities in Appalachia* (Lincoln: University of Nebraska Press, 2000), 84–134. See also J. David Smith, *The Eugenic Assault on America: Scenes in Red, White, and Black* (Fairfax, VA: George Mason University Press, 1993).

23. Excerpted from Marks, *Human Biodiversity*, 85.

24. Excerpted from ibid., 88.

25. Ibid., 88–89.

26. Ibid., 89–95.

27. The following discussion is eclectically based on, first, Franz Boas's writings, especially Franz Boas, "The Limitations of the Comparative Method in Anthropology," *Science* 4 (1896): 901–8, *The Central Eskimo* (Lincoln: University of Nebraska Press, 1964 [1898]), *Anthropology and Modern Life* (New York: Norton, 1928), and *Race, Language, and Culture* (New York: Free Press, 1940); and, second, more general descriptions of Boas's role within the overall emergence of anthropology—see, for example, Douglas Cole, *Franz Boas: The Early Years, 1858–1906* (Seattle: University of Washington Press, 1999), Melville Jean Herskovits, *Franz Boas: The Science of Man in the Making* (New York: Scribner, 1953), George W. Stocking, *Race, Culture, and Evolution: Essays in the History of Anthropology* (New York: Free Press, 1968), and *The Ethnographer's Magic and Other Essays in the History of Anthropology* (Madison: University of Wisconsin Press, 1992).

28. Boas, *Anthropology and Modern Life*, 20.

29. The following discussion on race relies heavily on Boas, *Anthropology and Modern Life*; Marks, *Human Biodiversity*; and Ashley Montagu, *Man's Most Dangerous Myth: The Fallacy of Race*, 6th ed. (Walnut Creek, CA: AltaMira Press, 1998).

30. Boas, *Anthropology and Modern Life*, 63.

31. Ibid., 30.

32. For a comparative survey of blood-type frequency distribution around the world, see A. E. Mourant, Ada C. Kopec, and Kazimiera Domaniewska-Sobczak,

The Distribution of the Human Blood Groups and Other Polymorphisms, 2nd ed. (London: Oxford University Press, 1976).

33. Marks, *Human Biodiversity*, 130.

34. My discussion of sickle-cell anemia here is a bit oversimplified, especially in regard to changes in these populations (and their diaspora) due to the introduction of modern medicine. For an easily read and broadly based discussion of how sickle-cell anemia and a host of other diseases can be understood within an evolutionary and biomedical framework, see Randolph M. Nesse and George C. Williams, *Why We Get Sick: The New Science of Darwinian Medicine* (New York: Times Books, 1994).

35. See, for example, Montagu, *Man's Most Dangerous Myth*. Cf. Smedley, *Race in North America*.

36. Excerpted from Marks, *Human Biodiversity*, 50.

37. Boas, *Anthropology and Modern Life*, 18.

38. Audrey Smedley, "The Origin of Race," *Anthropology Newsletter* 38 (September 1997): 50, 52.

39. Ibid.

40. See Baker, *From Savage to Negro*, 119.

41. See, for example, ibid., 150–63.

42. See Carolyn Fluehr-Lobban, "Anténor Firmin: Haitian Pioneer of Anthropology," *American Anthropologist* 102, no. 3 (2000): 449–66; Elisabeth Tooker, "Lewis H. Morgan and His Contemporaries," *American Anthropologist* 94, no. 2 (1992): 357–75; L. G. Moses, *The Indian Man: A Biography of James Mooney* (Urbana: University of Illinois Press, 1984), especially 222ff.; and Baker, *From Savage to Negro*.

43. Baker, *From Savage to Negro*, 100.

44. See Cornell West, *Race Matters* (Boston: Beacon Press, 1993).

2

Anthropology and Culture

Much has happened in American anthropology since Boas, his students, and his contemporaries established anthropology as a professional discipline in its own right. Suffice it to say that, as you might expect, human biology and culture became the primary concern of modern anthropology in the years following World War II—and it continues to be the primary focus today. Anthropology is now a discipline concerned mostly with understanding human beings through a careful and comparative study of biological differences and similarities as well as cultural differences and similarities. Anthropologists are today broadly concerned with these differences and similarities—both past and present—on local and international scales.

The four major subfields of anthropology.

As modern anthropology flourished in the twentieth century, it began to develop into four main subdisciplines: **biological** or **physical anthropology**, **archaeology**, **linguistic anthropology**, and **cultural anthropology**. Although these subfields are split into sub-subfields and sub-sub-subfields, each of these areas today focus on a particular component of the human experience. Biological or physical anthropology focuses on human biology, archaeology centers on human technology and material culture, linguistic anthropology concentrates on language, and cultural anthropology addresses culture. Although I will focus primarily on culture throughout this book, I'd like to look briefly at the way its study fits within the overall discipline of anthropology.

FROM BIOLOGY TO CULTURE TO APPLICATION: ON THE SUBFIELDS OF ANTHROPOLOGY

Let's start with physical or biological anthropology. This field is concerned primarily with human biology. But biological anthropologists conceptualize human biology in very broad terms. From the social problem of race to the actual biological complexity of populations, from disease to health, from heredity to genetics, from bone structure to cell structure—biological anthropology does many different things. A unifying concept in biological anthropology, however, is biological change, or evolution. Through this lens, biological anthropologists seek to understand biological changes over the long and short terms. Biological anthropologists take up as subjects the evolution of the human species as well as the evolution of the latest influenza virus. Moreover, they seek to understand human biological variation within the larger framework of the biological variation found among all animals. Just where humans fit in the overall scheme of biological evolution remains an important question for deciphering how we are both similar to and different from other animals (like our closest living relatives, chimpanzees and gorillas).

Archaeology shares many of its research methods with biological anthropology (such as the archaeological dig) but diverges from the study of human biology to focus on human technology or **material culture** (i.e., materials that human beings purposefully create either as tools to adapt to their environments or as meaningful expressions of their experience). To put it simply, the key concept in archaeology is the **artifact**, an object created by humans. But the point is not about collecting artifacts, like a treasure hunter might do. Archaeologists place these artifacts within larger social contexts to *infer* and *understand* human behavior. Thus, from religion to economics, from small

Language involves much more than the spoken word. We use a variety of symbols—sounds, gestures, and body language, for example—to impart meaning when we communicate with others. Many linguistic anthropologists thus seek to understand language as a process of communication inextricably bound to social contexts. Photo by Danny Gawlowski.

villages to large cities, from weapons of war to arts and crafts, from the development of agriculture to the fall of civilizations, from human exploitation of the environment to human adaptation to the environment—archaeologists use artifacts situated in their larger social context to uncover the secrets of human society in both the past and the present.

Linguistic anthropology focuses exclusively on **language** because of its central role in defining who we are as humans. In a general sense, we depend on language like no other animal to survive. And as we use it to communicate complex ideas and concepts, language is, to be sure, at the very heart of culture. As such, it is a rich source for expressing the diversity of human experience. In a more particular sense, the whole range of an individual society's collective experience is contained in language. The word for *love* in English, for example, is translated as "respect" in another language. Knowing this helps linguistic anthropologists understand that not everyone sees the world in the same way, and our diversity of languages reflects and, many linguists say, *shapes* our uniqueness.

The idea that language not only reflects but can also shape how we think and how we act—sometimes called the *Sapir-Whorf hypothesis*—is an important concept for understanding differences across cultural groups. Ideas about "love" or "respect"—to continue with the same example—may index similar human feelings, but their historical use and development within particular cultural contexts help linguist anthropologists understand how certain feelings are thought about and acted upon differently. Very interesting stuff indeed.

Because language can mean both spoken and nonspoken discourse, a central concept in linguistics is **communication**: in anthropological terms, communication is the use of arbitrary symbols to impart meaning. This means that certain sounds or gestures have no inherent meaning in and of themselves: we assign meaning to them and through them impart meaning to others. For example, a belch at the dinner table is considered a rude gesture among polite company in the United States; apparently, it communicates a compliment in some other countries. Or consider how a slight nod of the head may mean yes among most Americans; the same gesture might be meaningless among non-English speakers who use other gestures to communicate an affirmative response nonverbally. It's not the gesture of nodding or the sound of belching itself but rather the meaning *behind* the gesture or sound. Thus, from sounds and gestures to the composition of language families, from the history of words to their ongoing evolution, from the different ways men and women communicate to how power structures are transmitted through spoken language, linguistic anthropologists seek to understand the intricacies of human communication within larger social contexts (both past and present).

Finally, let's turn to cultural anthropology. Cultural anthropology—often called **sociocultural anthropology**—shares with anthropological linguistics a focus on human communication. But its central, driving concept, culture, is much broader in scope. While we may popularly think of culture as synonymous with groups or the values and attitudes of those groups, in an anthropological sense, culture is a shared and negotiated system of meaning informed by knowledge that people learn and put into practice by interpreting experience and generating behavior.[1] This is a mouthful—and based on several different anthropological definitions and understandings of culture (see note 1 at the end of the chapter)—but don't worry about apprehending exactly what I mean by this just yet. I will go into more depth later. For now, let's say simply that culture is the lens through which we all view the world; at the same time, culture is that which produces the human differences found in our world. What makes American society different from, say, French society is culture; what makes the feel of one town different from another is culture; what makes my family different from yours is culture. In the same sense we all share similarities in culture, like the questions surrounding the meanings of birth, marriage, inheritance, or death. This is the stuff of cultural anthropology.

From gender roles to the cultural construction of race, from music to the social construction of violence, from politics to economics, from law to the concept of freedom—cultural anthropologists study culture to understand the powerful role it has in our lives.

While biological anthropology, archaeology, and linguistic and cultural anthropology now constitute the four so-called subfields, some anthropologists identify a fifth subfield of anthropology called **applied anthropology**— the application of anthropology to human problems. Unlike the other subfields, applied anthropology is more of a perspective, an approach that is applied in all areas of anthropology, from biological anthropology and archaeology to linguistic and cultural anthropology. From forensic anthropologists (who apply biological anthropology to solve, for example, murder cases) to cultural resource-management archaeologists (who apply archaeological research to federal and state mandates to preserve the archaeological and historical record for the future) to medical anthropologists (who apply biological, linguistic, and cultural anthropology to address health problems), the work of anthropology in the public realm is indeed multifaceted.

ANTHROPOLOGY HERE AND NOW

A well-established application of anthropological knowledge to human problems is forensic anthropology, in which anthropologists may apply anthropological knowledge to legal cases that involve the identification of human remains. Much of what we know about identifying human remains has been the direct result of research carried out at so-called body farms, places where human decomposition is studied and documented. One of the most widely known locations is the Forensic Anthropology Center at the University of Tennessee, Knoxville. You can learn more about the center and its various and ongoing studies of human decomposition at fac.utk.edu.

CHECK IT OUT!

HOLISM AND COMPARATIVISM

How do anthropologists make sense of all of this varied information about humans? Doesn't a focus limited only to biology or culture leave us with an incomplete picture of the human experience in all of its complexities? Indeed, could Boas have formulated his critique of social evolution and race without understanding humans in both biological and cultural terms?

To be sure, anthropology is an extremely broad and far-reaching discipline. But two main concepts organize the subfields into a larger whole: **holism** and **comparativism**. First, holism. *Holism* is a perspective that emphasizes the whole rather than just the parts. In general, the *holistic perspective*—as it is also called—pushes an understanding of the big picture that can often be lost by focusing solely on details. Thus, in anthropology, holism encourages us to understand humans as both biological and cultural beings, as living in both the past and the present. Elucidating the relationships in all that is human is especially important to holism.

Holism, of course, is inherent to anthropology. But, as a driving concept behind both the theory and practice of the field, holism reminds us that regardless of whether we are biological, archaeological, linguistic, or cultural anthropologists, anthropology is ultimately concerned with understanding the human condition in *all* its complexities. As such, anthropologists realize that there are a number of ways to understand these human complexities, from literature and art to science and mathematics. Indeed, literature, art, science, and mathematics are each a distinct area of study that leads us to understand human beings in a unique way. Taken together, they give us a greater understanding of the whole.

Anthropology, then, continues to be heavily influenced by the sciences (biology, physics, chemistry) as well as the humanities (history, literature, music). For example, while biological and archaeological anthropology can heavily depend on the scientific method, linguistic and cultural anthropology can heavily depend on the interpretive method (which is also common in fields like historical and literary studies). There are thus anthropologists who consider themselves scientists and anthropologists who consider themselves artisans, or both. But regardless of our individual methodologies or interests, most anthropologists realize that, ultimately, we are part of a much larger disciplinary project. Anthropology is indeed much broader than the sciences or humanities taken by themselves.

While holism is the philosophical construct that underlies anthropology, a broadly based approach called comparativism makes the holistic perspective possible. *Comparativism* is, simply, the search for similarities and differences between and among human beings in all of their biological and cultural complexities. On some levels, we do this all the time. We regularly compare ourselves with others, with other religions, or with other ways of life; consequently, we define for ourselves how we are similar and different from others. But in anthropology, comparativism is the use of diverse information from all the subfields (both biologically and culturally based) from many different populations to make generalizations about the complexity of human beings. Thus, in anthropology, to "compare" is to understand the general trends that make human life what it is, from evolution to language to society. Without comparison, we become lost in the details. And, in the end, comparativism is the method that makes holism possible.[2]

Anthropology, the subfields, applied anthropology, holism, comparativism—I know this is a lot to think about. But what does it all mean? These organizing concepts are important because they constitute the conceptual tools that anthropologists use to critique simplistic notions of human diversity—a critique begun by those like Boas and carried out by succeeding generations of anthropologists. Anthropology, the subfields, applied anthropology, holism, and comparativism are thus core concepts that anthropologists use to build a more complex understanding of human biology and culture.

DEFINING CULTURE

So what is culture, anthropologically speaking? Among anthropologists, culture has a different meaning from the way that "culture" is used in everyday English. When we think of culture, what comes immediately to mind might include various traditions, customs, beliefs, ceremonies, foods, or the kinds of clothes people wear.

This idea of culture comes closest to one of the first culture definitions used by anthropologists. It was written in 1871 by an early British anthropologist named Edward Burnett Tylor. Tylor wrote, "Culture . . . taken in its wide ethnographic sense is that complex whole which includes knowledge, belief, art, morals, law, custom, and any other capabilities and habits acquired by man as a member of society."[3] For Tylor, the differences between human societies could be identified by their differences in customs, morals, or beliefs.

Although he developed his definition of culture to elaborate the stages of social evolution (he used culture synonymously with civilization, for example),
Tylor's definition helped to hint early on that behavior, or knowledge, or customs, or habits were primarily learned rather than inscribed in our biology.

With Boas and modern anthropology, Tylor's definition of culture took
on new meaning outside the framework of social evolution—a meaning close
to the idea of culture most often used in English today. This definition was
one that anthropologists employed for many years; it was common in introductory textbooks until the 1950s and 1960s and in some continues even
today. And for good reason. To be sure, we can recognize differences between
ancient Greeks (who often buried their dead) and ancient Parsees (a people
of southeast Asia who once exposed their dead to the elements), differences
between the Bedouin (a Middle Eastern people whose men may have multiple
wives) and the Pahari (a people in northwest Nepal whose women may have
multiple husbands), differences between Southern Baptists (who live mostly
in the southern United States and often encourage witnessing to the "unsaved") and Primitive Baptists (who also live mostly in the southern United
States but often discourage witnessing to the unsaved), and so forth. We can
say that these observable differences rest in differences in culture.

Tylor's definition of culture, however, emphasizes things and expressions.
This is to say that, whether we are identifying different burial customs, marriage
practices, or beliefs, we are identifying the by-products or *artifacts* of culture,
not culture itself. And this is where things get a little more complicated.

An old Buddhist saying reminds us, "The finger that points at the moon is
not the moon." That saying is relevant here. It means that we should not be
fooled into thinking that the messenger is the message or that the means that
point us to an end are the end itself. In the same way, we should not be fooled
into thinking that the by-products or artifacts of culture are culture itself.
Instead, they point us to deeper human meanings. For many anthropologists,
then, culture is the *meaning behind* that which humans produce. Morals,
beliefs, customs, or laws are things; the significance that humans *give* these
things is meaning. For example, the American flag is not American culture,
but its negotiated meanings are—that is, the American flag can be said to
point us to a deeper national conversation about what it means to be American. Of course, this is something over which people discuss, debate, and
argue. And this is the point: American culture is not static; it is not a thing or

a group of things. It is a complex system of meaning created and maintained by people. And the same can be said for all systems or networks of interacting people who inscribe meaning on experience.

Let me put this a little more succinctly by returning to the culture definition that I offered earlier. In an anthropological sense, *culture* is a shared and negotiated system of meaning informed by knowledge that people learn and put into practice by interpreting experience and generating behavior. At this point, I'd like to focus on different parts of this definition to elaborate just what I mean here. Let's start with a *shared and negotiated system of meaning*.

Culture as a Shared and Negotiated System of Meaning

To begin with, a system refers to a group of interacting or interrelated parts that operate in relation to one another. In reference to culture, those parts are (of course) people. For these *human* parts to interrelate as a meaningful system, however, there must be a broad base of shared (but not necessarily equally agreed-on) meanings. At any point where people can communicate and negotiate these shared meanings, culture is at work. When we speak of American culture, for instance, we reference a system of interacting people who share, within certain limits, a common experience. But that experience, of course, can be widely diverse. In the context of American society (read, "system"), diverse people thus interact with each other on many different levels and in many different contexts, where they communicate and negotiate to varying degrees an American experience and in turn engender American culture. We can say the same for the workings of Japanese culture, New York City culture, or even "university culture." Conversely, we can say that the interrelated parts—the people—are not the culture. The interrelated parts are, in broad terms, human societies, which, as a necessary condition for culture, give rise to various "systems of meaning."

This is not to say, however, that these various systems of meaning that we call "culture" are necessarily circumscribed by clear boundaries, like geographical or political borders. Indeed, they overlap, intersect with, and compete with one another. Thus, culture is better understood as a process. The parts that make up the system—people—are not puppets or stick figures; people like you and me constantly negotiate meaning with ourselves and others. The ever-changing culture of the Internet is a good example (and an equally good analogy for culture).

Although a symbol like the American flag (seen here in a Hispanic nightclub in Evansville, Indiana) represents the United States, it in no way captures the full range of diversity within American culture. Indeed, this symbol means different things for different people. Photo by Danny Gawlowski.

So, just as we can talk about American or Japanese culture or university culture or Internet culture, we can also talk about something as particular as family culture. Although clear cultural differences between families emerge between those living in, say, Brazil and Korea, different families *within* a society also have their own systems of meaning that make them unique and different from one another. In my own family, for example, telling stories was always an important part of dinnertime conversation, which often lasted for hours. My parents were farmers as children, and because this kind of dinnertime conversation was so important in their childhood, they carried the tradition with them when they left the farm. Telling stories is, of course, not unusual, but the particular stories that were told related to a particular experience that we shared, a system of meaning that we constructed and reconstructed each time we had dinner (especially when we argued about the details or meaning of a story). Today, when we gather, in many ways these stories make us who we are; they are our collective memory or, in an anthropological sense, our collective (and negotiated, debated, and contested) system of meaning—in a word, our culture.

Just as we can talk about something as familiar as family culture, we can also talk about culture that is less familiar. Take the peculiar and exotic culture of stock car racing. Yes, the culture of stock car racing. Here's one that I just do not understand. Although I have had folks explain it to me more than once, I have never fully understood why people would watch cars go around and around and around a track. You get my point—it makes little sense to me, but it is culture nonetheless: stock car racing has a system of shared and negotiated meanings. I'm not quite sure what it is, but it exists.

I used to say the same thing, incidentally, about demolition derbies. I could never understand why people would want to watch drivers destroy their cars—that is, until I went to a demolition derby (which included a *combine* demolition derby) in the rural Midwest. I could not keep my eyes off of it. There was just something about watching these old cars—and then these old combines—completely destroy one another. Once again, I'm not exactly sure what the shared meanings are, but they exist, and so does the culture of demolition derbies.

A combine demolition derby in the rural Midwest. Photo by author.

All of this is to say that culture—as a shared and negotiated system of meaning—permeates every aspect of our lives. Whether we are talking about families, American flags, universities, or cars (driven fast or destroyed), each involves a system of meaning. The goal in the anthropological study of culture is to uncover the shared and negotiated systems of meaning behind something like a demolition derby. But as I have already suggested, anthropologists also try to understand that such a system of meaning exists in conjunction with other systems of meaning. Indeed, as humans we enter and exit through a multitude of these systems each day, often without even thinking about it. While we can talk about family, stock car racing, or demolition derby culture, these systems exist within a larger American culture, which, in turn, exists within a larger world culture.

Culture as Informed by Knowledge

Each of these systems is *informed by knowledge.* In a general sense, knowledge is the process of learning and discovery; knowledge is understanding gained through experience; knowledge is grasping something in the mind with certainty. But in a particular sense (once again, in the context of my culture definition discussed here), knowledge exists in the *minds* of any people who share and negotiate culture. In our families, for instance, we share, communicate, and negotiate knowledge about "being" parents, "being" children, or "being" siblings. It's in our minds. We use this knowledge to interpret each family experience and to generate acceptable behavior within this context. Of course, we use this knowledge in conjunction with a larger and broader range of sophisticated knowledge to interact in a variety of other meaningful systems besides the cultures of our families.

When speaking a particular language, to present another example, we use a complicated knowledge to generate and interpret sounds—to write and interpret the symbols that we call letters, words, sentences, and paragraphs. We use this same range of knowledge to place words together in a prescribed grammar and syntax and to create and re-create new sounds, words, and expressions. The word *hello*, for instance, was apparently created along with the telephone. Alexander Graham Bell proposed that people use *Ahoy!* to answer the phone, but Thomas Edison's choice of *hello* caught on. Today, we use the word not only to answer the telephone but also to greet someone face to face in everyday interaction.[4]

Yes, here we have culture—a system of meaning informed by shared knowledge that we use whenever we are on the phone. We use this knowledge, of course, without even thinking about it. Indeed, we are deeply cultural beings. In our minds, cultural knowledge is both unconscious and conscious. On the one hand, much of the knowledge we have and use is implicit and unspoken; people are usually unaware of this knowledge and do not communicate it verbally. The rules of language are perfect examples. When we use *hello* to answer the phone, we don't think about where *hello* comes from or what it means; we take it completely for granted. On the other hand, much of our cultural knowledge also exists explicitly on a conscious level: it is shared knowledge that people are usually aware of and can talk about. Cultural traditions or rules are perfect examples. When we go to a formal dinner, for instance, we consciously know and talk about the fact that it is inappropriate to show up in shorts and a T-shirt. ("You're not going to wear *that*, are you?" my wife would ask.)

Of course, conscious and unconscious knowledge work together; they represent opposite ends of the same continuum. That is, that which we take for granted can and may move into the arena of conscious knowledge and vice versa. At one time people were very much aware of the strangeness of the new telephone word *hello* and talked to one another about its use. But over time, it entered into the realm of unconscious knowledge. Today, people use *hello* on the phone and in face-to-face interaction as though it has always existed.

Culture as Learned

Understanding that systems of meaning are informed by knowledge, we must also understand that this knowledge is primarily learned. To learn something literally means to acquire knowledge. In reference to culture, the process of learning necessarily implies that the vast majority of cultural knowledge is not inherited or inscribed in our biology. This is important—we are not *born* with culture. We learn it. Although all humans have the biological capacity for language, for example, the many different languages we all speak are learned through experience, study, practice, and trial and error. This is the stuff of learning, and it is something that all culture has in common. So while all people may not share the same language, we all share the language-learning process.

Even our common human biology is affected by cultural knowledge that we impose on our biology. In America, we tend to marry within so-called racial groups, thus reproducing certain observable characteristics, like skin color. We also learn to see ourselves as part of a racial group with associated behaviors, we learn to recognize and reproduce the boundaries between these racial groups, and we learn perceptions that define our interpretation of our own and other racial groups' behavior.

Another powerful example of how we learn to impose cultural knowledge on biology is eating. All humans face the biological need to nourish their bodies with food. But *when* to eat (such as after sundown during Ramadan) or *how* we eat (such as the custom of talking during dinner in much of the United States or remaining silent during a meal, which is the custom in some Native American communities) or *what* we eat (whether it is curdled milk [cheese] or insects) is each intimately tied to what we learn through a limited range of experience. Even the idea that a particular food or drink tastes good or bad is acquired: although tasting involves a biological reaction, our minds learn to cast that biological reaction in a certain way, associating pleasant or unpleasant sensations with certain foods or drinks.

In the same way that we learn to mold basic biological needs, we also learn to forge our vision of the world around us. Morality, or that which we consider to be right and wrong, is an example. We *learn* that burying our dead to dispose of them is right and correct, or we learn, as was the custom in some ancient cultures, that eating our dead to reintegrate them into our own living bodies is the right and proper thing to do. We *learn* that it is morally right to have one spouse, or we *learn*, as is also the custom in some groups, that it is right and responsible to take your spouse's unmarried siblings as spouses. We *learn* that it is morally wrong to kill another human being, or we *learn* that it is acceptable to kill another human being during war.

All of this learning—whatever its form—must take place within a system of meaning. Because we learn from others, learning is an active social process that people put into practice all the time. Anthropologists often call this process of learning culture **enculturation**. Enculturation often refers to the passing of cultural knowledge to children, but enculturation is a constant and ongoing process; indeed, it goes on throughout our lives. Very recently, both children and adults have learned how to use computers, for example; our society now takes them so much for granted that we can barely imagine our

Enculturation is an incredibly powerful process. Photo by Danny Gawlowski.

lives without them. When learning what's cool and what's not, we are being enculturated. When we learn the grammar, syntax, and meanings of a new language, we are being enculturated. Indeed, you are being enculturated as I impart to you the language of anthropology.

Culture as Practice

In order to serve the workings of "culture"—that is, as a shared and negotiated system of meaning—people must put this learned knowledge into practice. We put this knowledge into practice by *interpreting our own and others' experience* in everyday social interaction, which in turn we use to shape our actions (i.e., *generate behavior*). Still a tall order? Let's begin with the experience part of this equation.

Every human life is composed of experience; indeed, constant encounters with the world around us carry us from birth to death. These encounters with the natural and cultural environment are what we call experiences. These experiences are not completely raw encounters—they don't happen in a vacuum. From the time we are born, all new experiences are viewed through the lens of previous experiences. And those previous experiences help to de-

ANTHROPOLOGY HERE AND NOW

YouTube, of course, is a repository of experience where people
the world over share and negotiate meaning on a daily basis. The
ever-evolving culture of YouTube is one of the topics of study
for an anthropologist whom *Wired* magazine has called "the
explainer": Michael Wesch (Kansas State University), who has
several well-known and award-winning YouTube videos himself.
Check out his webpage at www.michaelwesch.com.

CHECK IT OUT!

termine how the new experience will be shaped, interpreted, and understood.[5]
When, for example, I went to my first demolition derby, I approached it with
a set of prejudices and assumptions. I had encountered and experienced it
only on television, and watching it from that distance it seemed to me ir-
responsible and careless. Understand that I came from a Southern Baptist
"waste-not, want-not" background in which destroying things for the sake
of having fun was beyond wasteful—it was sinful. Although I have not considered myself a Baptist since I was a teenager, the experience of having been
reared as such shaped my encounter with the demolition derby, regardless of
whether I liked it. But my one experience of witnessing demolition firsthand
changed my perception from judgment to curiosity. That experience forced
me to rethink how I viewed the derby. Now when I encounter a demolition
derby, I see it in a new way. I cannot say I completely understand it, but I can
appreciate it differently.

This is a simplified example, but I mention it here to point out that so
much of our knowledge about the world around us is derived from our experience. We then use that knowledge (learned either consciously or uncon-
sciously) to interpret every successive experience. What's more, these new
experiences are framed not only by our own previous experiences but also
by the larger experience (or, simply put, history) of the particular groups in
which we interact. Think about it. In this vast system of meaning we share,
our personal experiences intermingle with the personal experiences of others

in a much larger system of meaning that transpires in everyday social interaction, which, of course, occurs on a number of levels.[6]

Furthermore, in the context of this culture definition, "interpreting experience" refers to both the way we interpret the experience of self within a particular culture and how we encounter and experience others. When, for example, we decide that eating insects is gross, that marrying more than one spouse is wrong, or that demolition derbies are sinful, we are viewing these cultural practices through the lens of our experiences, through our own enculturation into particular groups. And this is exactly how culture works: we learn and share knowledge that we use to interpret our own experiences as well as the experiences of others. (I'll return to this issue a little later.)

Now, on to the behavior part. In the context of my culture definition, *behavior* means to act or conduct oneself in a specified way. Of course, knowledge shapes those actions, but beyond this, our systems of meaning become enacted, embodied, and practiced through behavior, which we in turn negotiate with others in the context of society. When we pick up the phone and say hello, we are putting a particular system of meaning into action—that is, we are acting out knowledge that exists in our minds. When someone dies and we follow a prescribed way of disposing of the body, we (the living, that is) are enacting systems of meaning—extending that which is in our minds into the actions of our very bodies, over and over again, shaping and reshaping the process from generation to generation.

I am, of course, using behavior in a much wider sense than a simple reaction to a stimulus. When talking about the anthropological concept of culture, behavior implies a far broader range of actions and practices. Indeed, behavior is what makes experience real; it forges culture into the diversity of human activities found in the world.

Because all human behavior exists within a larger system of meaning, a particular human action carries no meaning in and of itself. Behavior always arises in a specific context. Anthropologists James P. Spradley and David McCurdy put it this way: "Culture is . . . the system of knowledge by which people design their own actions and interpret the behaviors of others. It tells an American that eating with one's mouth closed is proper, while an Indian, from south Asia, knows that to be polite one must chew with one's mouth open. There is nothing preordained about cultural categories; they are arbitrary. The same act can have different meanings in various cultures. For example, when adolescent Hindu boys walk holding hands, it signifies friendship, while to Americans the same act may suggest homosexuality."[7]

Reading Spradley and McCurdy's words, other examples come to mind. When we cross our fingers and hold them next to our head in the United States, we are often expressing hope. Yet the same action in parts of highland New Guinea can imply something altogether different: it is an insult having sexual connotations.[8] For many Americans, when we look straight into the eyes of someone while we are talking to them, it means that we are listening; it is the polite thing to do. To look away while you are talking might suggest you are trying to hide something. But in some Native American communities, looking straight into the eyes of someone while talking to them would be considered rude.

These brief examples illustrate how actions and practices can have different connotations in different social contexts and in different systems of meaning. It is not the action itself that has meaning; it is the context within which that action occurs. This is what is meant by *arbitrary*. And, to reiterate the point one last time, *human behavior does not carry meaning in and of itself.* Any particular human action exists within larger systems of meaning, and we call those systems of meaning "culture."

While the examples that I have used are individual and eclectic, behavior in the cultural sense can also imply composites of traits or patterns that are repeated throughout a particular society or culture, traits like aesthetics, values, beliefs, traditions, and customs—the "things" of culture that Tylor originally identified as culture itself. And here we come full circle—but we arrive at a different place from the point that initiated my discussion of culture. While Tylor's "things" are cultural artifacts, they are not *merely* things. Because people ascribe meaning to these things and interpret and reinterpret them across time and space, they can both reflect and shape culture. Think of the movie and television industries, for example, which are very fond of asserting that their media merely (and *only*) "reflect" American culture. Frankly, this is nonsense. In a world where corporations spend billions on ad campaigns because they know they affect people's buying behavior, the expressions generated by movies and television also have an enormous impact on the contours of our lives. From the way we remember our pasts (think about all those World War II movies you watched growing up) to the way we define and stereotype others (think of all those movies about "Indians") to the way we admire and emulate the rich and famous (think of all those talk shows)—over and over again, we integrate these expressions into our negotiated systems of meaning.[9] Indeed, the artifacts of American culture—as in any culture—are not *just* things. The movie and television industry is just one example. *All* of us are born and enculturated into previously existing composites of traits like aesthetics, values, beliefs, traditions, and customs that, in turn, compel us to act, think, and behave in specific prescribed ways. In a word, these composites of traits carry **power**: the far-reaching process of influence (that can be expressed directly or indirectly, implicitly or explicitly), which mediates how and what we learn, the knowledge we use to interpret experience and generate behavior, and even how we interact with one another. Just *how* we integrate these composites of traits into our individual lives and negotiate individual meanings with larger, complex cultural systems is a problem in which many anthropologists have great interest.[10]

Human behavior does not carry meaning in and of itself. Any particular human action exists within larger systems of meaning that we call culture. Photo by Danny Gawlowski.

Now you should more fully understand what culture, in an anthropological sense, is. It does include the things that humans produce (as in Tylor's definition), but ultimately these things or artifacts are always couched in a *shared and negotiated system of meaning informed by knowledge that people learn and put into practice by interpreting experience and generating behavior.* This definition of culture should make more sense at this point. Are you still having a hard time putting your finger on just what culture is? Are you getting that uncomfortable feeling that culture may be messy and unwieldy? Congratulations! You have arrived. Culture is nebulous rather than absolute, chaotic rather than harmonious, dynamic rather than idle, ubiquitous rather than esoteric, complex rather than simple. It is, because people are.

STUDYING CULTURE

Given that culture is nebulous, chaotic, dynamic, ubiquitous, and complex, how do anthropologists actually know what they know about culture? What are the conceptual tools they use to go about *understanding* the culture concept in all of its complexities? More important, what are the conceptual tools that we need to appreciate the power of culture in human life?

First and foremost, the concepts of culture, holism, and comparativism all work together. You will recall that holism is a perspective that emphasizes the whole rather than the parts. When it comes to culture, holism emphasizes understanding how the parts of culture work together to create a larger system of meaning. The interrelations among a society's history, politics, and economics are examples. We can't really understand one part, history, without understanding the other parts, politics and economics. This is holism, plain and simple. In the study of culture, to focus only on economics, for example, is to miss larger patterns. Anthropologist James L. Peacock puts it this way: "To think holistically is to see parts as wholes, to try to grasp the broader contexts and frameworks within which people behave and experience. One such framework is culture. Anthropology is concerned not only with holistically analyzing the place of humans in society and in nature but also, and especially, with the way humans construct cultural frameworks in order to render their lives meaningful."[11]

Take the study of American culture. To understand such a complex system, we would want to take into account the history and development of this individual nation-state, its economics and politics, as well as its individual traditions, values, or customs *and* how they interact with one another as a system, which of course includes the American people themselves. If we wanted to understand a smaller part of American culture, like religion, we would want to take into account all the components of religious belief in America—from Catholicism to Protestantism, from Islam to Judaism, from fundamentalism to atheism. We would also want to take into account how religious belief is negotiated in this country, its deeper meanings to American identity, and how it spills over into other realms of American experience, like politics. Still further, if we wanted to focus on the culture of one particular religion in the United States or even the culture of a particular church, once again we would want to take into account its every part and *how it interacts* with other parts as a system.

Here's another example. Since the time I was an undergraduate, I have had an interest in **ethnomusicology**, an area of study that combines aspects of both musicology and anthropology to understand the role and meaning of music cross-culturally. Ethnomusicologists don't just study music, however. As a group, ethnomusicologists try to understand in a holistic way the larger human complexities of music, which is a cultural universal—that is, all human groups practice an expression that they separate from that which is spoken, an expression that we call in English "music." Ethnomusicologists (and other social scientists who study music) try to understand how musical expression in each case spills over into other areas of human activity and meaning. They do, because it always does.

Over and over again, music expresses and shapes deeper meanings about, for example, national, regional, or ethnic identity (think about the national anthems of modern nation-states); music expresses and shapes solidarity (think about the use of "We Shall Overcome" in the civil rights movement); music expresses and shapes political agendas (think about the use of pop songs in U.S. election campaigns); music expresses and shapes protest and rebellion (think about punk music of the 1970s and 1980s); music expresses and shapes religious belief (think about the fact that people use music in almost every religious tradition); music expresses and shapes the buying and selling of commodities (think about advertising); music expresses and shapes human emotion (think about the use of music in the movie and television industry); and music even expresses and shapes how we think about ourselves (think of the radio stations you listen to or the music collections you own). In each case, if we focused only on the sound of music itself, we would miss its significance and power in other realms of human life and meaning. To understand music, then, we must understand the larger contexts in which music expresses and shapes human activity.

To look for such connections between parts is holism. Yet, as might be apparent, holism is an insurmountable goal in many respects; it can seem completely overwhelming, especially when we consider that almost every human system is part of another larger system, which is in turn part of a still larger system. We could very well take the study of music or American culture to the point of infinity. With this in mind, you may very well ask: Can we ever grasp the wholeness of culture? Can we ever understand every component of a system as complex as American or world culture? Indeed, when we consider that understanding all the subtle nuances of a single individual is nearly impossible, how can we presume to know as much about an entire group or society? Anthropologist James L. Peacock answers: "Holism is an important but impossible ideal. You cannot see everywhere or think everything. You must select and emphasize. To do this, you must categorize and make distinctions. Only in this way can you analyze and understand."[12]

Anthropologists thus approach culture with the philosophy of and struggle for holism but realize that ultimately one must focus on parts, parts that— when compared to other parts—point us in the direction of understanding larger human issues. Hence, anthropologists often study a particular church to make inferences about the role of religion in human life, or they study one kind of music to understand music's role within a particular society, or they study a small group of women in a rural village to understand larger issues of gender in human life. In each case, an individual study enters into conversation with other anthropological studies that, when taken together, have something to offer our understandings of religion, music, or gender, respectively.

Each of these studies, which focus on the particular, points us in the direction of holism, which in turn points us to a deeper understanding of culture. But just like the saying "The finger that points at the moon is not the moon," we realize its incompleteness—that we are always *in the process* of understanding culture.

ANTHROPOLOGY HERE AND NOW

Anthropologists may study the particular to gain insight into larger human issues. Take, for example, the work of cultural anthropologist Celeste Ray (University of the South), who studies Irish holy wells: sacred springs or waterholes associated with cures for particular illnesses, often dedicated to unofficial Irish saints, many of whom were local holy women. Ray suggests that well-side rituals have something to tell us, not only about Irish religious praxis, but also about the endurance of local and regional beliefs and practices within internationally embraced faiths. You can learn more about Ray's research from *National Geographic* (which includes an audio interview with Ray) at newswatch.nationalgeographic.com/tag/celeste-ray.

CHECK IT OUT!

This does not mean that anthropologists, or anyone for that matter, can *never* attain a clear understanding of culture. It is as James Peacock says: "[C]ulture is not a physical thing but an attitude, a way of viewing the world. We can describe indications of a certain cultural pattern—people hurrying or loitering as clues to their assumptions about time, for example—but culture itself is an abstraction that we make based on such indications. There is nothing wrong with an abstraction so long as we recognize it for what it is."[13]

In this way, holism reminds us that the very concept of culture is an abstraction; it is *not a thing*, as I have already established. Yet Peacock implores us to remember that culture, although an abstraction, "can nonetheless have reality and power in experience."[14] This is why anthropologists often focus on the particular, on small communities, or on a few people— sites where culture is embodied, enacted, experienced, and in turn negotiated—on an intimate human level.[15]

Anthropologist Philippe Bourgois, for example, lived and studied with over two dozen crack dealers in East Harlem for five years. By studying the particular among a very few in a small community, Bourgois was able to point us toward an understanding of the way worldwide economic patterns are articulated in the lives of users and dealers in an underground economy, how the use of violence becomes meaningful to success in the illegal drug trade, and how dealers respond to and shape larger drug markets. When reading Bourgois's work, we realize that the users and dealers he describes are a very small component of a much larger culture of illegal drug use and trade. Yet we also realize that Bourgois's study does *point us in the direction of understanding the larger culture of illegal drug use and trade.*[16] Each anthropological study is like this. Although focusing on one particular *part*, it points us to broader discussions.

This is where comparativism comes in. In order for the part to have relevance in a broader conversation about culture, we must compare. Recall that in the general study of anthropology, *comparativism* means to search for similarities and differences between and among human beings in all their biological and cultural complexities. In the study of culture, this approach concentrates on comparing varied cultural descriptions from around the world to make generalizations about human beings and the role of culture in human life. In the study of culture, this comparative perspective is called **ethnology** (which is sometimes used synonymously with *cultural anthropology*). Thus, while anthropologists may study an individual culture—like families in Japanese society or Protestant churches in the southern United States—their ultimate purpose is to advance a deeper understanding of larger cultural issues. These issues might include race and ethnicity; religion; politics and economics; kinship, marriage, and family; ecology; gender; or the nature of violence, conflict, and peace. These understandings in turn help to address such questions as the following: Why do people differ? What can we learn about others and ourselves by studying the wide range of culture? Why do we find universals in all societies—like religion or music or taboos against incest? Why is marriage found everywhere? Why do people create social hierarchies—between the rich and poor, for example—over and over again? Exploring these questions through the framework of ethnology means taking into account all that we know about culture.

This means that in the study of culture the particular is always struggling against the general and vice versa. On the one hand, while we may emphasize how culture is different from one group to the next, it is important to understand that all culture shares similarities (like the common problems presented by the food quest). On the other hand, while we may recognize that all culture has common elements, it is important to recognize that culture also has unique qualities (consider the ways people define "good" and "bad" food). Thus, in order to understand culture both particularly and generally, we must try to understand culture in all its complexities. We struggle to see parts in larger cultural contexts (holism), and we push for understanding the comprehensive role of culture in people's lives without losing sight of its particular expression in human experience (ethnology).

With that said, however, I am reminded of my earlier discussion about the role and limits of experience in the definition of culture. Holism and ethnology are difficult to recognize in the first place because people characteristically generalize and compare on the basis of their own experience. They often see the parts and connections they *want* to see. As the German philosopher Arthur Schopenhauer once said, "Every man takes the limits of his own field of vision for the limits of the world." Indeed, many people the world over believe their own religion to be the *right* religion, or they say that the music of other people all sounds alike, or they think that all people are essentially the same or, at the other extreme, that nobody is like them. Departing down the road of culture requires that we look at two more concepts that, when fully understood and properly balanced, make holism and ethnology possible: ethnocentrism and cultural relativity.

Let's take an extended look at these two concepts. **Ethnocentrism** is the tendency to view the world from the basis of one's own experience. On a very fundamental human level, we cannot help but be ethnocentric. It is a fact of every human life. Our experience is limited, and what exists outside the limits of that experience is foreign and strange (like, for me, the culture of stock car racing). But more than this, the cultural knowledge, customs, traditions, values, and ideas with which we are enculturated have enormous power in defining how we will continue to encounter, experience, and understand the world around us. Often we are completely unconscious that the way we live and experience the world fashions our ethnocentrism. Indeed, ethnocentrism is so basic to our being that we may not even realize just how powerful it can be. Many Americans, for example, are often unaware of how culturally specific "notions of beauty" shape their views of themselves and others. And those views can have powerful implications: studies have illustrated that these notions of beauty can affect things like popularity, employment and hiring decisions, and even student evaluations of their professors. In one interesting study, researchers found that "attractive professors consistently outscore

Culturally specific notions of beauty shape how we perceive and enact personal beauty. Photo by Danny Gawlowski.

their less comely colleagues by a significant margin on student evaluations of teaching."[17] Of course, the physical qualities that make some professors "attractive" and others "less comely" are neither universal nor uniform; our attributions of attractiveness are rooted in ethnocentrism, shaped by very powerful cultural, often unconscious, ideas about what constitutes beauty.

Realizing the power of ethnocentrism is the first step toward understanding the bias that we carry in our studies of culture. No one can be completely bias free. But everyone can, first, recognize that they are ethnocentric and, second, seek ways to understand culture outside their own view of the world. Put another way, we must shift ethnocentrism from the unconscious to the conscious realm of knowledge.

Unchecked, ethnocentrism can prevent us from understanding the larger questions of culture. Unconscious ethnocentrism can inform our conscious judgments of other peoples and other cultural practices. Ethnocentrism often tells us that our view of the world is right and that other ways of looking at the world are wrong or weird. When, for example, we hear of other people who eat, say, dogs as food, we cringe. For many of us, dogs are little people in furry suits, and to eat one is tantamount to cannibalism. We cannot stand back from our own ideas about who and what dogs are. We are not interested in why other people may not view dogs in the same way, and so we jump to conclusions, as did many social evolutionists: anyone who would eat dogs must be, in our minds, savage.

But let's look more deeply into what eating dogs might mean to others. Cheyenne-Arapaho—a Native American group living in western Oklahoma—are known to eat dogs sometimes. Paradoxically, many Cheyenne-Arapaho view their dogs like other Americans, as little people in furry suits. Nevertheless, once a year, some Cheyenne-Arapaho choose to ritually, as a group, eat dogs.

Cheyenne-Arapaho today tell an old story about a time when they were starving to death, and their dogs came forward and told the people that they would give their lives for food so that the Cheyenne-Arapaho might live. Today, each year, at their annual sun dances, the Cheyenne-Arapaho thus ritually eat a dog to remind them of this event—that their dogs paid the ultimate price. Dogs, then, were and are much more than little people in furry suits. Seen in this light, it appears to be a very different thing when we step outside of our ethnocentrism, doesn't it?[18]

Unchecked ethnocentrism can get in the way of understanding other people and other cultural practices. Indeed, when ethnocentrism is taken to the extremes of overt prejudice, racism, bigotry, or hatred—as it so often is—we miss not only the deeper intricacies of culture but also the commonality of human experience. And, as a result, we ourselves become more set apart and less human.

How do we overcome our own ethnocentrism, an ethnocentrism that is so intrinsic to the human experience? When we consider the reasons some Cheyenne-Arapaho might eat dogs from *their* perspective, we are using the conceptual tool of cultural relativity. Cultural relativity is the second part of the conceptual foundation that allows us to study culture through the frameworks of holism and ethnology.

Cultural relativity, you will recall from my discussion of Boas, is the idea that each society or culture must be understood on its own terms. It does not mean that we necessarily agree with every cultural practice that we come across; it means that if we really want to *understand* how culture works, we must look at culture from the viewpoints of those who create, maintain, and experience it, not from our own.

Take, for example, Bourgois's work with inner-city drug dealers. Bourgois did not condone the selling of drugs or the brute violence on which the culture of dealing illegal drugs often rests. Instead, Bourgois approached the drug dealers through the framework of cultural relativity rather than judgment so that he could understand how the culture of selling crack really works. After five years of living and studying on the street, Bourgois began to understand drug dealers as people struggling to survive on the margins of American society. He wrote that the drug dealers had "not passively accepted their structural victimization. On the contrary, by embroiling themselves in the underground economy and proudly embracing street culture, they are seeking an alternative to their social marginalization."[19]

While Bourgois came to these understandings through cultural relativity without succumbing to ethnocentrism, he also directly witnessed overt acts of violence. Understanding this "culture of terror" was critical to understanding how this component of street culture worked; it also reinforced Bourgois's conviction that the illegal drug trade and its accompanying attributes of violence were deeply detrimental to American society. While the drug dealers had found ways to survive in the inner city, they also had "become the actual agents administering their own destruction and their community's suffering."[20]

ANTHROPOLOGY HERE AND NOW

You can learn more about Philippe Bourgois's work—including his latest studies of homelessness and drug addiction—at philippe bourgois.net.

CHECK IT OUT!

Bourgois's intimate five-year study would not have been possible without the use of cultural relativity. Yet, like ethnocentrism, cultural relativity can also be taken to extremes. Some might be tempted to just say we can make no judgments about others or their cultural practices. Hypothetically, it would be nice if we didn't have to make judgments about other people. Yet what do we do with the knowledge of *actual* human behavior in our world? What do we do with the ongoing human practices of violence, slavery, genocide, or the exploitation of others? Take, for example, violence against women. Rape, sexual assault, harassment, or the international trafficking of women sold into prostitution rings are hard facts of both local and international culture.[21] To simply sit back and say, "Well, that's the culture and we really shouldn't judge or seek to change it," is to take cultural relativity to an extreme.

Let's take another difficult example: **genocide**, the extermination of one group of people by another. Genocide is a dark underside of many, many societies around the world. We may be most familiar with Nazi Germany, but the practice is not by any means unusual human behavior, past or present; unfortunately, it has cropped up throughout human history and is still relatively common among human beings.

In the twentieth century alone, which includes well-known genocides such as Nazi Germany (six million), Stalin's Soviet Union (ten million), and Khmer Rouge Cambodia (two and a half million), estimates of those who perished as a result of genocide range as high as twenty-eight million. But consider the figures of genocides from just 1950 to 2000. From 1955 to 1972, the Sudanese army eradicated five hundred thousand southern Sudanese people. In 1971, in Bangladesh, the East Pakistan army murdered about three million people. In 1972, in Burundi, Tutsis killed around two hundred thousand Hutus, and in Rwanda, in the course of a few months in 1994 alone, Hutus exterminated well over five hundred thousand Tutsis. Think about that last example: five hundred thousand people murdered in the course of a few months. In 1994, five hundred thousand people would have comprised a small to midsize U.S. city, like Nashville. Imagine that, over the course of a few months, the people living in Nashville were gone. Vanished. Wiped off the face of the earth. While, in all, the Tutsis and Hutus would, by the end of the century, account for the deaths of well over a million people, this peculiar human phenomenon has spared no particular region of the world. From North and South America to Eurasia to Africa, genocide is a phenomenon that all humans share in their collective past.[22]

While anthropologists study this phenomenon to gain better understandings of the culture of violence, it does not mean that we can sit back and say, "Well, it's their culture, and we shouldn't judge or seek to change it." In the study of genocide and its relation to the culture of violence, the real questions become these: How do we address this kind of human violence on a worldwide level? Is it natural or cultural? If it is socially and culturally constructed, how can we work to change people's attitudes about each other? While recognizing the complexities of human differences, how can we build bridges of understanding between people?

These kinds of questions are becoming all the more important as we move toward the global village. People are being forced to answer for actions like genocide in forums such as the World Court at The Hague. Here, different groups of people come together and decide that, for example, slavery should not be tolerated regardless of its role in a particular society or culture. The UN Universal Declaration of Human Rights declares in its fourth article that "[n]o one shall be held in slavery or servitude; slavery and the slave trade shall be prohibited in all their forms."[23] Yet slavery still exists in our world, from forced labor in China to the ongoing slave trade in Sudan.

Of course, people have always negotiated their own moralities with other people. But, unlike the past, groups today are having to negotiate what they might consider natural and right (such as enslaving others) with those who consider it wrong on an international scale. As anthropologist Carolyn Fluehr-Lobban writes, "The exchange of ideas across cultures is already fostering a growing acceptance of the universal nature of some human rights, regardless of cultural differences."[24]

Ethnocentrism and cultural relativity, then, can be incredibly complicated to balance, both in the study of culture and in the negotiation of culture on a worldwide level. Coming to understand the complexities of ethnocentrism and cultural relativity is a vital and ongoing process, one that is informing and shaping not only the study of culture but also the cultural knowledge of human survival itself.

SUMMING UP: LESSONS FROM DEFINING AND STUDYING CULTURE

So what do we do with our understanding of culture? Culture's role in human life is enormous. Yet popular ideas about culture are often limited to traditions, customs, or habits. Although these "things" are indeed part of culture, they are only a small part of a larger equation that can lead us to understanding human beings in all their complexities. And because human beings are complicated, so, too, is culture. Living in today's complex world thus means that we are increasingly called on to understand culture in much more complicated ways—from our daily interactions with others to the relationships

The uncritical acceptance of cultural relativity may actually hinder our common efforts to address complex, multifaceted global problems. Indeed, all the world's citizens increasingly find themselves having to evaluate their cultural practices in light of our rapidly changing and ever more integrated world. Nelson Mandela (center), for example, has argued that addressing Africa's AIDS epidemic is more than just educating the public; people must also change conventional cultural practices that augment the spread of this infectious disease. Photo by author.

between nation-states on the world stage. Not until we understand culture in its broader framework can we approach complex human problems and reach for their complex solutions. Understanding the power of culture can thus offer us a powerful tool for understanding and creating change in our own lives and in our own communities.

With this said, let's briefly review. You'll recall that culture is a shared and negotiated system of meaning informed by knowledge that people learn and put into practice by interpreting experience and generating behavior. To put this another way, remember the following:

- Culture is a system of meaning (the system is made up of parts—that is, people).

- Culture is shared and negotiated among and between people.
- Culture consists of knowledge.
- Culture is learned through enculturation.
- In practice (i.e., in everyday social interaction), culture frames experience (and vice versa).
- In practice (i.e., in everyday social interaction), culture generates behavior (and vice versa).

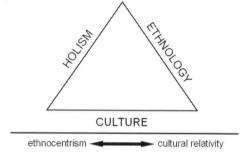

A model for understanding the complexities of culture.

Remember that understanding the actual complexities of culture proceeds through a philosophical lens that balances culture with holism and ethnology (i.e., comparativism as applied to the study of culture), which, in turn, rests on the ever-evolving balancing act between ethnocentrism and cultural relativity. This is where understanding culture in an anthropological sense resides. Although anthropologists use a philosophical model, they also apply a distinct methodology for approaching the study of culture. This methodology is called ethnography, and it is the subject of the next chapter.

NOTES

1. This culture definition (and my following discussion of culture in the section "Defining Culture") is based on several sources. My focus on culture as a negotiated system of meaning is informed by Gregory Bateson, *Steps to an Ecology of Mind* (San Francisco: Chandler, 1972); James Clifford, *The Predicament of Culture* (Cambridge, MA: Harvard University Press, 1988); Clifford Geertz, *The Interpretation of Cultures* (New York: Basic Books, 1973), and *Local Knowledge: Further Essays in Interpretive Anthropology* (New York: Basic Books, 1983); and Renato Rosaldo, *Culture and Truth: The Remaking of Social Analysis* (Boston: Beacon Press, 1993). My focus on cultural knowledge is revised from James P.

Spradley, ed., in *Culture and Cognition: Rules, Maps, and Plans* (San Francisco: Chandler, 1972), 6–18, and especially *The Ethnographic Interview* (New York: Holt, Rinehart and Winston, 1979), in which Spradley states, "[C]ulture . . . [is the] acquired knowledge that people use to interpret experience and generate social behavior" (5). This perspective has precedence with Ward Goodenough's writings— see, for example, "Cultural Anthropology and Linguistics," in *Report of the Seventh Annual Round Table Meeting on Linguistics and Language Study*, ed. P. L. Garvin (Washington, DC: Georgetown University Monograph Series on Language and Linguistics, no. 9, 1957), and *Culture, Language, and Society* (Menlo Park, CA: Benjamin/Cummings, 1981). My departure from the rules of culture and elaboration of experience and practice of culture (especially in the discussion that follows) is informed primarily by Pierre Bourdieu, *Outline of a Theory of Practice*, trans. R. Nice (Cambridge: Cambridge University Press, 1977), which I pose here within the context of an introductory discussion. See also Michael Jackson, ed., *Things As They Are: New Directions in Phenomenological Anthropology* (Bloomington: Indiana University Press, 1996), and Victor W. Turner and Edward M. Bruner, *The Anthropology of Experience* (Chicago: University of Illinois Press, 1986).

2. For a deeper discussion of these issues, see James L. Peacock, *The Anthropological Lens: Harsh Light, Soft Focus* (Cambridge: Cambridge University Press, 1986), especially 1–47.

3. Edward B. Tylor, *Primitive Culture*, vol. 1 (New York: Harper & Row, 1958 [1871]).

4. "You Say Hello, I Say Ahoy," *All Things Considered*, National Public Radio, March 19, 1999.

5. See Edward M. Bruner, "Experience and Its Expressions," in Turner and Bruner, *The Anthropology of Experience*, 3–30.

6. Ibid.

7. James P. Spradley and David W. McCurdy, eds., *Culture and Conflict: Readings in Cultural Anthropology*, 8th ed. (New York: HarperCollins, 1994), 4–5.

8. Paul Wohlt, personal communication, 2000.

9. A plethora of studies have explored how media affects behavior—much of it conducted by the advertising industry. For clearly written and provocative discussions about the relationships of the movie and television industry to culture, see, for example, Sissela Bok, *Mayhem: Violence as Public Entertainment* (Reading,

MA: Addison-Wesley, 1998); Conrad Philip Kottak, *Prime-Time Society: An Anthropological Analysis of Television and Culture* (Belmont, CA: Wadsworth, 1990); and Scott Robert Olson, *Hollywood Planet: Global Media and the Competitive Advantage of Narrative Transparency* (Mahwah, NJ: Lawrence Erlbaum Associates, 1999). For discussions that take up the effect of the television and movie industry within even larger frameworks of business and economics, see, for example, Thomas Frank, *The Conquest of Cool: Business Culture, Counterculture, and the Rise of Hip Consumerism* (Chicago: University of Chicago Press, 1997).

10. I am, of course, referring to the complex and far-reaching study of culture and power. Anthropologists have drawn inspiration from a number of different theorists, including Max Weber (see, for example, *The Theory of Social and Economic Organization* [New York: Oxford University Press, 1947 (1925)]), Émile Durkheim (see *The Rules of the Sociological Method* [New York: Free Press, 1938 (1895)]), Karl Marx (see *Capital: A Critique of Political Economy* [London: Sonnenschein, 1887 (1867–1894)]), Antonio Gramsci (see *Selections from the Prison Notebooks of Antonio Gramsci* [London: Lawrence and Wishart, 1971]), Michel Foucault (see *Power/Knowledge: Selected Interviews and Other Writings* [New York: Pantheon Books, 1980]), and Pierre Bourdieu (see *Language and Symbolic Power* [Cambridge, MA: Harvard University Press, 1991]), among many others.

Anthropologists have thus elaborated power in a diversity of ways, including as the physical domination of one person or group over another (via Weber), as inscribed in social institutions (via Durkheim), as originating in modes of production (via Marx), as emergent in the rise of hegemony (via Gramsci), as a discursive process in the social construction of reality (via Foucault), or as a deeply symbolic practice (via Bourdieu).

11. Peacock, *The Anthropological Lens*, 17.

12. Ibid., 19–20.

13. Ibid., 20.

14. Ibid., 23.

15. For a deeper discussion, see Peacock, *The Anthropological Lens*, 11ff.

16. See Philippe Bourgois, *In Search of Respect: Selling Crack in El Barrio* (Cambridge: Cambridge University Press, 1995).

17. Gabriela A. Montell, "Do Good Looks Equal Good Evaluations?" *Chronicle of Higher Education*, October 15, 2003.

18. Eugene Blackbear Jr., "Ceremonial Aspects of the Sun Dance and Sweat Lodge Rituals as They Relate to Contemporary Wellness" (paper presented at "Affects on Wellness: A Holistic Approach," Indian Health Service, Anadarko, Oklahoma, October 27, 1993).

19. Bourgois, *In Search of Respect*, 143.

20. Ibid.

21. See United Nations Population Fund, *The State of World Population 2000* (New York: United Nations Population Fund), especially chapter 3, "Violence against Women and Girls: A Human Rights and Health Priority."

22. Michael N. Dobkowski and Isidor Wallimann, *Genocide in Our Time: An Annotated Bibliography with Analytical Introductions* (Ann Arbor, MI: Pierian Press, 1992); Israel W. Charny, ed., *Encyclopedia of Genocide*, 2 vols. (Santa Barbara, CA: ABC-CLIO, 1999); Isidor Wallimann and Michael N. Dobkowski, eds., *Genocide and the Modern Age: Etiology and Case Studies of Mass Death* (Syracuse, NY: Syracuse University Press, 2000).

23. United Nations, "Universal Declaration of Human Rights," General Assembly Resolution 217 A (III), December 10, 1948.

24. Carolyn Fluehr-Lobban, "Cultural Relativism and Universal Rights," *Chronicle of Higher Education*, B1–B2, June 9, 1995.

3

Ethnography

In the previous chapter, I introduced an anthropological definition of culture, its driving concepts, and the philosophical constructs within which anthropologists focus their studies of culture. I stressed how this involves understanding holism and ethnology, concepts that rest on balancing the deeper complexities of ethnocentrism and cultural relativity. In this chapter, I will go further in my discussion of anthropology's unique approach to studying culture. What I have in mind is anthropology's distinctive method for investigating and exploring the intricacies of culture as well as its approach to writing about culture, a method called **ethnography**.

In the comparative study of culture (or ethnology), anthropologists depend almost exclusively on ethnography to make broad generalizations about human beings. Indeed, without the particular descriptions of culture, we cannot very well presume to make cross-cultural comparisons about human behavior or the role of culture in people's lives generally. Thus, because of its importance to the field of anthropology (especially sociocultural anthropology), ethnography is a multifaceted approach in its own right. Like the culture concept, it has broad theoretical and philosophical underpinnings. To address ethnography and its theoretical and philosophical underpinnings, I'd like to return to my anthropological story.

BRITISH SOCIAL ANTHROPOLOGY AND BRONISLAW MALINOWSKI

Although most anthropologists associate the development of modern American anthropology with Boas, many associate the development of modern ethnography with Bronislaw Malinowski.[1] About the same time Franz Boas was molding American anthropology around cultural relativity and historical particularism, Polish-born British anthropologist Bronislaw Malinowski put forward a new way of writing descriptions of culture. Malinowski influenced British social anthropology in ways that paralleled Boas's influence in the United States. Like Boas, he advocated living with a particular people for long periods of time; unlike Boas, he set forth what became known as a *systematic* way of theorizing, practicing, and writing ethnography within an anthropological framework.

Malinowski was, in many ways, embroiled in the same kinds of discussions as Boas. Malinowski's response to the social evolutionists was what he called "the native's point of view." The goal of ethnography, wrote Malinowski, was "to grasp the native's point of view, his relation to life, to realize *his* vision of *his* world."[2] Like Boas, he believed that in order to understand another society, you had to live with the so-called natives, put aside your own judgments about them, and seek to understand their culture from their point of view. But, unlike Boas, Malinowski placed the search for the "native's point of view" squarely within a systematic method.

In his famous book *Argonauts of the Western Pacific* (based on his four-year study with the Trobriand Islanders in the western Pacific from 1914 to 1918 and published in 1922), Malinowski argued that doing ethnography should be based, at the very least, on three foundations. He summarized them as follows:

1. *The organisation of the tribe, and the anatomy of its culture* must be recorded in firm, clear outline. The method of *concrete, statistical documentation* is the means through which such an outline has to be given.
2. Within this frame, the *imponderabilia of actual life,* and the *type of behaviour* have to be filled in. They have to be collected through minute, detailed observations in the form of some sort of ethnographic diary, made possible by close contact with native life.
3. A collection of ethnographic statements, characteristic narratives, typical utterances, items of folk-lore and magical formulae has to be given as a *corpus inscriptionum*, as documents of native mentality [emphasis in original].[3]

For Malinowski, then, doing ethnography should center, first, on the sound documentation of culture and its structure; second, on documenting actions and behaviors that articulate culture in experience through the use of field notes; and, third, on documenting the cultural knowledge of the natives from their point of view, information often gathered through the use of formal and informal interviews.

When Malinowski wrote this, many British anthropologists, like their American counterparts, focused their ethnographic studies on exotic non-Western societies. Doing so presented the most formidable challenges to the prevailing ideas of social evolution. And, like its American counterpart, British anthropology came to be known for its focus on non-Western peoples. This is why Malinowski used the word *tribe*. This focus on the tribe, of course, is diminished today—especially because anthropology as a whole now attends to culture both distant and close, both Western and non-Western, both exotic and familiar. Nevertheless, Malinowski's call for ethnographers to record culture's organization and structure through concrete documentation had an important impact on the development of ethnographic methodology.

In developing these methods, Malinowski was implicitly responding to the norm for going about a study of non-Western peoples, a norm for describing "exotic others" that had been dominated by, on the one hand, missionaries, soldiers, or colonial authorities and, on the other hand, scholars who did "touch-and-go" surveys of local groups. Most social evolutionists, for example, did little fieldwork (i.e., living and studying in a local community) and more often than not used broad-ranging reports from military exploits, missionary descriptions, or colonial records to interpret other cultural practices and to construct their evolutionary models from a distance. Living with so-called savages or barbarians was neither necessary nor desired. For example, the famous British anthropologist James George Frazer wrote thirteen volumes on the so-called savage mind and how those beliefs and customs represented an early developmental stage of social evolution. But when asked if he had ever seen or talked to any of these savages, his answer was an emphatic "God forbid!"[4]

Like Boas, Malinowski argued that a true cultural description could be undertaken only through the medium of direct experience. But living with the natives of a particular society and appreciating their "native's point of view" was not enough. Malinowski argued that writing about culture should also be a systematic undertaking, one characterized by the ongoing documentation of the expressions of culture imparted by detailed observations, field notes, and interviews; it should not be characterized by the interpretations of culture from the viewpoint of, for example, a missionary, a soldier, or a colonial authority. For Malinowski, these latter accounts were bound to be limited. Only by using a relativistic method that discerned "the native's point of view" as based on direct, unbiased evidence could a "scientific" study of culture be made. From Malinowski's point of view, the **ethnographer**, the anthropologist who undertakes ethnography, could write an unbiased, objective description of another culture only through determined adherence to this model.

Many contemporary anthropologists contend that constructing a "scientific" or purely objective description of culture is impossible (we are, after all, only human, and there is that problem of human bias, ethnocentrism). Nevertheless, Malinowski reinforced the growing consensus among anthropologists in both Europe and the United States that a description of culture must be based on direct participation and observation and, further, that writing an ethnographic account demanded that the ethnographer, in Malinowski's words, "must show clearly and concisely . . . which are his own direct observations, and which [are] the indirect informations that form the bases of his account."[5]

With that said, however, there is another component of this point we must examine: Malinowski's statement about *the organization of the tribe and the anatomy of its culture*. Malinowski was advocating a method for describing culture, but he was also advocating a particular assumption, philosophy, or theory of culture—a theory of culture that still informs ethnography today.

Malinowski argued that each part of culture had a purpose for its existence. The "stuff," or artifacts, of culture—actions, behaviors, beliefs, customs, or traditions—existed within the framework of cultural institutions like politics, economics, or family and kinship. For Malinowski, culture ultimately fulfilled a function; it somehow served basic human needs, needs that were universal to the human condition. He argued, for example, that the magical beliefs of the Trobrianders were not some primitive form of religion representative of an earlier stage of civilization. Instead, Trobriand religious beliefs and practices had a function; they fulfilled the basic human need to address the uncertainty of life.

The Trobrianders traveled regularly from one Pacific island to another, trading goods in a western Pacific exchange network. Their travel, which took place in boats, was uncertain and dangerous. The Trobrianders, consequently, used magic to ensure safe travel. And Malinowski argued that the

For Bronislaw Malinowski, although particular cultural practices could differ markedly in their expressions, their function was one and the same. Each fulfilled some purpose. Practices like Trobriand magic or Christian prayer (pictured here), Malinowski suggested, thus served a basic psychological need to address the uncertain. Photo by Danny Gawlowski.

Trobrianders' magic fulfilled a basic human need—that is, the psychological need to address the uncertain.

In this way, the Trobriand practice was no different from the Christian use of prayer, which puts a particular uncertainty "in God's hands." For Malinowski, although the *expressions* of Trobriand belief and Christian belief differed markedly, their *function* was one and the same. They each fulfilled some purpose. And both institutions served a basic human psychological need by dealing with the uncertain. The Trobriand belief in magic, it turns out, is rather logical, as is the Christian belief in prayer.

Today, anthropologists would argue that systems like religion—although they serve obvious purposes—are a little more complicated than this. Nevertheless, Malinowski's argument that culture is functional remains intrinsic to the culture concept (e.g., recall that brute violence is a function of the underground drug trade, as mentioned in the previous chapter). Moreover, the concept of functionality remains intrinsic to the *practice* of ethnography. Contemporary ethnographers still approach culture with the assumption that cultural practices serve a purpose and engender meaning in some way or another.

The fundamental assumption that culture works as a system echoes the holistic perspective. In British social anthropology, this assumption first began to solidify around Malinowski and his contemporaries (e.g., A. R. Radcliffe-Brown). For Malinowski, the Trobrianders' belief in magic did not exist in a cultural vacuum. Such practices were connected to an extensive system of exchange among islands, a system of exchange that the Trobriand islanders called the **Kula**.

Simply put, the Kula was an extensive network consisting of trading partners scattered throughout several western Pacific islands. While Trobrianders traded many things, the Kula centered on the trade of two particular items: arm shells and shell necklaces, which traveled through the island villages in a very predictable fashion. The arm shells traveled from island to island in one direction, and the shell necklaces traveled from island to island in the other direction. Both items were highly desirable, and all economic exchange seemed to follow in the wake of their trade.

For Malinowski, the system functioned to integrate the islands into a larger social and political system. The traded items—arm shells and shell necklaces—had no inherent value in and of themselves, but the Trobriand

ANTHROPOLOGY HERE AND NOW

The study of human systems of exchange and their relationship to other realms of life—like that of Malinowski's Kula—has long been a staple of anthropological study. In a recent ethnographic work on Wall Street, anthropologist Melissa Fisher (New York University) observes the first generation of highly successful women working on Wall Street. Fisher describes how individuals forge identities and successes within socioeconomic and political contexts, linking global markets and struggles for gender equity. You can learn more about her ethnography, *Wall Street Women*, at www.dukeupress.edu/Wall-Street-Women.

CHECK IT OUT!

islanders assigned economic meaning to them. They were highly desirable because of attributes such as age (many had been in the network for many, many years) or previous ownership. In this way, Malinowski inferred that Trobriand exchange was not "primitive" or "savage" but very much like Western systems of exchange, which were also built around arbitrary meanings assigned to objects that have no inherent value in and of themselves (e.g., money, which is only paper). Although the Kula was much smaller than exchanges between nation-states, the value that Trobrianders assigned to arm shells and shell necklaces was no more arbitrary than the value that we might assign to antiques, old paintings, or Elvis's underwear (which, if you had them, would be very valuable indeed).

Malinowski's point was to illustrate that from religion to economics, people construct systems that have a function (i.e., a purpose for their existence) *and* that are intimately interconnected with other systems of meaning. In the Kula, magic, for example, was intimately tied to the exchange of goods; without it, moving from island to island trading arm shells and shell necklaces was just too dangerous. Malinowski wrote that the Kula "presents several aspects closely intertwined and influencing one another. To take only two, economic enterprise and magical ritual form the inseparable whole, the forces of magical belief and the efforts of man molding and influencing one another [in the trade of the arm shells and shell necklaces]."[6] Thus, while Malinowski argued that each cultural institution functioned to serve basic human needs (which are universal), he also argued that these institutions—like religion, economics, or politics—functioned as a whole, a whole called "culture."

Malinowski's theoretical approach to culture thus firmly articulated holism in the *written description* of culture. If parts make up the whole (which we call culture), then it follows that an ethnography must describe this, Malinowski reasoned. Consider, for example, how Malinowski organized his ethnography on the Trobriand islanders. He split the book into twenty-two chapters. Each chapter was designed to elaborate the parts of the system. He began with the people themselves, then moved on to summarize the Kula, and beginning with chapter 4 he set out to describe each part of the Kula trading network: from the building of canoes to the act of sailing, from the ceremonies around the Kula to the actual face-to-face economic exchanges, and from the legends and myths surrounding the Kula to the practice of magic. All the chapters are designed to point toward the last, chapter 22, titled "The Meaning of the

Kula," in which Malinowski summarizes a point that he makes all along—that each part acts in concert to compose the logical whole that is the Kula.

Today, many ethnographers reject Malinowski's assumption that culture is a clearly bounded system. Instead they focus, for example, on one aspect of culture like religion or economics or politics. And they now assert (as I did in the previous chapter) that culture exists on multiple levels and that boundaries between various cultural systems are murky at best. To represent culture as a bounded, functional system like Malinowski once did is, thus, less common today. Nevertheless, the theoretical assumption that culture works as a system still remains intrinsic to the culture concept and in turn remains intrinsic to how anthropologists approach ethnography as both a field method and a method of writing.

All told, British "functional" ethnographies such as Malinowksi's became archetypes for writing ethnography. Indeed, the form would come to dominate the way anthropologists—not just in Britain but all over the world—would write about culture as a meaningful system. Thus, while ethnography developed as a field method, it also developed as a very particular genre of literature. As a method of participating, observing, taking field notes, and interviewing, ethnography evolved as a challenge to social evolutionists and the conviction that the culture of the "savage" was less logical than the culture of the "civilized." For its day, the emergence of this kind of ethnography was radical stuff. Indeed, this very simple method is *still* radical stuff. (Think about debates about poverty. The people we hear from in this debate are not those struggling to get by; for the most part, we hear from politicians, "experts," and other so-called talking heads who for the most part have never experienced real and prolonged poverty.)

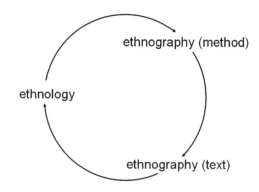

Ethnography is both a field method for studying culture and a way of writing about culture. As a written genre, it informs ethnology, which in turn informs newer questions about culture, which ethnographers explore through firsthand ethnographic fieldwork.

ethnography (method)

ethnology

ethnography (text)

As a particular genre of literature, the written ethnography remains a distinctive literary approach for understanding culture. Because the written ethnography gives us insight into the "native's point of view" one description at a time, it also informs our larger theoretical and ethnological understanding of human behavior and meaning.

Ultimately, then, ethnography is meant to inform the larger debate about the role of culture in people's lives everywhere. It feeds ethnology, which in turn feeds newer questions about culture that ethnography has a unique ability to address. Indeed, the interplay between ethnography and ethnology is a system unto itself that has a greater purpose. It is just as Malinowski wrote many years ago:

> In grasping the essential outlook of others, with reverence and real understanding . . . we cannot but help widening our own. We cannot possibly reach the final Socratic wisdom of knowing ourselves if we never leave the narrow confinement of the customs, beliefs and prejudices into which every man is born. Nothing can teach us a better lesson in this matter of ultimate importance than the habit of mind which allows us to treat the beliefs and values of another man from his point of view. Nor has civilised humanity ever needed such tolerance more than now, when prejudice, ill will and vindictiveness are driving each European nation from another, when all the ideals, cherished and proclaimed as the highest achievements of civilisation, science and religion, have been thrown to the winds. The Science of Man, in its most refined and deepest version should lead us to such knowledge and to tolerance and generosity, based on the understanding of other men's point of view.[7]

ETHNOGRAPHY AS A FIELD METHOD TODAY: ON PARTICIPANT OBSERVATION

Now that I have established the theoretical and philosophical underpinnings of ethnography as story, I'd like to look more deeply at how contemporary anthropologists go about studying culture through a field method inherited from Boas and Malinowski—among many others. Today, we call this field method **participant observation**: the systematic approach involving long-term participation, observing, taking field notes, and interviewing the natives of a particular society, community, or group (whether tribal, racing, demolition, or corporate).

First, participation. Anthropologists still contend that firsthand experience is critical if you seek to understand culture from the viewpoint of those who live within it. Anthropologists contest the notion that we can understand culture thoroughly by touch-and-go surveys, interviews, or observation alone. Philippe Bourgois—recall the anthropologist who wrote the ethnography on drug dealers—points out that a good deal of scholarly knowledge about illegal drug using and dealing is generated by brief interviews or surveys, many of which assume that users and dealers are honestly disclosing full information on the illegal drug trade. Just like Malinowski and Boas, Bourgois challenged the depth of conventional knowledge about taking and selling illegal drugs through the simple method of participation.[8]

I say that participation is simple. But is it? *Is* it simple to pack up and head off to encounter another world for an extended period of time? This is expected of anthropologists who want to study culture. Bourgois, for example, left his relatively comfortable life in Manhattan and moved into East Harlem, where, with his wife and son, he lived for five years.

Participation in another society, community, or group is often an arduous and demanding task, especially when the community or group is so distant from your own experience (like, for me, stock car racing). Although participation sounds simple and straightforward, actually getting to know another group and its accompanying cultural practices can be a complicated task— not to mention the amount of preparation that goes into beginning such an endeavor (I'll come back to this below). Most anthropologists would agree with ethnographer Melinda Bollar Wagner, who writes that "participant observation proceeds through certain stages, whether it occurs in a faraway land with a culture very different from the ethnographers' own or whether it occurs in their native lands. The labels [anthropologists] use to identify these stages vary, but I think it is valid to say that [ethnographers] tend to experience the stages of *making entrée, culture shock, establishing rapport*, and *understanding the culture*" [emphasis in original].[9]

In her ethnography *God's Schools: Choice and Compromise in American Society*, Melinda Bollar Wagner outlines the way she approached the study of fundamentalist Christian schools through this experiential framework. As a scholar of American religious experience, she appreciated that although she differed in her views about religion and education, understanding Christian schools from the viewpoint of the fundamentalist Christians who ran them was an important component of understanding, in turn, the diverse components of religion in the United States. But she wasn't a member of this community. How to get in? How to start?

Wagner explains that she made entrée into the group through a former student who had become a Christian schoolteacher. After attending a secular teaching conference together, Wagner began to ask her former student about Christian schools and her faith. After some time, Wagner was able to gain access to this world through her former student.[10] Like many anthropologists, Wagner entered the group through what anthropologists call an informant or **consultant**—that is, someone who informs and regularly consults on the ethnographer's understanding of a particular community's culture. Although ethnographers will often have many consultants, those who help the anthropologist enter a particular community often become "key consultants" (simply, the ethnographer's *main* consultants).

From Boas and Malinowski to Bourgois and Wagner, getting to know key consultants is critical to doing ethnography. In addition to allowing us to enter into their lives, ultimately, key consultants make possible the understanding of their community's culture. Should I embark on an ethnography on the culture of stock car racing, I would have to gain entrée by getting to know people who are part of it. In other words, I would have to get to know fans who go to every race and those fans who just go periodically. I would have to get to know the racers themselves as well as the pit crews. I would have to get to know the food vendors as well as the ticket scalpers. If I wanted to understand this system of meaning, then I would have to gain access to it from its many different parts—that is, the people who make the participants' culture real in experience. For example, anthropologist James Todd studies the culture of stock car racing in America and its connection to wider issues of race (i.e., "whiteness"), regionalism (i.e., the American South), and capitalism (i.e., how the sport is marketed). Although his ethnographic study of NASCAR necessarily meant becoming intimately familiar with drivers and fans, Todd's research methodology also called for studying NASCAR as an assemblage of the many groups that make the sport meaningful by producing and consuming it. In attempting to "trace the complex ways NASCAR is shaped, made and understood," Todd researched "born-again Christians, tourists, historians, traveling vendors, marketing directors, corporate executives, museum curators, race team specialists, celebrities, public relations officials, television reporters, and newspaper beat-writers."[11]

Anthropologist James Todd (right) talks with NASCAR driver Mike Wallace. Although Todd spent countless hours doing participant observation at NASCAR racetracks, his research took him far afield to garages, campgrounds, church services, corporate offices, meetings with marketing executives, and even the memorial for legendary driver Dale Earnhardt. "My research," he says, "became about documenting the specific narrative forms and devices, as well as the political economies and organizational politics, through which this complex and fascinating entity—both corporation and community—reproduces both itself and a specific version of American regionalism." Photo by Don Coble.

Making entrée, however, can be even more involved than just meeting and getting to know consultants. One doesn't merely decide on a research topic or group to study and then just "show up" in the field. Many ethnographers spend much time reading prior ethnographies and other reports, surveying their study's feasibility, preparing their research design (i.e., how their ethnographic work will proceed in the field), crafting research questions (i.e., lining out what questions they will ask their consultants as well as the larger theoretical questions in which their study fits), and seeking funding. And in addition to all this, anthropologists must often gain permission to do their

research from governments, organizations, local communities, or group leaders. Todd, for example, had to gain official permission from NASCAR and
the sport's racetracks, who fortunately granted all-access credentials for his
study. Some anthropologists are less fortunate: often they may have to wait
years for permission to conduct their studies, and even then their activities
may be closely watched or supervised. To be sure, governments implement
laws around which all ethnographers must negotiate. Bourgois, for example,
worked within the law, never himself directly engaging in the illegal drug
trade or its accompanying culture of violence. Aside from these obvious restrictions, anthropologists are bound to ethical standards set by the discipline
of anthropology and the institutions within which anthropologists work. Anthropologists are obligated to tell their consultants why they are participating
in their lives and *what* they are studying. Moreover, they must always put
their consultants' safety and welfare ahead of a study.[12] Gaining entrée into a
particular society, community, or group, then, is always mediated by certain
restrictions and constraints—both legal and ethical.

I mention this because within any discipline—medicine, for example—
there are limits on each and every study. Because of this, it follows that there
are limits to gaining entrée, and in turn there are limits to the participation
part of the ethnographic equation. Nonetheless, direct participation remains
the predominant way anthropologists go about doing ethnography. And key
consultants make this possible.

Gaining entrée, however, is only the beginning. As Wagner suggests, gaining entrée is often directly followed by **culture shock**—the meeting of two or
more systems of meaning in the *body*, expressed as anxiety, inappropriate behavior, or physical illness. Simply put, once ethnographers enter a particular
cultural scene, they often experience, in a very personal way, the differences
between themselves and the people they are studying. They may have a very
uncomfortable feeling about customs and traditions that are not their own,
they may feel acutely out of place, they may make mistakes in their behavior
when they do not know the cultural rules, or, in the extreme, they may even
experience physical ailment or illness.

Perhaps the most common form of culture shock is expressed in the behavioral mistakes ethnographers make long before they learn to understand
the community they are studying. In the case of Melinda Wagner, she initially
attended Christian school meetings in plain clothes, thinking that it would be
most appropriate to what she perceived were fundamentalist Christian ideals.

But she quickly discovered that her plain clothing was out of place, especially among other women whose clothes were more colorful and flashy.[13]

In a study that I did as an undergraduate on drug addiction and recovery, I attended Narcotics Anonymous meetings to get a sense of the recovery process. At my first meeting, I started taking notes, as any anthropologist might when doing fieldwork. The meeting came to an abrupt halt and all eyes turned to me; everyone wanted to know what I was doing. Because anonymity is such an important foundation of Narcotics Anonymous, my behavior of taking notes was highly inappropriate. Was I a reporter? A cop?

Bourgois tells a story with potentially life-threatening consequences in which he made the terrible mistake of publicly embarrassing one of his consultants—a man he calls Ray—by asking him to read a newspaper article in front of his friends. Unbeknownst to Bourgois, Ray could not read. Bourgois writes that "Ray's long-buried and overcompensated childhood wound of institutional failure had burst open. He looked up; regained his deadpan street scowl, threw down the paper, and screamed, 'Fuck you Felipe! I don't care about this shit! Get out of here! All of you's!'"[14] Several days later, Ray told Bourgois, "Felipe, let me tell you something, people who get people busted—even if it's by mistake—sometimes get found in the garbage with their heart ripped out and their bodies chopped into little pieces . . . or else maybe they just get their fingers stuck in electrical sockets. You understand what I'm saying?"[15]

Another very common form of culture shock is the anxiety felt when you encounter cultural practices with which you are not familiar or cultural practices that make you feel uncomfortable. In the case of Melinda Wagner, being "witnessed to" was among the earliest cultural practices that made her feel uncomfortable.[16] In another ethnographic study, of the occult, Wagner details how the language the participants used initially made her feel marginal and peripheral to the group. Although their language was English, their vocabulary was completely foreign to her.[17]

Many anthropologists have written about this initial anxiety of not knowing what to do, how to act, or how to respond to cultural practices that are completely different from their own. Although anthropologists try to remain culturally relative, anthropologists are, after all, human beings. For anthropologists, as for all humans, experiencing culture shock is a natural part of encountering cultural diversity because it is derived from our own ethno-

Philippe Bourgois in East Harlem, where he conducted his ethnographic fieldwork for In Search of Respect: Selling Crack in El Barrio. *The graffiti is a memorial to a slain youth in East Harlem. Photo by Oscar Vargas.*

centrism (which we can never totally escape). Culture shock is important to consider because it often marks that ambiguous space between the various systems of meaning that we call "culture." Indeed, when we are passing from our own comfort zones into worlds with which we are unfamiliar, we should *expect* to experience culture shock. But as anthropologists James P. Spradley and David W. McCurdy write, "Culture shock and ethnocentrism may . . . stand in the way of ethnographers. . . . Immersed alone in another society, the ethnographer understands few of the culturally defined rules for behavior and interpretation used by his or her hosts. The result is anxiety about proper action and an inability to interact appropriately in the new context."[18]

Although culture shock almost always characterizes the earliest stages of fieldwork, most anthropologists eventually learn to overcome it. They learn the rules for appropriate cultural behavior and get over their initial anxiety or their inability to interact with others. Yet culture shock does not completely disappear; it always remains a part of the learning process of fieldwork. As Melinda Wagner writes, culture shock "waxes and wanes, taking its turn with rapport."[19]

This brings me to the next component of participation: establishing rapport—the development of relationships with members of a society, community, or group characterized by mutual trust. In the case of Melinda Wagner, after some time she found herself blending into the community of fundamentalist Christian schools. As people began to trust her intentions and appreciate that she was not there to judge them but to understand their cultural practices, Wagner was accepted as an observing member of the schools in which she studied. More and more, she was asked to participate in school functions and activities, even those that were very intimate, like prayer.[20]

The same was true for Bourgois. Initially, he had trouble convincing drug dealers that he was not an undercover police officer. After some time, however, he gained his consultants' trust and began recording their conversations on tape. Anthropologists Dorothy and David Counts, who wrote *Over the Next Hill: An Ethnography of RVing Seniors in North America*, gained entrée and established rapport with RVing seniors relatively quickly and joined the "Escapees RV Club," after which they became full members of the community as they traveled around North America trying to understand why RVing is such an important part of postretirement life in America and Canada.[21] (Like the culture of stock car racing, this is another one that I just cannot understand. Perhaps when I retire. . . .)

Establishing rapport moves the ethnographer from outsider to an insider of sorts. Most of the time, however, the anthropologist remains marginal. For example, in my own study of Narcotics Anonymous, I was eventually incorporated into the group, invited to closed meetings that are not open to outsiders, and asked to share with the group my thoughts about drug addiction. Yet I had not experienced drug addiction and recovery personally. And from the viewpoint of my consultants, my lack of personal experience meant that there were some things about drug addiction I would never understand. Because of this lack of experience, I was always on the margins of the Narcotics Anonymous community in which I studied.

My experience of living and studying with Kiowas—a Native American group who live in southwestern Oklahoma—was and is in many ways very different. After living and studying in the community off and on for several years, many of my Kiowa hosts insisted that I was an insider of sorts by virtue of my long-term participation in their community. Over the years, I developed lasting friendships with many Kiowa people, many of whom took me as a relative (i.e., as a son, brother, uncle, or nephew) and often referred to me in their language as Koy-ta-lee (which means "Kiowa boy"). Although I was not born in their community, today many Kiowa people nonetheless refer to it as my home away from home. And in many ways, it *is* my home. My friends and relatives there have been an important part of my life, influencing not just my anthropological work but also my personal life; indeed, they have even changed how I see, interpret, and understand the world.[22] (My Kiowa friends and consultants and I recognize, of course, that although we may refer to the Kiowa community as "my home," I am still nonetheless marginal to their community—being a white guy and all.)

I mention this because I want to point out that although anthropologists may study a particular society, community, or group for a specified period of time (a year, for example), many establish rapport in communities for a lifetime. This is because establishing rapport often turns into friendship, and friendship is characterized by long-term and ongoing intimate relationships. Such experiences are by no means unusual. Melinda Wagner and her consultants, for example, maintained their friendship long after the ethnography on Christian schools was finished—even though they differed in their religious and philosophical beliefs.[23]

Just as culture shock and establishing rapport work in concert, so do establishing rapport and what you'll remember Wagner calling "understanding the culture," which is a process whereby the ethnographer moves from ethnocentrism and culture shock to an appreciation and understanding of the shared and negotiated system of meaning that, again, we call culture. This happens, first and foremost, through careful documentation and study, which I'll come to shortly, but suffice it to say now that most ethnographers assume that this understanding is never complete and is always tentative and ongoing. Indeed, we can never presume to understand another society, community, or group in all its complexities. Nevertheless, "understanding the culture" relies heavily on establishing rapport with consultants who open a window for us into their community from the "native's point of view." As Melinda Wagner writes about her own participant observation, "It is exhilarating to learn about an unknown culture one-on-one from other people."[24]

Yet from an ethnographic point of view, "understanding the culture" does not rely on *experience* alone. As important as it is to the ethnographic method, experience is not enough. Experience may give us an intuitive understanding of cultural practices, for example, but, as anthropologists, we must ultimately translate this experience into the written ethnography. To do so requires close attention to a larger system of meaning that we call culture—one that frames, bridges, and articulates the experience of *others*, not just ourselves. To do this, ethnographers rely heavily on observation and interviews.

Recall that Malinowski insisted that ethnographers must document culture to understand it. Today, most ethnographers recognize that documentation includes observing yourself, your own biases, and how your own ethnocentrisms shape your perception and your developing understandings. It also includes documenting the public life of others, which ethnographers often do through the medium of field notes. The "typical" ethnographer is often and regularly taking notes on all that is observed and experienced. These notes are recorded in a variety of ways—in field notebooks, on laptop computers, or even as sound files on portable digital recorders. However they are registered, field notes must, as Wagner writes, "start with what was seen, heard, tasted, smelled, and felt."[25] With this in mind, some ethnographers keep a diary (for documenting self) and a separate collection of field notes (for documenting observations of cultural practices). Others, however, reject this arbitrary separation. They recognize that, ultimately, all documentation—because it is seen through the eyes of the observer—is subjective. Nevertheless, ethnographers take notes on their observations (both of self and others) in the same way that you might take notes during a workshop or while reading. The process is very similar.

Observations of self and others, however, are incomplete without the interview. Engaging consultants in regular and ongoing conversation—either informally or formally—is the most critical component of ethnographic research.[26] It allows ethnographers, first, to check and recheck the validity of their observations and, second, to gain a deeper understanding of cultural practices from the native's point of view as it is articulated by the members of a particular group. Ultimately, the interview is extremely important because field notes are constructed from the viewpoint of the ethnographer; they do not tell us very much about the native's point of view. They only point us in that direction.

Regularly engaging consultants in conversation allows us to confront the ethnocentrism projected by our own experience. Often we come to believe that because we have experienced something with other people, our experience of that thing was the same as everyone else's. Through conversation, we discover how our own experience is different from the experience of our consultants. Here, in the space of conversation, the ambiguity of shared experience breaks down and differences emerge.[27] Anthropologist Marjorie Shostak, for example, lived with and studied among the !Kung people—a nomadic hunting-and-gathering people who today, for the most part, live in settled communities in southern Africa. Her primary research interest revolved around the life of a particular !Kung woman. In her ethnography *Nisa: The Life and Words of a !Kung Woman*, Shostak describes how her intensive conversations with Nisa helped to elaborate the point that although the two shared similarities by virtue of being women, their differences were very particular to their own societies. From sex and marriage to childbirth and family, Nisa illustrated for Shostak how being a woman in !Kung culture and being a woman in American culture could not be reduced to a common experience based entirely on a common biology (as is sometimes assumed in cross-cultural studies of women).[28]

ANTHROPOLOGY HERE AND NOW

Some of the most interesting and engaging collaborative ethnography carried out today is done by the Neighborhood Story Project in partnership with the University of New Orleans. A community-based book writing project that utilizes collaborative ethnographic approaches, teams of community members and NSP staff work together to research and write "our stories told by us." Take a look at their work and their many successful books and other story projects at www.neighborhoodstoryproject.org.

CHECK IT OUT!

In addition to conducting interviews and along with field notes, contemporary ethnographers use a variety of other methods—including drawing maps, doing archival research, taking photographs, administering questionnaires, and charting kinship and other community relationships.[29] For example, in much of my own ethnographic research, I have built on the ethnographic interview and the dialogic research process it engenders, using the method of **collaborative ethnography**, an approach that systematically engages consultants in the process of both practicing fieldwork *and* writing ethnography

Student ethnographer Jessica Booth interviews Pastor Martel Winburn Sr. for the collaborative ethnography The Other Side of Middletown: Exploring Muncie's African American Community. *Photo by Danny Gawlowski.*

(see the following section).[30] This collaborative method can deploy a variety of approaches to achieve this end—like the use of focus groups, community editorial boards, community forums, and ethnographer/consultant teams (who go about doing ethnographic research and writing together).[31] I'll come back to collaborative ethnography below, but ultimately the collaborative method, like most ethnographic methods, points back to establishing cultural understandings on intense and ongoing conversation with our consultants.

In sum, then, ethnography proceeds (through participation) from gaining entrée to culture shock to establishing rapport. "Understanding the culture" builds on direct experience and participation, but ultimately it is based on intense observation and employing a variety of ethnographic methods, the most important of these being engaging others in conversation. Thus, participant observation, taken broadly, allows us to understand the similarities and differences of culture on a very personal, intimate, and particularistic level.

ETHNOGRAPHY AS A GENRE OF LITERATURE TODAY: ON THE WRITTEN ETHNOGRAPHY

Understanding culture through the process of fieldwork and writing about culture as ethnography are two very different things. Participant observation may reveal to us an implicit understanding of culture, but writing about it forces us to make that understanding explicit. In writing an ethnography, we are forced to ask the questions: How do we go about describing another society, community, or group as we begin to understand it more deeply? How do we transform "understanding the culture"—as partial or emergent as it might be—into a written text?

As I mentioned earlier, anthropologists write within the bounds of a particular genre of literature. At one time, anthropologists addressed the problem of describing culture by elaborating each of its presumed components, like Malinowski did. But, as I mentioned, most anthropologists today reject the notion that culture can be split up into clearly bounded parts; very few ethnographies are currently written this way. Nonetheless, ethnographies, like all genres of literature, are still composed of chapters, paragraphs, and sentences, which are still arranged within an ethnographic tradition characterized by its own set of assumptions and goals that define the boundaries and contours of the ethnographic text.

Although anthropologists now write ethnography with a plethora of objectives in mind, two definitive goals of ethnography still concern, first, the call to illustrate cultural diversity and the power of culture in people's lives and, second, the call to teach us something about ourselves—as individuals, as groups, and as societies (wherever they may be situated).[32]

With that said, I'd like to explore these points more thoroughly by returning to my anthropological story. First, on the call to illustrate cultural diversity and the power of culture in people's lives. In the decades following Malinowski's pivotal work with the Trobriand Islanders, many ethnographers (among them, Boas and his students) questioned the effectiveness of Malinowski's theoretical approach to cultural function—namely, that it was based entirely on psychological needs. Although from a Western or academic point of view this explanation might appear reasonable (which was perhaps Malinowski's strongest point, made to a broad readership), the explanation was very much situated with *the ethnographer's* point of view. Take Malinowski's explanation of magic, which he argued was a function of the universal psychological need to address the uncertain. This psychologically based approach really has more to tell us about ourselves and the assumptions we make about our own *disbelief in magic* than about the "native's point of view." Although Malinowski set forth a radical idea at the

16

extensively the Trobriand point of view, in the end he
.. ıιs ethnography through a powerful ethnocentric framework:
..c that *presumes* that magic "can't be real" and seeks instead to explain it
through rational models.[33] (I'll take this up again in chapter 7.)

Of course, ethnographers past and present cannot help but be ethnocentric—they are, after all, forging culture into texts that are very culturally
specific to a Euro-American tradition of writing.[34] And everyone, everywhere, is ethnocentric. Even so, many ethnographers began to wonder how
people explained their own cultural practices in *their* own minds, in *their*
own terms, and how this was different from outsiders' explanations. If the
goals of ethnography are to illustrate cultural diversity, these ethnographers
asked, doesn't ethnography have a role in elaborating non-Western ways of
explaining cultural expressions like magic or religion or economics?[35] The
Trobrianders, for example, do not explain magic through Western psychol-
ogy. They have their own reasons and justifications for it, and we should seek
to understand them as deeply as the very practice of magic itself.

By the 1950s and through to the 1970s, many ethnographers had become
increasingly interested in how people articulated and shaped meaning in
their own lives as actors in a cultural system. While culture shaped people's
experience, how did, conversely, people shape and reshape this larger system
of meaning in which they lived? The central task of the ethnographer began
to concern understanding how cultural practices like magic articulated meaning to the people who practiced it, not how it took on meaning, for example,
within a psychological model imposed by the ethnographer.

One type of ethnographic research model that chose this method of writing
about culture was called **ethnoscience**—ethnography that focuses on recording the knowledge of culture as articulated through language. Ethnoscientists
distinguished this kind of knowledge production (how the Trobrianders
would explain magic, for example) from that which imposed explanations
from the outside (how Malinowski explained Trobriand magic in terms of
universal function). They referred to the former as "emic" knowledge and the
latter as "etic" knowledge.[36]

Perhaps one of the best-known anthropologists to embrace and disseminate this methodology—to students, in particular—was anthropologist and
ethnographer James P. Spradley, who wrote that

[e]thnography alone seeks to document the existence of *alternative* realities and to describe these realities in their own terms. Thus, it can provide a corrective for theories that arise in Western social science. . . .

Ethnography, in itself, does not escape being culture-bound. However, it provides descriptions that reveal the range of explanatory models created by human beings. It can serve as a beacon that shows the culture-bound nature of social science theories. It says to all investigators of human behavior, "Before you impose your theories on the people you study, find out how those people define the world." Ethnography can describe in detail the folk theories that have been tested in actual living situations over generations of time. And as we come to understand personality, society, individuals, and environments from the perspective of other than the professional scientific cultures, it will lead to a sense of epistemological humility; we become aware of the tentative nature of our theories and this enables us to revise them to be less ethnocentric.[37]

Spradley thus argued that we students of culture should discover the explanations grounded in the societies, communities, or groups we study without succumbing to our own ethnocentric perspectives. To do this, Spradley reasoned, like most ethnoscientists, that language was among the most powerful ways to discover how others map the world around them, generate behavior, and articulate and interpret experience.[38]

I used Spradley's model in my first ethnographic projects as an undergraduate college student. I found that members of Narcotics Anonymous used words and expressions that are particular to their shared culture of drug addiction and recovery. Words like "being addicted," "being clean," or "Let Go and Let God" had specific meanings to them. By interviewing my consultants about these expressions, I was able to better understand how these expressions were specific to *their* experience and in turn how these expressions reflected and shaped a larger system of meaning around which drug addiction and recovery revolved. Thus, language did not just provide me a window into drug addiction and recovery from their point of view; importantly, it *also* provided me the categories on which to base the writing of my ethnography. Instead of organizing the ethnography around my own presumptions about the "parts of culture," I organized it around the categories that my *consultants* used in their speech.

In its day, this approach to doing and writing ethnography distinguished ethnoscience as the "new ethnography."[39] Around the same time that ethnoscience was dubbed the "new ethnography," another approach to studying and writing about culture would powerfully inform how anthropologists would write ethnography (in fact, much more so than ethnoscience). It was called **symbolic anthropology**, and it also emerged in the 1950s and continued through the 1970s. It was similar to ethnoscience in its focus on individual action within culture, but it also focused on how people actively negotiate cultural symbols—that is, cultural expressions (both verbal and nonverbal) to which people assign meaning. Instead of just focusing on experience as articulated by language, symbolic anthropologists focused on how experience was also articulated in public rituals or ceremonies (like national holidays), key symbols (like a nation's flag), or cultural metaphors (like a national pastime).[40] How people *negotiated* experience through these symbols was the primary concern for symbolic anthropologists.[41] And symbolic anthropologists wrote their ethnographies in a way that reflected this—an entire ethnographic text might be based on a single holiday, a nation's flag, or a national pastime (or the interrelations of all three).[42] The point, however, was not to focus entirely on the symbol itself; the heart of the matter concerned how the symbol points us to deeper cultural meanings defined by and negotiated among people (in both spoken and nonspoken communication). American movies, for example, have a lot to tell us about American culture. They have very similar story lines because they carefully (or not so carefully) play on key elements of American culture—our assumptions about romantic love, for example, or our deep cultural attachment to the conflict between good and evil. By focusing on American movies as ethnography, we can learn much about American culture: how people interpret and negotiate these cultural symbols and how these expressions in turn affect the ways people think about and act on the meaning of their lives.[43]

Symbolic anthropology is important for us to consider because one symbolic anthropologist, Clifford Geertz, almost single-handedly set into motion a change in the way ethnographers would approach the writing of ethnography as primarily an interpretive endeavor.[44] Geertz argued that cultural forms like a public ritual, a nation's flag, or a single holiday are symbolic systems around which people essentially build cultural stories, stories that people regularly engage to *tell themselves something about themselves*. Let's return

Baseball is not just an athletic activity; the sport has also become a powerful symbol that points to deeper cultural meanings. Photo by Danny Gawlowski.

to American movies—they're perfect examples. In our movies, we extol over and over again a particular idea about, for instance, the nature and consequences of romantic love, and we never seem to tire of it.

Given that cultural or symbolic forms are essentially culturally based stories, Geertz argued that the method of writing ethnography should proceed with this assumption in mind. Understanding culture is like reading a book. Both books and cultural systems are composed of symbols that are *read* and *interpreted*. "The culture of a people is an ensemble of texts . . . ," wrote Geertz in 1973, "which the anthropologist strains to read over the shoulders of those to whom they properly belong."[45] Ethnographers, Geertz implied, should see themselves as interpretivists, or translators of culture.[46] And because any cultural form can have a plethora of interpretations and can be "read" from many different viewpoints, Geertz added that ethnography, and thus ethnology, was better cast as a kind of "dialogue"—a metaphor for ethnography that seemed much better suited to the humanities than to the natural, physical, or lab sciences.[47]

In making this argument, Geertz cast Boas's "cultural relativity" and Malinowski's "native point of view" in a new light and thus inched ethnography into the realm of literature and the interpretive arts. He opened ethnography up to a much broader range of writing methods and approaches. By the 1980s and 1990s, many ethnographers had pushed Geertz's model, called **interpretive anthropology**, even further toward literature and art: they began to experiment with traditional modes of ethnographic writing, experimentations that sought to represent more fully the complexities of both doing and writing ethnography.[48] Anthropologist and ethnographer Barbara Tedlock, for example, combined traditional ethnography with literary approaches to "the autobiography" and "the novel." In her ethnography *The Beautiful and the Dangerous: Dialogues with the Zuni Indians*, she allows the story about her friendship with her Zuni hosts to frame the narrative much as would an autobiography or novel. Instead of approaching culture as a clearly bounded system, she takes us along her own process of coming to know Zuni people over several years. Tedlock leads the reader to understand that coming to know another group or community is a process, one ultimately formulated by the intimate relationships between the ethnographer and the ethnographer's hosts.[49]

Such experimentation in representing culture as a meaningful, symbolic system would eventually come to dominate ethnographic writing. Indeed, this **experimental ethnography** is in many ways still with us today.[50] But importantly, this experimentation has given rise to a wide variety of forms. Take collaborative ethnography, which I mentioned earlier in this chapter. In this approach, ethnographers and consultants may work together to define research questions, outline the trajectory of a particular study, and even cointerpret the research results as they emerge. Ethnographers have experimented with this participatory method (as it is sometimes called) for many years, but unlike other participatory approaches, collaborative ethnography also involves consultants in the process of writing ethnography. As such, the approach mobilizes the diverse experiences, perspectives, and interests of both ethnographers and consultants to collaboratively research and write ethnography.[51] For example, when I was an associate professor of anthropology at Ball State University (BSU), I developed an interest in the famous "Middletown" studies of Muncie, Indiana (where BSU is located), first initiated by Robert and Helen Lynd in their 1929 book *Middletown: A Study in Modern American Culture*. My interest eventually coincided with that of local African American activist and former Indiana state legislator Hurley Goodall, who was interested in redressing the absence of African American experience in the original Middletown study as well as in subsequent studies of Muncie. If Muncie somehow represented a typical

American city—as some have claimed of "Middletown USA"—then why, asked Goodall, were African Americans absent from that story?[52]

A collaborative museum exhibit, community-university theater production, and historic photograph project engendered further discussion about these issues between Goodall, Muncie community members, myself, folklorist Elizabeth Campbell, and other BSU faculty and students—namely, about how a collaborative ethnographic approach might amend this problem in the Middletown literature.[53] Our discussions eventually led to the collaborative ethnography *The Other Side of Middletown* (a good deal of which was written by undergraduate students in collaboration with Muncie community advisers).[54] As described in the book, faculty, students, and community members together explore the undocumented history of Muncie's black community, the enduring legacy of race and racism in small-town America, and the many facets of contemporary African American experience in Middletown, including—as in the original 1929 study—work and home life, schooling, leisure, and religious and community activities. Within this framework, the ethnography unfolds as a collaboratively inscribed conversation about race relations past and present, engaged by both black and white students, faculty, and community members—all of whom are struggling together to understand the deeper experiential complexities of race in Muncie, in particular, and more generally in America.[55]

Student ethnographer Michelle Anderson discusses the evolving Other Side of Middletown *text with community adviser Dolores Rhinehart. Photo by Danny Gawlowski.*

ANTHROPOLOGY HERE AND NOW

You can access many of the actual interviews conducted by the students who wrote *The Other Side of Middletown* via Ball State University's Digital Media Repository, posted at libx.bsu.edu/cdm/landingpage/collection/MidOrHis (click on "Other Side of Middletown Oral Histories" to access the audio recordings and their accompanying transcripts).

CHECK IT OUT!

Because *The Other Side of Middletown* partnership embraced a very particular dialogue, about a very particular set of issues, among a very particular group of participants, this individual collaborative ethnography is rather unique in its form. This is not unlike most collaborative ethnographies: they reflect the contours of very specific experiments and consequently can be, like other experimental forms, widely diverse. Given this, though, collaborative ethnography and other experimental approaches to writing ethnography share basic assumptions about the interpretive approach to culture as ushered in by Geertz.

By challenging anthropologists to view ethnography through an interpretive lens, then, Geertz and experimental ethnographers since have reminded us that whether we are the ethnographer or the reader of ethnography, we always approach the ethnography through our own experience. This is the base from which we ultimately interpret our own and others' experiences. Writing and reading ethnography allows us to broaden our interpretive lens by understanding others' points of view, but ultimately we—the ethnographer and the reader of ethnography—are part of the process of interpretation.[56] Simply put, from doing *and* reading ethnography, we can also gain an understanding of ourselves—as individuals and as societies—which brings me to the second key purpose or goal of ethnography.

Geertz and experimental ethnographers were not the first to make this point, of course. Indeed, the second goal of ethnography that I mentioned earlier, to teach us something about ourselves, has always been implicit to the goals and purposes of ethnography. One has only to recall the implications behind Malinowski's previously cited quote: "In grasping the essential outlook of others, with reverence and real understanding . . . we cannot but help widening our own."[57] It was one of Boas's students, Margaret Mead, who made this second purpose of ethnography explicit in the writing of ethnography.[58]

In 1928, Mead wrote *Coming of Age in Samoa*, an ethnography about adolescence among the Samoans in the South Pacific. She approached Samoan adolescence much as Boas approached the Inuit or Malinowski approached the Trobrianders, but, importantly, Mead added a whole section to her ethnography to suggest what understanding adolescence in Samoa should mean for Americans.[59]

Up until Mead's study, scientists and laypeople alike generally assumed that adolescence was primarily a biological experience; thus, it followed, the experience of adolescence was the same everywhere. By this logic, every human teenager could expect to go through a turbulent period wrought by rapid changes in the body. Yet Mead found that Samoan teenagers had a very different experience with adolescence. Instead of a turbulent time characterized by dread and discomfort, Samoan adolescence was something to which both children and parents looked forward. Mead thus illustrated that adolescence was a cultural construction; although the biological changes were similar between Americans and Samoans, the adolescent experience certainly was not. Following Boas, she argued that the behavior Americans associated with adolescence was not biologically based but rather specific to American culture.

Mead directed the book at Americans, particularly educators and parents. She argued that because culture was learned, Americans could learn to deal with adolescence differently than they had before. If the Samoans could experience adolescence with ease, so could Americans. Adolescence did not have to be a turbulent, rebellious passage from childhood to adulthood. We could reshape it because it was learned and shaped by culture.[60]

Mead's book was widely read in the United States through the 1950s and 1960s. Like other ethnographies, her work illustrated cultural diversity and the power of culture in people's lives, but, importantly, her ethnography also represented an explicit critique of American society. The way Mead chose to describe culture placed ethnography within a genre of literature that sought directly to challenge Americans' understandings of themselves—a technique often called **cultural critique**. It was as much about Americans as it was about Samoans.[61]

Mead's book was harshly criticized for overstating the case that the adolescence experience was completely culturally determined.[62] But both her approach to writing (especially writing to an audience outside the discipline
of anthropology) and her approach to cultural critique (especially of the
ethnographer's "home" society, wherever situated) have profoundly affected
ethnographic writing; this is especially so today, as ethnographers seek ways
to articulate a larger and more relevant cultural critique to a broader readership.[63] Indeed, although cultural critique is not always an explicit purpose of
each ethnography, as it was in Mead's *Coming of Age in Samoa*, it remains at
least implicit in the writing of each. For example, in my first ethnography,
The Power of Kiowa Song, I offer a cultural critique of prevalent American
perceptions of Native Americans to establish a foundation for exploring the
power of Kiowa song from the viewpoint of my Kiowa consultants. I describe
how my own teenage experience in the Boy Scouts of America and American Indian hobbyism (a popular movement involving mostly white Anglo-
Americans focused on Native American dancing and singing) served as the
backdrop for my entrance into the field of anthropology in my early twenties.
The assumptions that I carried into the Kiowa community as a result of my
Boy Scout and hobbyist experience differed profoundly from the way my
Kiowa consultants lived and interpreted their own lives. I approached Kiowa
people with a whole set of complex assumptions about American Indians,
assumptions that had much more to do with me and my background than
with Native American experience. I presented this narrative, alongside critical
dialogues with Kiowa consultants, to advance a cultural critique of this nearly
universal problem in our society, a problem that truly prevents most Americans from understanding Native American cultural diversity on deep levels.
For many Kiowas, I found out, those deeper levels had little to do with popular ideas of Indians, revolving instead around understanding the importance
and power of language, narrative, and song in contemporary Kiowa culture.[64]

ETHNOGRAPHY'S LESSON: WHAT'S IT GOOD FOR?
In this chapter, I suggested the importance of noticing and understanding the
complexities of culture. While we may appreciate the concept of culture itself,
the study of culture is incomplete without ethnography. In that ethnography
struggles to present the "native's point of view" (albeit imperfectly) from a diversity of locales, perspectives, and writing approaches, it ultimately presents

Cultural critique is an important part of much ethnography. In The Power of Kiowa Song, *for example, I argue that much of the imagery surrounding Indians centers on how Americans privilege what they can see—and what they expect to see—over other senses. Indeed, many Americans continue to found their knowledge of Indians on reified observations rather than on engaging the experience of Native American communities through other means. In the Kiowa community of southwestern Oklahoma, for example, the power of what can be heard—particularly language, narrative, and song—often takes precedence over what can be seen. Individuals entrusted to disseminate this Kiowa "world of sound," like singers (shown here), can be thus enormously important to the community. Photo by author.*

us with "basic data" of how people actually share and negotiate meaning in their everyday lives. Consequently, it teaches us something about ourselves.

In this way, ethnography's approach is distinctive: we learn about ourselves as we learn about others; conversely, we learn about others through learning about ourselves. When all is told, ethnography extends to us the actual complexities of human life—our own and others—transforming perceptions of one another (based on passing intuitions and ethnocentrism) to deeper understandings of one another (based on the philosophy of knowledge that we call "culture"). Melinda Bollar Wagner sums it up: "Ethnography," she writes, "promote[s] understanding among people by creating a description of one culture that will let members of another culture understand it better. Cardboard cutout stereotypes of a culture and its people give way to more well-rounded portraits, complete with contradictions and inconsistencies."[65]

NOTES

1. For a more sophisticated discussion of these processes, see, for example, George W. Stocking, *The Ethnographer's Magic and Other Essays in the History of Anthropology* (Madison: University of Wisconsin Press, 1992).

2. Bronislaw Malinowski, *Argonauts of the Western Pacific* (New York: Dutton, 1922), 25.

3. Ibid., 24.

4. See James L. Peacock, *The Anthropological Lens: Harsh Light, Soft Focus* (Cambridge: Cambridge University Press, 1986), 106.

5. Malinowski, *Argonauts of the Western Pacific*, 15.

6. Ibid., 515.

7. Ibid., 518.

8. Philippe Bourgois, *In Search of Respect: Selling Crack in El Barrio* (Cambridge: Cambridge University Press, 1995), 12.

9. Melinda Bollar Wagner, *God's Schools: Choice and Compromise in American Society* (New Brunswick, NJ: Rutgers University Press, 1990), 218.

10. Ibid., 218–19.

11. James Eugene Todd, personal communication with author, July 25, 2005.

12. American Anthropological Association, *Revised Principles of Professional Responsibility* (Washington, DC: Author, 1990).

13. Wagner, *God's Schools*, 220.

14. Bourgois, *In Search of Respect*, 21.

15. Ibid., 22.

16. Wagner, *God's Schools*, 220–21.

17. Melinda Bollar Wagner, *Metaphysics in Midwestern America* (Columbus: Ohio State University Press, 1983), 191–92.

18. James P. Spradley and David W. McCurdy, *Conformity and Conflict: Readings in Cultural Anthropology*, 8th ed. (New York: HarperCollins, 1994), 16.

19. Wagner, *God's Schools*, 221.

20. Ibid., 221–28.

21. Dorothy Ayers Counts and David R. Counts, *Over the Next Hill: An Ethnography of RVing Seniors in North America* (Toronto: Broadview Press, 1996), 1–14.

22. See Luke E. Lassiter, *The Power of Kiowa Song: A Collaborative Ethnography* (Tucson: University of Arizona Press, 1998), especially 17–65.

23. Wagner, *God's Schools*, 221ff.

24. Ibid., 229.

25. Ibid.

26. See Clifford Geertz, "'From the Native's Point of View': On the Nature of Anthropological Understanding," in *Local Knowledge: Further Essays in Interpretive Anthropology* (New York: Basic Books, 1983), 55–70.

27. Cf. David Hufford, "Ambiguity and the Rhetoric of Belief," *Keystone Folklore* 21, no. 1 (1976): 11–24.

28. Marjorie Shostak, *Nisa: The Life and Words of a !Kung Woman* (New York: Vintage Books, 1981).

29. See, for example, H. Russell Bernard, *Research Methods in Anthropology: Qualitative and Quantitative Approaches*, 4th ed. (Walnut Creek, CA: AltaMira Press, 2005).

30. See, for example, Luke Eric Lassiter, *The Chicago Guide to Collaborative Ethnography* (Chicago: University of Chicago Press, 2005).

31. For a more in-depth discussion, see Luke Eric Lassiter, "Collaborative Ethnography and Public Anthropology," *Current Anthropology* 46, no. 1 (2004): 83–97.

32. George E. Marcus and Michael M. J. Fischer, *Anthropology as Cultural Critique: An Experimental Moment in the Human Sciences* (Chicago: University of Chicago Press, 1986).

33. See chapter 7 and David Hufford, "Traditions of Disbelief," *New York Folklore Quarterly* 8 (1982): 47–55. See also the following notes on ethnoscience.

34. See Edward Said, *Orientalism* (New York: Vintage Books, 1979).

35. See, for example, Ward H. Goodenough, "Componential Analysis," *Science* 156 (1967): 1203–9.

36. See Kenneth L. Pike, "Emic and Etic Standpoints for the Description of Behavior," in *Language in Relation to a Unified Theory of the Structure of Human Behavior* (Glendale, CA: Summer Institute of Linguistics, 1954), 8–28. Cf. Robbins Burling, "Linguistics and Ethnographic Description," *American Anthropologist* 71, no. 4 (1969): 817–27; Charles O. Frake, "The Ethnographic Study of Cognitive Systems," in *Anthropology and Human Behavior* (Washington, DC: Anthropological Society of Washington, 1962), 72–93; James P. Spradley, ed., *Culture and Cognition: Rules, Maps, and Plans* (San Francisco: Chandler, 1972); Stephen Tyler, ed., *Cognitive Anthropology* (New York: Holt, 1969); William Sturtevant, "Studies in Ethnoscience," *American Anthropologist* 66, no. 3, pt. 2 (1964): 99–131; and Oswald Werner, "Ethnoscience," *Annual Review of Anthropology* 1 (1972): 271–308.

37. James P. Spradley, *The Ethnographic Interview* (New York: Holt, Rinehart and Winston, 1979), 11.

38. Ibid.

39. See William Sturtevant, "Studies in Ethnoscience." But see Marvin Harris, "Emics, Etics, and the New Ethnography," in *The Rise of Anthropological Theory* (New York: Thomas Y. Crowell, 1968), 568–604.

40. See, for example, Sherry Ortner, "On Key Symbols," *American Anthropologist* 75, no. 5 (1973): 1338–46.

41. See, for example, Victor Turner, *Schism and Continuity in an African Society: A Study of Ndembu Village Life* (Manchester, UK: Manchester University Press, 1957).

42. See, for example, William Aren, "Professional Football: An American Symbol and Ritual," in *The American Dimension: Cultural Myths and Social Realities* (Sherman Oaks, CA: Alfred Publishing, 1976).

43. For fuller discussions and examples of symbolic approaches to culture, see Herbert Blumer, *Symbolic Interactionism: Perspective and Method* (Englewood Cliffs, NJ: Prentice Hall, 1969); Clifford Geertz, *The Religion of Java* (Chicago: University of Chicago Press, 1960); James L. Peacock, *Rites of Modernization: Symbolic and Social Aspects of Indonesian Proletarian Drama* (Chicago: University of Chicago Press, 1968); and Victor Turner, *Dramas, Fields, and Metaphors: Symbolic Action in Human Society* (Ithaca, NY: Cornell University Press, 1974).

44. Clifford Geertz, *The Interpretation of Cultures* (New York: Basic Books, 1973).

45. Ibid., 452.

46. Ibid., 3–30.

47. Geertz, "'From the Native's Point of View,'" 55–70.

48. See Marcus and Fischer, *Anthropology as Cultural Critique.*

49. Barbara Tedlock, *The Beautiful and Dangerous: Dialogues with the Zuni Indians* (New York: Viking, 1992). Admittedly, I am glossing the larger critique levied against Geertz, especially his evasion of how natives of a culture actually articulated meaning to themselves. See, for example, James Clifford and George E. Marcus, eds., *Writing Culture: The Poetics and Politics of Ethnography* (Berkeley: University of California Press, 1986).

50. See George E. Marcus and Michael M. J. Fischer, *Anthropology as Cultural Critique: An Experimental Moment in the Human Sciences*, 2nd ed. (Chicago: University of Chicago Press, 1999).

51. For a discussion on how collaborative ethnography fits within larger participatory approaches, see Luke Eric Lassiter, "Moving Past Public Anthropology and Doing Collaborative Research," in *Careers in Applied Anthropology: Advice from Practitioners and Academics*, ed. Carla Guerron-Montero (Washington, DC: American Anthropological Association, 2008), 70–87.

52. For a more in-depth discussion of the evolution of *The Other Side of Middletown* project, see Luke Eric Lassiter, "Introduction: The Story of a

Collaborative Project," in *The Other Side of Middletown: Exploring Muncie's African American Community*, ed. Luke Eric Lassiter, Hurley Goodall, Elizabeth Campbell, and Michelle Natasya Johnson (Walnut Creek, CA: AltaMira Press, 2004), 1–24.

53. Ibid., 4–5. See also Lee Papa and Luke Eric Lassiter, "The Muncie Race Riots of 1967, Representing Community Memory through Public Performance, and Collaborative Ethnography between Faculty, Students and the Local Community," *Journal of Contemporary Ethnography* 32, no. 2 (2003): 147–66.

54. For a student retrospective of the project, see Michelle Anderson, Sarah Bricker, Eric Efaw, Michelle Johnson, Carrie Kissel, and Anne Kraemer, "Whose Book Is It Anyway? Challenges of the Other Side of Middletown Project," *Anthropology News* 45, no. 7 (2004): 18–19.

55. This brief description is excerpted, in part, from Luke Eric Lassiter, "2005 Margaret Mead Award Remarks" (paper presented at the sixty-sixth annual meeting of the Society for Applied Anthropology, Vancouver, British Columbia, March 2006). See www.sfaa.net/mead/lassiter.html.

56. See Geertz, *The Interpretation of Cultures*, and *Local Knowledge*. See also James Clifford, *The Predicament of Culture: Twentieth-Century Ethnography, Literature, and Art* (Cambridge, MA: Harvard University Press, 1988); Clifford and Marcus, *Writing Culture*; and Renato Rosaldo, *Culture and Truth: The Remaking of Social Analysis* (Boston: Beacon Press, 1993).

57. Malinowski, *Argonauts of the Western Pacific*, 518.

58. Marcus and Fischer, *Anthropology as Cultural Critique*, 1–16.

59. Margaret Mead, *Coming of Age in Samoa* (New York: Morrow, 1928).

60. Ibid.

61. Marcus and Fischer, *Anthropology as Cultural Critique*, 1–16.

62. See Derek Freeman, *Margaret Mead and Samoa: The Making and Unmaking of an Anthropological Myth* (Cambridge, MA: Harvard University Press, 1983).

63. See, for example, George E. Marcus, *Critical Anthropology Now: Unexpected Contexts, Shifting Constituencies, Changing Agendas* (Santa Fe, NM: School of American Research Press, 1999).

64. See Lassiter, *The Power of Kiowa Song*, especially part I.

65. Wagner, *God's Schools*, 217.

ETHNOLOGY: SOME HUMAN ISSUES

4

History, Change, and Adaptation

On the Roots of Our World System

Recall that in chapter 2, I suggested that while anthropologists may study an individual society, community, or group—like families in Japan or Protestant churches in the southern United States—their ultimate purpose is to advance a deeper understanding of larger cultural issues, issues like race and ethnicity; or religion; or politics and economics; or kinship, marriage, and family; or ecology; or gender; or the nature of violence, conflict, and peace. When it comes to the ethnological study of culture, these are the larger human issues in which anthropologists are ultimately interested. This is because the similarities of culture that bridge the human experience are best understood through comparison, which highlights larger human patterns and relationships.

Now in part II of this book, I initiate a discussion about the larger realm of human cultural issues. We can compare these issues cross-culturally—an approach, you'll remember, that is built on ethnography. In the next three chapters, I plan to introduce three of the many human cultural issues that anthropologists explore: gender, marriage/family/kinship, and religion. But first I need to clarify the larger context within which all human issues reside: a larger, evolving **world system**.

We all know that our world is becoming smaller every day, that we live in an incredibly complex and multifaceted world, and that **globalization** is a fact of twenty-first-century life. But I'd like to tell the story from an anthropological point of view, one that takes into account the historical trajectory of this world system, and one that includes a consideration of all the world's

Scene from a Beijing Walmart. Photo by Danny Gawlowski.

societies that have lived within it, both past and present. Many anthropologists argue that the world system as we know it today, including its politics and economics, is a larger, evolving world culture. This will be our theoretical point of departure.[1]

IN THE BEGINNING: ADAPTATION, CULTURE, AND HUMAN SUBSISTENCE

The culture of the world system in which we live today springs from events that were set into motion ten thousand to twelve thousand years ago with the development of **agriculture**. Although our modern world is couched within the more recent history of **industrialism** and **capitalism**, the seeds of the human problems that we face today—including overpopulation, poverty, hunger, inequality between rich and poor, and accelerated ethnic conflict—were planted long ago. But I'm getting ahead of myself.[2]

To give you an idea of where I'm going with this, I plan to discuss human adaptation before and after agriculture, the ramifications of a settled life (particularly the interdependence created by economic trade as a result), the constant rise and fall of complex civilizations, the problem of growing populations, and, finally, how the rise of our current world system can be understood within this cultural framework, a framework that is still evolving.

My intention is to offer you the larger cultural context in which all the world's people now live. We must understand and appreciate this larger cultural context before we start on our more intensive and particularistic study of gender, marriage/family/kinship, and religion.

Like all good anthropological stories, the story about the world system is a story of constant fluctuation and change; it's a story about biological and cultural adaptation, selection, and reproduction. Like all other living organisms, human beings have continuously evolved physical and behavioral characteristics that allow them to survive and reproduce. And, like all other living organisms, our past and present relationship with the physical environment is mediated by the complex evolutionary workings of natural selection, variation, and other biological processes (see chapter 1). But unlike most other living organisms, the relationship between human beings and the environment is also mediated by another process: culture.

Recall for a moment the definition of culture offered in chapter 2: culture, in an anthropological sense, is a shared and negotiated system of meaning informed by knowledge that people learn and put into practice by interpreting experience and generating behavior. Although I have used, and will again use, this definition of culture broadly in the upcoming chapters, for now it is sufficient to say that people, in a general sense, use knowledge that they have learned from their experience in the physical environment to survive, and they pass this knowledge through social means to succeeding generations. Indeed, as human beings, we are absolutely dependent on this culturally based process. Infants are not born with the knowledge of how to hunt or how to build a fire or how to cook; they are not born with the knowledge of how to converse, read, or use a computer; they are not born with the knowledge of how to treat illness or heal disease. No, the human *collective* (in a general sense) remembers this knowledge for survival. Without it, we perish. To survive, we reproduce, change, and add to this knowledge, passing it from generation to generation. Technically, this process is called **cultural reproduction** (as compared to biological reproduction), and it appears to have emerged as an adaptation in human evolution around two million years ago among early ancestors of modern *Homo sapiens* (that's another story, however).[3] Since then, culture has been that which, like natural selection, mediates our relationship with the surrounding environment—no matter who we are. It is the middleman, the matchmaker, the liaison between us and the surrounding environment.

Culture is not just adaptive to human survival; it also generates maladaptive practices. For example, mountaintop removal (shown here)—literally, the removal of mountaintops to access coal—has brought about devastating and irreversible damage to both the environment and the local communities surrounding mountaintop removal sites. Photo by Vivian Stockman, courtesy of Ohio Valley Environmental Coalition.

Of course, culture is not always adaptive. Culture often produces and reproduces maladaptive practices, practices that threaten survival rather than enhance it (one need only think of environmental pollution). Generally, however, we use culture to adapt, to reproduce, and to survive in a way different from any other living creature. With culture, we have enormous flexibility (over the long haul) to adapt, reproduce, and change. Indeed, we have learned to adapt to nearly every possible climate; we now live and reproduce in almost every part of the globe. And this is where the real meat of my story is found.

GATHERING, HUNTING, AND MOVING: ON FORAGING

The earliest known cultural adaptation began with what anthropologists call **foraging**, which may have begun as long ago as 1.5 million years—well before the emergence of *Homo sapiens*.[4] In cooperating groups, people gathered undomesticated plants and hunted wild animals (including those that swim and fly). They lived in small nonsettled groups (usually composed of fewer than a few dozen) moving from place to place. Men were usually but not exclusively the hunters (hunting both small and large game), and women were usually but not exclusively the gatherers (collecting wild plant food such as nuts, berries, or insects). The foraging diet consisted primarily of gathered foods; meat only supplemented this diet. This is why some anthropologists prefer to call this strategy "gathering and hunting" instead of the more popular nomenclature "hunting and gathering."[5]

It might sound like a bleak existence, but what anthropologists know about foraging may surprise you. Foraging is the most stable form of adaptation ever practiced by human beings. In fact, up until ten thousand to twelve thousand years ago, the entire world's population consisted of gatherers and hunters. Today, very few modern foragers remain, often because of forced settlement by modern **nation-states**.[6]

Much of what we know about foraging comes from intensive ethnographic study over the past several decades with these modern foragers. One group whom anthropologists have studied intensively since the 1950s are the !Kung or Ju/'hoansi (which means "real people") of southern Africa. The !Kung are part of a much larger population called the San, who today number well over ninety thousand, and although nearly all !Kung San were foragers in the 1950s, few hunt and gather full time today.[7] Nevertheless, one of the first things that shocked the world about the !Kung's foraging way of life was how healthy it was. Most scholars and laypeople alike had imagined gathering and hunting to be a nasty, brutish, day-to-day struggle. But, as it turns out, people like the !Kung had equally as good or even better diets than most modern Americans. Consider the following.

Richard Lee, an ethnographer who closely followed and measured the !Kung diet in the 1960s, concluded that "[m]eat and mongongo nuts comprised the major part of the diet, contributing 31 and 28 percent of the weight respectively. About 20 species of roots, melons, gums, bulbs, and dried fruits . . . made up the remaining 41 percent of the diet. In all, the work of the Ju/'hoansi made available a daily ration of 2,355 calories of food energy and 96.3 grams of protein to each person. . . . The caloric levels were more than adequate to support the Dobe population and to allow the people to live vigorous, active lives without losing weight."[8]

ANTHROPOLOGY HERE AND NOW

The lives of San peoples—today living in countries in southern Africa such as Namibia and Botswana—have changed dramatically since the times when they were extensively studied as foragers in the mid-twentieth century. Many anthropologists who studied and worked directly with the San have also worked as advocates during these transition times, helping to develop projects that directly benefit the San and other indigenous peoples of the region. One such organization is the Kalahari Peoples Fund, which has launched a variety of projects, ranging from water and land development to linking San people with computers and the Internet. You can learn more about the organization and their various projects at www.kalaharipeoples.org.

CHECK IT OUT!

Another thing that shocked many people about the !Kung and other foragers was the relatively small amount of work they put into getting what they needed to survive comfortably. This was another thing that Lee studied closely. On average, all the work that men did in a week—including hunting, making tools, and "housework" (i.e., as Lee writes, "food preparation, butchery, drawing water and gathering firewood, washing utensils, and cleaning the living space")—averaged to 44.5 hours; all the work that women did—including gathering, making tools, and "housework"—averaged to 40.1 hours. The combined average for both men and women was 42.3 hours.[9] When you compare this to our own work lives, in which we now work forty to sixty hours per week (if not more) just at our workplace, not including housework (like cutting the grass or cleaning the bathroom or repairing things), the foraging lifestyle of the !Kung begins to look rather undemanding, doesn't it? In fact, it is (or was). Lee reported that the vast majority of the !Kung's time was spent in leisure: eating, resting, playing with the kids, and visiting. "In summary," wrote Lee, "we have learned from the study of Ju/'hoan subsistence that despite the popular stereotype [of foragers], the Ju do not have to work very hard to make a living. In assuming that their life must be a constant struggle for existence, we succumb to the ethnocentric notions that place our own

Western adaptation at the pinnacle of success and make all others second or third best. Judged by these standards, the Ju are bound to fail. But judged on their own terms, they do pretty well for themselves."[10]

When compared with dozens of other studies on foragers, it seems that what Lee learned about the !Kung was also true for other foragers.[11] We now know that, in general, people (both individuals and societies) work today far more than we ever have. This was true fifty years ago; it also seemed to be true hundreds of years ago and even thousands of years ago. With the emergence of agriculture, people started working more and more to get what they needed to survive, and the trend hasn't stopped. But I'm getting ahead of myself again. Back to foraging. It may surprise us that the !Kung and other foragers did not work as much as we might think to get what they needed to survive comfortably, and, in addition, they were amazingly healthy. It may surprise us even more that they did not suffer disease on the same levels as did people in the Middle Ages or during the industrial revolution or even in today's world. Their secret was mobility. Although there were perhaps thousands of San people, for example, they never lived in one spot as a single population (until very recently). Recall that one of the characteristics of a foraging way of life is that people live in small, nonsettled, mobile groups, moving from place to place. This was the case for the !Kung San: they lived as small mobile groups gathering and hunting and did not move about as one giant mass. So because the !Kung—like most foragers—never gathered as a population in one locale for any extended period of time, any one disease could not easily flourish and spread. Although a communicable disease could affect one or more of these small mobile groups, wiping out a few dozen people, the disease could not spread to the population as a whole because of the demographic and geographic distance between the smaller, mobile populations.[12] Anthropologists have a name for this type of organization—that is, for foragers who live in small unsettled mobile groups. They call it a **band.**

While the band is often associated with small, mobile, foraging groups, the band also describes a particular social, political, and economic organization. When people are organized in this way—moving about in small mobile groups, like the !Kung once did—certain social, political, and economic patterns manifest repeatedly. Interestingly, in almost every foraging society known to anthropologists, social, political, and economic relations have very similar characteristics.[13] Consider the following three patterns.

First, in a social sense, these bands are not haphazard collections of a few dozen people; they are almost always organized around **kinship**. That is, everyone in a particular band is related to almost everyone else either through birth or marriage. Social ties *between* bands, however, are also based on kinship. Men and women can marry outside their own band, for example, because they may be too closely related to those in their own band. This cements the ties between bands, each of which is connected to other bands through kinship ties.[14]

Second, politically speaking, leadership in bands is very loosely defined. Leadership decisions are most often made by elder members of the band (usually men). Beyond gender, the leadership role is determined by age, individual skill, and accumulated respect; it is not predetermined (through birth, or royalty, for example), as it can be in other societies. Because the band is relatively egalitarian, any elder can be a leader. (There are exceptions to this rule, but rarely do we find, for instance, the passing of a leadership role from father to son, as we find in agricultural societies.) While a band leader may make decisions about where to camp or when to hunt, these same leaders have no *real* power: they cannot make others follow orders against their will. In case of conflict, any person can leave one band and join any other band, feeling right at home with close or distant relatives. Among most foraging bands like the !Kung, the social and political makeup of any one band is constantly changing because of this fluidity of people.[15]

Third, and finally, the overall health and survival of a band heavily depends on a particular kind of economic exchange. What I mean by *economic* here is that which concerns how resources are *obtained* and *distributed* between and among people. Within the band, all resources that become available to any one individual (hunted meat, gathered fruits) pass through a system called **reciprocity**, the exchange of goods and services between two or more people without the use of money.

Let me explain exactly what I mean by this. Among foragers like the !Kung, when all the men in a particular band go hunting, everyone understands that not everyone will bring back a kill. Whoever does bring back a kill must share it with the entire group. To put it personally, if I don't bring back a kill this time, my brother may, and my family and I will get some of it; when I bring back a kill, I also share it with everyone.

We could say that the property of any one person belongs to the whole band. But this reciprocity is not some cool "commune thing." It's a little more complicated than that. In some foraging groups, for example, sharing is moderated by closeness to certain relatives—that is, the more closely related you are to me, the better selection of meat you might get from my kill. But, as in so many other things, what goes around comes around, and the sharing tends to even out over the long haul in most foraging societies. Thus, reciprocity is a system of exchange that lies at the very heart of the way a foraging band survives. Without this exchange of goods and services (and the constant expectation of reciprocation), the social and political system of the band breaks down, along with everything else—including well-balanced diets and short workweeks. I need to point out that reciprocity works in a variety of ways and that foragers can also engage in other forms of reciprocal exchange, like trade. Of course, all humans—including you and me—engage in reciprocity all the time (as when we invite someone over for dinner and then they invite us), but, importantly, foragers depend on reciprocity for their very survival.[16]

THE DOMESTICATION OF PLANTS AND ANIMALS

About ten thousand to twelve thousand years ago, a few human groups began to abandon the exclusive use of foraging and to take up the practice of domesticating plants and animals for food. I write *the practice of domesticating* because everything we know about foragers points to the probability that humans most likely knew about **domestication** long before but chose not to practice it. For example, foragers like the !Kung have apparently known about farming for hundreds, if not thousands, of years from their contacts with settled peoples. But they never took it up. After all, why should they take the time to grow food when they could just gather it? It takes more effort to grow your own food than to gather and hunt for it.[17]

Why *did* foragers start domesticating plants and animals for food? A good many anthropologists believe that it was not until humans were forced to start settling—forced by the need of more food to feed growing populations. Remember that humans have always been, in almost all cases, in contact with other humans; we know of no group that has been isolated from any other group long enough to be considered a completely isolated population. As foraging bands grew larger and larger, they needed more and more land on which to hunt and gather. But these lands were also being used by other foragers. As foragers moved from camp to camp, hunting and gathering on vast expanses of land, competition for land and resources increased, and people started settling down to raise their own food. Although it took more work, the returns were high. A population growing crops, for example, could feed more people on less total land than that needed by foragers. More food for more people, however, did not necessarily mean better-quality food for higher numbers of people. There was, in the end, a price to be paid for this higher production.[18] But more on that later.

The domestication of plants and animals probably first emerged as a way to subsidize foraging. Anthropologists identify two different but closely related adaptive strategies that did just this: **horticulture** (or *swidden agriculture*) and **pastoralism** (or *herding*). The former involves the small-scale, nonindustrial cultivation of plants (often with crop rotation); the latter involves the domestication, control, and breeding of a specific herd of animals. *Horticulturalists* (people who practice horticulture) and *pastoralists* (people who practice pastoralism) are still found throughout our world, and anthro-

A woman and her twin daughters aerate a manure pile in preparation for spring planting in the mountain village of Walabi in Yunnan Province, China. Photo by Danny Gawlowski.

pologists have studied them extensively, but their numbers, like foragers, continue to dwindle as nation-states seek to integrate horticulturalists and pastoralists (often forcibly) into a larger **political economy**.[19]

Horticulture and pastoralism produced larger populations than did foraging, and some of these populations were settled in one spot for long periods of time. But this did not mean that mobility was suddenly halted. Many pastoralists, for example, have remained nomadic until the present. Economically, horticulturalists and pastoralists depended heavily on reciprocity, just like foraging bands of hunters and gatherers. Politically, kinship still played an important organizational role among both horticulturalists and pastoralists. But beyond these similarities, there were important differences.[20]

Unlike foragers, large families in time and space—called **descent groups** or **lineages**—could (and today, in many cases, still do) have power above and beyond any one individual. While individual leaders had not previously had much power, the descent groups to which they belonged often did. That is, the descent groups extended beyond the boundaries of any one settled village of horticulturalists or any one nomadic pastoralist band. And they could use their dominance to control resources (such as land), influence decisions, or resolve conflict in ways that a band leader working alone could not.[21]

Aside from descent groups, horticulturalists and pastoralists also organized themselves through other political means that transcended individual communities, political organizations that might have little to do with kinship. Religious societies and warrior organizations found among many historical Native American societies are examples: although people might be related in a particular warrior or religious organization, membership was determined by virtue of being a warrior or a particular kind of religious practitioner, not necessarily by being related.[22] Anthropologists call this kind of integration—in which different settled or nomadic communities are united through descent groups or common organizations (like warrior or religious societies)—a **tribe**. We could certainly say that the foraging bands like the !Kung are unified by connections among relatives, but among so-called tribes, the integration of communities can be much more formal than that found in most bands.[23]

AGRICULTURE AND THE EMERGENCE OF THE STATE

Horticulture and pastoralism set the stage for the large-scale domestication and cultivation of crops, an agricultural practice that emerged all over the world: in the Middle East, Eurasia, and Africa between seven thousand five hundred and twelve thousand years ago and in North, Central, and South America well over six thousand five hundred years ago.[24] With this emergence would eventually come the most complex forms of political and economic organizations: **states**.

These states did not just appear out of thin air, however. **Prestates**—which anthropologists often call *chiefdoms* or *kingdoms*—first developed by integrating horticulturalists, pastoralists, or other food producers (such as "intensive fishermen") into a hierarchical political and economic structure with a "chief," "lord," or "king" who occupied the highest position. People were ranked under this centralized leader, who could have considerable power and influence, much more than band or tribal leaders.[25]

An interesting example in the archaeological record is Cahokia, a city of mounds that existed where East St. Louis is located today.[26] Emerging around AD 1050, Cahokia consisted of thousands of people. It had collapsed by 1500, but at its peak, around 1150, more people lived at Cahokia (about twenty thousand people) than in London.[27] Like other chiefdoms, Cahokia was characterized by hierarchy: below the chief, an elite class of subchiefs (who were most likely related to the chief) ruled the leaders of family clans, who, in turn, ruled the commoners.[28] Not only was this ranking nominal, but it was also inscribed into the landscape: atop the largest mound—which, about one hundred feet tall, rose above everything and everyone else in the city—the chief administered Cahokia.[29]

ANTHROPOLOGY HERE AND NOW

You can learn more about Cahokia—its history as well as continuing research on the site—at www.cahokiamounds.org.

CHECK IT OUT!

Economically, the people who lived in prestates like Cahokia practiced reciprocity. But unlike foraging bands or tribal pastoralists or horticulturalists, some people had access to power, prestige, and even resources (such as food) that others did not, primarily because of their rank in the social order. This is

Cahokia Mounds, circa AD 1150. Courtesy Cahokia Mounds State Historic Site. Painting by William R. Iseminger.

where an economic system called **redistribution** comes into play. In this type of economic exchange, resources (e.g., crops at Cahokia) flowed into one central locale (e.g., the chief at Cahokia), and then they were redistributed again to support, for example, full-time warriors or religious specialists. (In some ways, the process works like taxes do today, although this modern practice is much more depersonalized.) Importantly, while resources flowed back out to the masses from the chief (though certainly not in the same form), the act of redistribution often increased the wealth, power, and prestige of the chief and his subordinates. Consequently, chiefs, lords, or kings often had the power to control land and resources in ways that tribal or band leaders did not.[30]

Chiefs, lords, and kings often maintained their political and economic domination through coercion and warfare.[31] In this regard, some so-called chiefdoms or kingdoms were very much like **ancient states**, which expanded through large-scale conquest. But, unlike chiefdoms or kingdoms, these early states consisted of much larger populations.[32]

Early states—hierarchical political systems characterized by centralized governments—arose primarily around large-scale agriculture and first emerged about five to six thousand years ago. Many of these developed independently of one another in places all over the world: Mesoamerica (Central America), South America, Africa, Mesopotamia, and Southeast Asia. These states had centralized power—that is, a consolidated authority was organized around a ruling bureaucracy rather than just one chief, king, or lord. For example, while Cahokia had a centralized authority—a chief—in the Mayan civilization of Central America (which collapsed around AD 900), a ruling body of individuals was spread throughout the state.[33] Like ancient Rome (also a state), the Mayans had bureaucrats who governed outlying towns and cities.

Political centralization was only the beginning, however. Integrating people within a centralized, ruling bureaucracy often included state-sponsored religion (the separation of church and state is a very recent phenomenon), the presence of a highly organized military (for both expansion and defense), reciprocity (as in bands and tribes), redistribution (as in chiefdoms or kingdoms), and **market exchange**—that is, the exchange of goods and services through the use of money. In times past, "money" included items such as shells, beads, animal skins, precious metals, and rice.[34]

The development of markets was especially important to the development of states. Indeed, the state depended (and today still depends) on market exchange (or in today's terms, import and export trade) to survive. For example, as people settled, their diets were increasingly limited to a few crops. They were able to produce more food for more people, but their diet had to be subsidized through trade. In addition, unlike foragers, who could just move to another locale when their food became scarce, agriculturalists were often stuck in one spot. When crops failed, food shortages ensued, making trade all the more important.[35]

The market, then, was (and is) an incredibly important factor in maintaining the state's political system. Ever since the first agricultural states emerged, they have depended on trade—internal or external—for their survival and maintenance. Human adaptation, politics, and economics, then, are intimately linked.[36] While there can be self-sufficient foragers, *there have never been any completely self-sufficient agricultural states.*[37]

AGRICULTURAL TRENDS AND THE MODERN WORLD: LESSONS FOR OUR TIME

As people moved from foraging to domestication (horticulture, pastoralism, and large-scale agriculture), political systems (e.g., leadership), economic systems (e.g., dependence on trade), and social systems (e.g., community size) got more complex. *Complex* here does not mean more developed but simply a much wider array of culturally governed relationships between and among people. For example, tribal political organization is more complex than band political organization because there are more political institutions (descent groups, warrior societies) through which people must navigate their lives. The state is much more complex than the band, primarily because the political economy that maintains a state—whether it be ancient or modern—is responsible for the survival of geometrically larger populations.

Some anthropologists have called the movement from foraging to domestication **cultural evolution**.[38] For contemporary anthropologists, evolution means only change—hence, cultural evolution means cultural change. To imply the more popular implication of evolution, progress, would misrepresent the facts. As humans adopted domestication, political and economic trends accompanied this change in adaptation. Among these were the growth of permanent settlements, an increase in population density, chronic food shortages (which were relatively low among foragers like the !Kung), a higher dependence on trade, full-time specialization (such as political leadership), and inequities in wealth. Such changes, of course, were ultimately brought on by a technology—agriculture—that involved harnessing food resources to support larger and larger populations.[39]

Heavy prices were paid for the adoption of agriculture, however—among them, worsened health, disease, and social inequality.[40] As people focused on

The scale, complexity, and effects of agriculture only continue to grow. Photo by Danny Gawlowski.

fewer types of crops, overall nutrition decreased. In addition, because people were living in close proximity, poor sanitation and its concomitant health threats became problems. The practice of trade helped spread disease across great distances, which could often have devastating effects within an agriculture state. In terms of social inequality, stored food helped to create, for the first time in human history, substantial economic divisions between groups of people. Indeed, the emergence of **class**—that is, the division of people into groups with differing access to resources—accompanied large-scale agriculture where, generally, no such grouping had existed among foragers.[41]

As I have already mentioned, one of the most dangerous undersides of agriculture is population growth—agriculture's "catch-22." As population increases, the need for high agricultural yields increase; as yields increase, populations increase, which brings about a need for even higher agricultural yields. Consequently, since the time when agriculture emerged, the world's population has steadily grown. As anthropologist John H. Bodley points out,

> The relatively rapid growth in population that accompanied and perhaps contributed to the adoption of farming is one of the most significant demographic events in human history. It marked the end of the long period of relative population equilibrium that foraging peoples established and initiated a period of almost continuous population growth and a rapid series of interrelated changes that led successfully to politicization, the emergence of large-scale urban culture, and finally the rise of industrial global cultures.[42]

About five hundred years ago, the Age of Exploration forged the links between the Old and New Worlds, and with the rise of industrialization, the world became fused into one international, global market economy. And with the increased mechanization of agriculture, the growth of manufacturing, the development of complex factory systems, and the expansion of urban centers, the populations of industrial societies exploded, increasing world populations exponentially. Since World War II, the rate of trade and consumption has increased as never before—and population has risen similarly. From 1950 to 2000, for example, the world's population doubled nearly two and a half times, from 2.5 billion to well over 6 billion people.[43] Today it's now over 7 billion.

The differences between ancient states and modern nation-states are significant, of course. Today, we live in nation-states that occupy every part of the globe, incorporate millions of people into multifaceted political systems, and integrate each and every economy into a **core** (the world's wealthiest and most powerful nation-states), the **periphery** (the world's poorest nation-states), and the **semiperiphery** (nation-states that mediate the flow of economic resources between the core and the periphery). People are moving from the periphery and semiperiphery to the core and from rural areas to urban centers as never before. Modern nation-states are facing unprecedented rates of immigration and emigration. Ethnic groups are in contact as never before, and, as referenced in chapter 2, the context of our world system is now forcing people with radically different cultural values, attitudes, and practices to negotiate their values, attitudes, and practices on an international scale—again, as never before. To be sure, we can no longer understand the complexities of people and the dynamics of culture outside this ever-emergent system.[44]

Modern nation-states and ancient states do share some characteristics. Although trade and the exchange of goods and services exist on a much broader and more complex level, and although international trade is for the most part framed by a capitalist world economy (with its own unique history), one characteristic persists: fragility. Exhaustion of resources, famine, social unrest, institutionalized inequality, food shortages, conquest, mass genocide—these are cultural artifacts of states that have led to their demise. When we examine the evidence, we see that throughout the past five or six thousand years, states have consistently risen and fallen because of political and economic pressures. The prestate Cahokia, for example, most likely collapsed because of the exhaustion of its surrounding resources, food shortages, and/or class conflict.[45] When states fall, survivors have presumably taken up less complex ways of organizing themselves—as foragers, pastoralists, or horticulturalists.

Today, however, the situation we face is very different from that of ancient states. In a relatively short amount of time, nation-states (and the international trade that supports them) have produced and reproduced larger and larger populations that can never go back in large measure to foraging, pastoralism, or horticulture. Because all the world's people are today integrated into a no-return political economy, we face some difficult questions in the twenty-first century, questions that humans have never had to face before, although the questions were generated long ago. Science writer Jared Diamond, who is most famous for articulating this point of view, puts it this way:

Archaeologists studying the rise of farming have reconstructed a crucial stage at which we made the worst mistake in human history. Forced to choose between limiting population or trying to increase food production, we chose the latter and ended up with starvation, warfare, and tyranny. Hunter-gatherers practiced the most successful and longest-lasting life style in human history. In contrast, we're still struggling with the mess into which agriculture has tumbled us, and it's unclear whether we can solve it. Suppose that an archaeologist who had visited us from outer space were trying to explain human history to his fellow spacelings. He might illustrate the results of his digs by a 24-hour clock on which one hour represents 100,000 years of real past time. If the history of the human race began at midnight, then we would now be almost at the end of our first day. We lived as hunter-gatherers for nearly the whole of that day, from midnight through dawn, noon, and sunset. Finally, at 11:54 p.m., we adopted agriculture. As our second midnight approaches, will the plight of famine-stricken peasants gradually engulf us all? Or will we somehow achieve those seductive blessings that we imagine behind agriculture's facade, and that have so far eluded us?[46]

We must recognize that living in modern nation-states (wherever they may be, however small or large) means that we are necessarily dependent on political and economic "others" (both individual people and individual societies) for our continued survival. The *real* threats to the survival of more than seven billion people have much more to do with politics and economics than with things like "moral decay," "lack of sufficient resources," or other popular assumptions. (For example, the core produces enough food to feed the entire world, but people are starving in the periphery and semiperiphery because of the political and economic inequities in distributing resources, not because there are too few resources to feed them.) Indeed, if this story about the evolution of the state has anything to teach us, it is this: self-dependence, self-sufficiency, and isolation are illusions. Nation-states simply cannot go it alone.[47]

Thus, the culture that mediates our relationship with the environment, writ on an international scale, is today powerfully shaped by political (state) and economic (market) systems. Our relationship with the environment and our survival within this environment cannot be considered outside this construct. It is, to put it simply, the larger cultural framework in which we live—whatever the "political" or "economic" form.

Members of a "peasant group" (gwoupman peyizan*) in rural Haiti participate in a peer education–based adult literacy program. Anthropologist Jennie M. Smith argues in her ethnography,* When the Hands Are Many: Community Organization and Social Change in Rural Haiti, *that foreign assistance agencies have much to learn from such groups about how to improve the ways that community development programs are formulated and implemented. Photo by Jennie M. Smith.*

Many anthropologists take very seriously the study of this larger cultural framework. They seek to understand how human groups—small or large—respond to and shape the processes of globalization on a daily basis. Biological and archaeological anthropologists are increasingly calling on all of us to recognize how the evolving physical, sociopolitical, and economic environment presents us with among the most important challenges of our time.[48] Linguistic and sociocultural anthropologists are increasingly calling on all of us to recognize the cultural complexities of integrating diverse peoples with diverse languages and backgrounds within common political and economic systems.[49] Ethnographers, especially, are increasingly calling on all of us to recognize the ways in which people in local communities can (and do) both mediate and resist the larger structural powers that dominate them and their lives.[50]

ANTHROPOLOGY HERE AND NOW

One of the many problems of globalization that anthropologists address today concerns how indigenous peoples may struggle to maintain their traditional ways of life. Issues such as border disputes, loss of land, differential access to resources, and tourism—to name just a few things—have made these traditional ways of life more difficult to sustain. Yet many peoples have found ways to negotiate and navigate globalization in diverse and dynamic ways. Anthropologist Charles Menzies (University of British Columbia) works on issues of cultural sustainability in indigenous and other local communities. He directs the Ethnographic Film Unit at the University of British Columbia, which uses "the language of documentary video to explore issues of environmentally and socially responsible resource use that prioritizes collaborative community-based projects." You can learn more about the unit and its various film projects at anthfilm.anth.ubc.ca.

CHECK IT OUT!

We are not entirely powerless. Ultimately, what this means for the study of cultural issues like gender, marriage/family/kinship, and religion is that our interconnections with others exist not only in our common biology or our common encounter with universal human problems (like the food quest) but also in a common political and economic world culture. Gender issues, for example, are not isolated issues; they are international issues and so are issues concerning marriage, family, kinship, or religion. Local actions are increasingly global actions and vice versa—so much so that a declaration like "think globally, act locally" might better be posed as "think globally, act globally."

NOTES

1. A profusion of literature takes up the history of the modern world system from a number of disciplinary perspectives. For a more thorough discussion of world-system theory, see, for example, Giovanni Arrighi, *The Long Twentieth Century* (London: Verso, 1994); Christopher Chase-Dunn and Thomas Hall, *Rise and Demise: Comparing World-Systems* (Boulder, CO: Westview Press, 1997); and

Immanuel Wallerstein, *The Modern World System: Capitalist Agriculture and the Origins of European World-Economy in the Sixteenth Century* (New York: Academic Press, 1974), and *Geopolitics and Geoculture: Essays on the Changing World-System* (Cambridge: Cambridge University Press, 1991).

2. This perspective has been most popularly articulated by Jared Diamond— see, for example, *The Third Chimpanzee: The Evolution and Future of the Human Animal* (New York: HarperCollins, 1992), 180–91, and especially *Guns, Germs, and Steel: The Fates of Human Societies* (New York: Norton, 1997). But archaeologists and other anthropologists have long argued that agriculture initiated a human way of life that continues to have a multiplicity of consequences today. Admittedly, I simplified this multiplicity for this introductory discussion. For more nuanced discussions of the complexities of agriculture and its consequences (as well as the diverse anthropological arguments surrounding its development), see Mark Nathan Cohen, *Health and the Rise of Civilization* (New Haven, CT: Yale University Press, 1989); Mark Nathan Cohen and George J. Armelagos, eds., *Paleopathology at the Origins of Agriculture* (Orlando, FL: Academic Press, 1984); Brian Fagan, *Floods, Famines and Emperors: El Niño and the Fate of Civilizations* (New York: Basic Books, 1999); Elman Service, *Origins of the State and Civilization: The Process of Cultural Evolution* (New York: Norton, 1975); Julian Steward, *Theory of Culture Change: The Methodology of Multilinear Evolution* (Urbana: University of Illinois Press, 1955); Joseph A. Tainter, *The Collapse of Complex Societies* (New York: Cambridge University Press, 1990); Leslie White, *The Evolution of Culture: The Development of Civilization to the Fall of Rome* (New York: McGraw-Hill, 1959); and Eric Wolf, *Peasants* (Englewood Cliffs, NJ: Prentice Hall, 1966).

3. For easily read introductions to the evolution of *Homo sapiens*, see Donald Johanson and Maitland Edey, *Lucy: The Beginnings of Humankind* (New York: Simon & Schuster, 1981), and Donald Johanson and James Shreeve, *Lucy's Child: The Discovery of a Human Ancestor* (New York: Avon, 1989).

4. Cf. Richard Lee and Irven DeVore, eds., *Man the Hunter* (Chicago: Aldine, 1968); G. Philip Rightmire, *The Evolution of* Homo erectus: *Comparative Anatomical Studies of an Extinct Human Species* (Cambridge: Cambridge University Press, 1990); and Robert J. Wenke and Deborah I. Olszewski, *Patterns in Prehistory: Mankind's First Three Million Years*, 5th ed. (Oxford: Oxford University Press, 2006).

5. See Frances Dahlberg, ed., *Woman the Gatherer* (New Haven, CT: Yale University Press, 1981).

6. For a fuller discussion, see Peter P. Schweitzer, Megan Biesele, and Robert K. Hitchcock, eds., *Hunters and Gatherers in the Modern World: Conflict, Resistance, and Self-Determination* (New York: Berghahn Books, 2000).

7. Richard Lee, *The Dobe Ju/'hoansi*, 2nd ed. (Fort Worth, TX: Harcourt Brace, 1993), 9–22.

8. Ibid., 59–60.

9. Ibid., 58.

10. Ibid., 60.

11. See, for example, Lee and DeVore, *Man the Hunter.*

12. Cf. George Armelagos and J. R. Dewey, "Evolutionary Response to Human Infectious Diseases," *Bioscience* 157 (1970): 638–44.

13. Steward, *Theory of Culture Change.*

14. Ibid.

15. Lee, *The Dobe Ju/'hoansi*, 61ff. Cf. Marjorie Shostak, *Nisa: The Life and Words of a !Kung Woman* (New York: Vintage Books, 1981).

16. For a fuller discussion, see Marshall Sahlins, *Stone Age Economies* (Chicago: Aldine-Atherton, 1972).

17. Much of the following discussion is based on Mark N. Cohen's *The Food Crisis in Prehistory: Overpopulation and the Origins of Agriculture* (New Haven, CT: Yale University Press, 1977).

18. Ibid.

19. See, for example, the recent works about the Nuer, pastoralists of eastern Africa. Among these are Jon D. Holtzman, *Nuer Journeys, Nuer Lives: Sudanese Refugees in Minnesota* (Boston: Allyn & Bacon, 2000), and Sharon Hutchinson, *Nuer Dilemmas: Coping with War, Money and the State* (Berkeley: University of California Press, 1996).

20. Steward, *Theory of Culture Change.*

21. See, for example, the literature on segmentary lineage systems, most notably E. E. Evans-Pritchard, *The Nuer: A Description of the Modes of Livelihood and Political Institutions of a Nilotic People* (New York: Oxford University Press, 1940), and Marshal Sahlins, "The Segmentary Lineage: An Organization of Predatory

Expansion," *American Anthropologist* 63 (1961): 322–45. But see also Adam Kuper, "Lineage Theory: A Critical Retrospective," *Annual Review of Anthropology* 11 (1982): 71–95, and Henry Munson, "On the Irrelevance of the Segmentary Lineage Model in the Moroccan Rif," *American Anthropologist* 91 (1989): 386–400.

22. See, for example, Robert H. Lowie, *Indians of the Plains* (Washington, DC: American Museum of Natural History, 1954).

23. See Marshall Sahlins, *Tribesmen* (Englewood Cliffs, NJ: Prentice Hall, 1968); Service, *Origins of the State*; and Steward, *Theory of Culture Change*. But see Morton Fried, *The Notion of Tribe* (Menlo Park, CA: Cummings, 1975).

24. For a discussion on the complications attendant on dating the emergence of agriculture—among other debates—see Bruce D. Smith, *The Emergence of Agriculture* (New York: W. H. Freeman, 1995). See also T. Douglas Price and Anne Birgitte Gebauer, *Last Hunters, First Farmers: New Perspectives on the Prehistoric Transition to Agriculture* (Santa Fe, NM: School of American Research Press, 1995).

25. For a more thorough discussion of prestates and their deeper complexities, see, for example, Timothy Earl, ed., *Chiefdoms: Power, Economy, and Ideology* (Cambridge: Cambridge University Press, 1991).

26. For a fuller discussion of Cahokia, see Timothy R. Pauketat, *The Ascent of Chiefs: Cahokia and Mississippian Politics in Native North America* (Tuscaloosa: University of Alabama Press, 1994), and Timothy R. Pauketat and Thomas E. Emerson, eds., *Cahokia: Domination and Ideology in the Mississippian World* (Lincoln: University of Nebraska Press, 1997).

27. Claudia Gellman Mink, *Cahokia: City of the Sun* (Collinsville, IL: Cahokia Mounds Museum Society, 1999), 24.

28. Mink, *Cahokia*, 20; see also Pauketat and Emerson, *Cahokia*, 3–5.

29. Mink, *Cahokia*, 24–25.

30. Elman Service, *Primitive Social Organization: An Evolutionary Perspective* (New York: Random House, 1962); see also Timothy Earl and J. Erickson, eds., *Exchange Systems in Prehistory* (New York: Academic Press, 1977).

31. See Robert Carneiro, "The Chiefdom as Precursor of the State," in *The Transformation to Statehood in the New World*, ed. Grant Jones and Robert Kautz (Cambridge: Cambridge University Press, 1981), 37–97, and Jonathan Haas, *The Evolution of the Prehistoric State* (New York: Columbia University Press, 1982).

32. For a full discussion of states, their emergence, and the consequences of their political economies, see Morton Fried, *The Evolution of Political Society: An Essay in Political Anthropology* (New York: Random House, 1967); Allen Johnson and Timothy Earle, *The Evolution of Human Societies: From Foraging Group to Agrarian State* (Stanford, CA: Stanford University Press, 1987); and Service, *Primitive Social Organization.*

33. See John S. Henderson, *The World of the Ancient Maya*, 2nd ed. (Ithaca, NY: Cornell University Press, 1997).

34. Sahlins, *Stone Age Economics.*

35. Cf. Cohen, *The Food Crisis in Prehistory* and *Health and the Rise of Civilization.*

36. For a more nuanced discussion of the market and its relationship to political economy, see, for example, Terence D'Altroy and Timothy Earle, "Staple Finance, Wealth Finance, and Storage in the Inka Political Economy," *Current Anthropology* 26 (1985): 187–206.

37. Cf. Johnson and Earl, *The Evolution of Human Societies.*

38. See, for example, ibid.

39. See White, *The Evolution of Culture.*

40. See, for example, Diamond, *The Third Chimpanzee*, 180–91.

41. Diamond, *The Third Chimpanzee*; see also Diamond, *Guns, Germs, and Steel.* Cf. Cohen, *The Food Crisis in Prehistory* and *Health and the Rise of Civilization.*

42. John H. Bodley, *Anthropology and Contemporary Human Problems*, 3rd ed. (Mountain View, CA: Mayfield Publishing, 1996), 151–52.

43. For a more detailed discussion of problems surrounding population growth, see Bodley, *Anthropology and Contemporary Human Problems* (especially chap. 6).

44. See Arrighi, *The Long Twentieth Century*; Chase-Dunn and Hall, *Rise and Demise*; and Wallerstein, *The Modern World System.*

45. Cf. Pauketat, *The Ascent of Chiefs*, and Pauketat and Emerson, *Cahokia.*

46. Jared Diamond, "The Worst Mistake in the History of the Human Race," *Discover* 8 (1987): 66.

47. Cf. Diamond, *Guns, Germs, and Steel.*

48. See, for example, Carole Crumley, ed., *New Directions in Anthropology and Environment: Intersections* (Walnut Creek, CA: AltaMira Press, 2001).

49. See, for example, Walt Wolfram, *American English: Dialects and Variation* (Malden, MA: Blackwell, 1998).

50. See, for example, Jennie M. Smith, *When the Hands Are Many: Community Organization and Social Change in Rural Haiti* (Ithaca, NY: Cornell University Press, 2001).

5

Sex, Power, and Inequality

On Gender

As human beings, we take a lot for granted. While we may appreciate that culture creates a world of meaning around us, we may still assume that our actions, behaviors, and thoughts are natural or right. We should appreciate that this, too, is a part of our ethnocentrism. Even with this knowledge, however, it can be difficult to break free from the assumptions we hold about the world. One of the more powerful assumptions currently is that of **gender**: human beings almost everywhere tend to think the differences between women and men are natural, inherent, and inborn. Even if they appreciate that culture establishes the contours through which we live our lives—from individual space to the institutions of economics or politics—people are less willing to extend such understandings to something as basic and, presumably, as biological as sex. Yet when we compare the world's societies, the vast differences we see among human expressions of gender conclusively illustrate that these differences are as much cultural as they are biological.

Take a classic example presented by anthropologist Margaret Mead in her 1935 book *Sex and Temperament in Three Primitive Societies*. In this well-known ethnographic study, Mead compared three tribes of New Guinea: the Arapesh, Mundugumor, and the Tchambuli. In each of these groups, men and women exhibited personality traits that were highly variable and very different from what Americans might expect. Arapesh women and men behaved in ways that Mead's readers may have expected American women to act: they displayed "a personality that . . . we would call maternal in its parental aspects, and feminine in its sexual aspects."[1] Mundugumor men and women, however, behaved in ways that many of Mead's readers might have expected American men to act—in the extreme: "Both men and women developed as ruthless, aggressive, positively sexed individuals, with the maternal cherishing aspects of personality at a minimum. Both men and women approximated to a personality type that we in our culture would find only in an undisciplined and very violent male."[2] In marked contrast to the Arapesh and the Mundugumor (both of whom downplayed the contrast between the sexes), among the Tchambuli, Mead found that, as in her contemporary American culture, men and women drew clear lines between the sexes, but, unlike Americans, Tchambuli harbored stereotypical attitudes about the sexes that were the exact opposite of 1930s American stereotypes: there was "a genuine reversal of the sex-attitudes of our own culture, with the woman the dominant, impersonal, managing partner, the man the less responsible and the emotionally dependent person."[3] In the end, Mead's study illustrated that culture had an enormous role in shaping the contours of the so-called sexes. "These three situations suggest, then, a very definite conclusion," wrote Mead. "If those temperamental attitudes which we have traditionally regarded as feminine—such as passivity, responsiveness, and a willingness to cherish children—can so easily be set up as the masculine pattern in one tribe, and in another be outlawed for the majority of the women as well as for the majority of men, we no longer have any basis for regarding such aspects of behavior as sex-linked."[4] For Mead, linking the behavior of women and men entirely to biology—seeing them as "sex-linked"—misses how culture shapes the behavioral profiles of "man" and "woman."

Although Mead's original studies have been criticized for overstating the case, countless others since have illustrated that culture constructs sexuality in ways radically different from the assumptions that place sex entirely within the realm of biology. Take, for example, religious practice. In many societies around the world, men and women may have separate access to the gods, take on separate religious functions, and even have separate expectations placed on their spiritual development. In all the major religions of the contemporary world, for example, priesthood roles have traditionally been the prerogative of men. That is no surprise. What may surprise you is how often religion corresponds with human sexuality—and in a number of different and interesting ways. In some Native American traditions, certain religious practices are the sole activity of men, who, as representatives of large families, are charged to pray for their entire tribe (both women and men)—a prayerful activity not engaged in by the women. Among many Pueblo tribes of the southwestern United States, for example, men attend the most sacred rituals held in the kiva—a room (usually underground) where these religious ceremonies take place.[5] Compare this with worship in mainstream America, where women constitute the majority of church membership. National opinion polls suggest that men as a whole are less devoted to their churches than women. Indeed, religion appears to be more important to women than men: women apparently pray more, and women more often and more deeply examine their faith, spiritual growth, and relationship to God. Although men may overwhelmingly hold priesthood roles, it turns out that women are the more "spiritual" sex in American churches.[6] People of the Ryūkyū Islands (just south of mainland Japan) would agree that females are more inclined toward spiritual matters than males. Ryūkyūan, an indigenous religion still practiced today, accords women a special ability to communicate with the supernatural. Women thus dominate religious rituals and even represent their families in prayer at the household hearth.[7] This attitude linking female sexuality with spirituality is also similar to some Hindu beliefs. Among the *hijras* of India, for example, men who want to take up worship of the mother goddess Bahuchara Mata must renounce their "maleness" by undergoing a castration ceremony before they can be considered a true *hijra*. After becoming a *hijra*, they take female names and adopt female dress and behavior.[8]

These examples suggest that religion can sometimes be as much about ideas surrounding human sexuality as about the search for spiritual meaning. Remember, we are not born with these ideas; rather, we learn them. Cross-culturally, then, the marriage of human sexuality with institutions like religion, politics, or economics is not really that surprising. But, interestingly, these examples also illustrate that men and women conduct their lives at the most basic and complex levels in reference to their ideas about human sexuality. Almost everywhere, with few exceptions (the Arapesh and the Mundugumor apparently being some of the few), women and men can have wholly different expectations placed on them, wholly different functions and roles, and often, as a result, wholly different lives.

Let's look at another example—an extreme one. Among several tribes of the South American Amazon and the New Guinea highlands, men and women live in separate houses. Women and their children live in their own

Among the hijras *of India, men who want to take up worship of the mother goddess Bahuchara Mata renounce their "maleness," take female names, and adopt female dress and behavior. Photo by Serena Nanda, author of* Neither Man nor Woman: The Hijras of India.

houses separate from men, who live in "men's houses." Women and men interact in everyday life, of course, but their relations are often suspect. In some tribes, men and women are said to thoroughly distrust one another; their sexual relations, for instance, are very infrequent. Unlike American society, in which the typical household is often established on a male-female (sex-based) marriage, in many tribes in these two regions the household is founded on a commonality with people of the same sex—unless, of course, they are under a certain age, as is the case with boys who live in their mother's houses but have not moved or been initiated into the men's houses.[9]

While this represents an extreme, these kinds of separations between women and men should not be all that surprising when we compare societies around the world. In actuality, men and women have regularly created sex-based groups, albeit on less extreme levels. For example, ethnographers and videographers Susannah M. Hoffman, Richard Cowan, and Paul Aratow report that in 1970s Kypseli (a small traditional Greek village), women and men clearly constituted separate groups in day-to-day life. During the day, men hunted, tended their fields (which they alone owned), and visited and transacted business in the village square (where women rarely, if ever, congregated). While the men were away from home, women's activities dominated the smaller village courtyards, where they gathered to visit and work. When the day came to a close, however, women lost control of the courtyards as the men returned and began visiting with each other. While the home was primarily the prerogative of women—that is, homes were given female names, owned by women, and were passed from mother to daughter—inside the home, men and women also had their own male and female sections. The inner parlor was the province primarily of men, and the kitchen was strictly a women's space. Religion, too, paralleled these divided worlds. In the village churches, men and women gathered as separate groups: men almost always sat closer to the church's altar, and women sat or stood in the back of the church.[10]

Although much has presumably changed in Greek villages like Kypseli since the 1970s, these patterns can remind us of our own American traditions. Think about our Thanksgiving holiday, when many Americans re-enact traditional values and assumptions about male and female groupings and the spaces in which they belong: women gather in the kitchen to cook, and men gather around the television to watch football. Yes, even in our

Men building a women's house in highland Papua New Guinea. From left to right, the house consists of a hearth room, pig stalls, and a bedroom for women and children. Photo by Ruth C. Wohlt.

so-called progressive times, it is hard to separate ourselves from our deeply held convictions about sexuality.

Contrast Kypseli with the village of Nazaré in Portugal. Here, a community of fishermen live in a working-class community that is in many ways very different from Kypseli.[11] Instead of men dominating public space, women do. In addition, women dominate private, domestic space as well. Ethnographer Jan Brøgger reports that men—who are the fishermen in this small Portuguese village—fish for their families. But their wives are responsible primarily for selling the fish in the public marketplace. In the home, there is no men's assigned space, as in Kypseli. Men are expected to wake in the morning, have a quick breakfast, and exit the home as soon as possible. At home they are considered "in the way"; in many respects they are marginal members of the home. That is, the working-class Nazaré are primarily **matrilocal**—after marriage, the newly married couple lives within the wife's family's household. Many a married man, then, enters a household entirely controlled by women who are related to one another—his wife, his wife's mother, his wife's married or unmarried sisters, and their children. Both he and his wife's father are considered "strangers" in the household: they are from altogether different families. And *their* families have no property rights in a home owned primarily by the women of the house. In other words, the entire space of the home is the prerogative of women. Coupled with women's dominance in the marketplace, Brøgger concluded that the working-class community of Nazaré (in contrast to the bourgeoisie of the village, who mirror the rest of Europe) represents a case in which,

> unlike the situation that traditionally prevails in both the United States and Europe, the women are also in charge of the economy outside the household. Many women among the stratum of fishermen are business-people in the true sense of the word. This unconventional division of roles between men and women makes the situation in Nazaré particularly interesting. . . . [T]he dominant position of women has important consequences for the conjugal [i.e., married] relationship and the family structure.[12]

Enough of the Nazaré and Kypseli, Thanksgiving, men's houses, sex-based religion, and Margaret Mead. I mention all these examples because of the questions they raise. Are women's and men's worlds always divided? Are they always characterized by power relations? Are men or women more often the

Chris Jorgenson

dominators of the other sex? These are questions I will take up shortly. But first, we need to nail down a basic, though often overlooked, distinction about human sexuality—namely, that between sex and gender.

SEX AND GENDER: UNDERSTANDING THE DIFFERENCE

First and foremost, these diverse examples illustrate that human sexuality—just like everything else—is shaped by culture. While human sexuality is a biological given, culture builds on this fundamental human similarity and assigns diverse behaviors, roles, and meanings to "male" and "female." Nazaré men are not born with the knowledge that they are "in the way" in their home or that they will live with their wife's family after marriage. They must *learn* this as they grow up. Boys in the Amazon or in the highlands of New Guinea—when they are taken to men's houses—are not born with the knowledge that they will *learn* in their induction ceremonies into the men's house. Women are not born with the inability to be priests; they *learn* that their lack of a penis prevents them from becoming leaders in certain churches. Women in Nazaré are not born with the knowledge that they will be responsible for selling fish in the market or that their husbands will live in their extended family household: they *learn* this from their mothers, aunts, or sisters. In the end, our respective cultural upbringings make sure that we take these differences for granted and that we deem these differences inborn, innate, and immutable. Natural.

With this in mind, we can make a clear distinction between sex and culture, or, more specifically, between biological sex and gender. **Biological sex** refers to the differences found among humans in male and female biology. These include universal, biologically based male and female differences, such as genitalia or the presence or absence of enlarged breasts. Exceptions include intersexed individuals born with biological attributes not typically male or female. But in all cases, people build on and interpret these biological differences within the framework of their own pasts, cultures, and experiences. Although human beings may be sexed male or female for biological reproduction, the biology of the sexes is the *foundation* on which humans build a variety of cultural behaviors, roles, and meanings from society to society and from culture to culture. And this leads us to gender, which is different from biological sex. While individual humans are sexed as reproductive organisms, **gender** refers to the way culture grafts meaning onto sexed individuals throughout their lives. This grafting is as diverse as humans themselves. Indeed, as anthropologist Carol P. MacCormack argues, "Gender and its attributes are not pure biology. The meanings attributed to male and female are as arbitrary as are the meanings attributed to nature and culture."[13]

If the meanings that are assigned to sex are arbitrary and random and depend on culture, then how and why does culture assign diverse behaviors, roles, and meanings to biological sex in the first place? The answer resides partly in how culture works, which, you'll remember from chapter 2, is inextricably bound to social interaction. We must associate with other people to reproduce ourselves, our societies, and our cultures from generation to generation. Because of this, we are always passing through life *in relation* to other people. From the time we are born, we are someone's child or grandchild, brother or sister, nephew or niece, friend or foe, student or teacher, mate, father or mother, uncle or aunt, or grandfather or grandmother. As human beings, we cannot escape this—whether we assign these categories to ourselves (e.g., personal identities) or whether others assign them to us (e.g., race).

None of these categories exist in a vacuum. They also give us the guidelines for defining how to interact with others. In some societies, young people are expected to treat the elders with respect; in other societies, young people are expected to upset the status quo set by their elders. In some societies, a married man is encouraged to develop a close relationship with his mother-in-law; in others, his mother-in-law is to be avoided at all costs. In some societies, our race determines how we should interact with members of other groups; in others, it even determines who we may and may not marry.

Being a member of certain groups and being expected to act in certain ways is fundamentally human. We are, after all, cultural beings. And because it so pervades our lives, gender weaves in and out of our social interactions: each and every person must negotiate a "gendered" position in society, no matter how or where they live. (This brings up an important point. Like everything else cultural, people *negotiate* their many culturally defined positions. And gender, of course, is an integral part of this cultural process.) In some societies, gender is considered immutable; in others, it is quite flexible. But whether immutable or flexible, our ideas about gender are always shaped by the groups of which we are a part. They always vary, if only by degrees, from people to people and from place to place.

Although human beings may be sexed male or female for biological reproduction, the biology of the sexes is merely the foundation on which humans build a variety of cultural behaviors, roles, and meanings that we learn to enact from the time we are born. Photo by Danny Gawlowski.

Let's briefly examine several **alternate genders**, ones that don't fit within our traditional male/female dichotomy. Many societies actually make room for a third or even fourth gender. I have already mentioned the *hijras* of India, in which emasculated men and intersexed individuals are accepted members of the group. Another case in point is the so-called *berdache*, or "two-spirit," of many Native American groups, biologically sexed males or females who reject or transcend traditional male or female roles. Although not as common in contemporary North American Indian communities as they once were (in no small part because of missionization and forced assimilation), ethnographers have recorded historical cases of a broad range of alternate genders in over 150 different North American Indian societies.[14] In many of these groups, individuals occupied a separate, often named, category from that of "man" or "woman." The majority of recorded cases document biologically sexed males who assumed female dress, occupations, and/or behaviors. But they did not have the same status as females; they inhabited an intermediate status, one often imbued with supernatural powers and/or responsibilities.[15] For example, among the Hidatsa—a northern Plains Indian tribe—the "man-woman," or *miati*, dressed and worked like Hidatsa women, but they also took on special religious and ceremonial roles. "Their roles in ceremonies were many and exceeded those of the most distinguished tribal ceremonial leaders," wrote ethnographer Alfred Bowers. "There was an atmosphere of mystery about them. Not being bound as firmly by traditional teachings coming down from the older generations through the ceremonies, but more as a result of their individual and unique experiences with the supernatural, their conduct was less traditional than that of the other ceremonial leaders."[16]

The *miati* assumed their separate status, unconventional ceremonial roles, and special associations with the supernatural through repeated dreams and visions that preceded and necessitated their gender transformations.[17] Such vision experiences encouraging or obliging gender transformations were common in many other Native North American groups as well, such as the Arapaho, Miami, and Ute.[18] Other documented cases of gender transformations also cite childhood interests in the activities of the other sex, which could develop over time.[19] Among the Mohave of the Greater Southwest, for example, women who were pregnant might dream that their children might become *alyha* or *hwame*, the gender variants for males and females, respectively. But it wasn't until those children began to express interests in the dress, activities, and behaviors of the other sex as they grew up that the alternate status became socially recognized.[20]

Like the Mohave, some groups, like the Cheyenne and Navajo, had variant gender categories for both males and females (having, in effect, four genders).[21] But even in societies with only one alternate gender (which in most cases was assumed by males) or no gender variants at all, some individuals (often female) could adopt the dress, occupations, and/or behaviors of the other sex without making a full transition into a separate, alternate gender category. In several Plains Indian tribes, for instance, women would at times assume masculine activities and/or behaviors without shifting their status as women. These "manly" or "manly hearted" women eschewed conventional female roles and extended their influence into male-dominated arenas of property ownership, ceremonial leadership, and even warfare.[22] When considered alongside the third gender variants available for males in many Plains groups, these alternatives "offered men and women opportunities," Standing

Rock Lakota and anthropologist Beatrice Medicine once noted, "for display-ing cross-sex talents in socially approved ways, and in doing so, they were probably essential to the psychological well-being of peoples who lived in societies with highly dichotomized gender expectations."[23] Indeed, the same could be said today for the many North American Native people who con-tinue to carve out spaces for "two-spirits"—the English nomenclature most often used today—within a larger society that, in most quarters (including in many contemporary Native communities), makes little room for alternatives when it comes to gender.[24]

ANTHROPOLOGY HERE AND NOW

Two-spirits continue to carve out space in our society, even in con-temporary Native communities, where their roles were tradition-ally more understood and accepted, although sometimes at great costs. *Two Spirits* is a documentary of a young Navajo teen, Fred Martinez, who was brutally murdered for his two-spirit identity. You can learn more about Martinez, the film, and alternate gen-ders the world over at www.pbs.org/independentlens/two-spirits.

CHECK IT OUT!

When we compare two-spirit manifestations in Native North America past and present with the *hijras* of India and with other societies around the world, it turns out that such gender variants are common cross-culturally. Still other instances include the *xanith* of Oman, who are said to exhibit both masculine and feminine characteristics; the *mahu* of Tahiti, men who, like the *hijras*, take on women's behavior and activities (but without emasculation surgery); and the "Sworn Virgins" of the Balkans, women who abstain from sexual relations and refuse marriage and motherhood to assume the dress and activities of men.[25]

These broad-ranging examples illustrate that gender can be highly variable and does not always correspond with biological sex: gender categories like "men" and "women" are not altogether rooted in biology. These categories might be better understood as opposite ends of the same continuum and

"Woman Jim" (also known as "Squaw Jim" and Finds Them and Kills Them) was a well-known bote *(a third gender role among the Crow of the northern Plains), famous for accomplishments as a warrior, artist, and religious and spiritual leader. Photo 1928, courtesy of the National Anthropological Archives, Smithsonian Institution (INV 00476400).*

alternate genders understood as points along that continuum. However genders are defined, they are based on people's creation and maintenance of culturally defined positions that they learn, share, negotiate, and put into daily practice.

GENDER AND POWER

In the context of everyday interaction, the culturally defined positions that we hold in relation to other people cannot be separated from the process of **power**. Indeed, these relations are often *defined* by power. Whether we are talking about a mother or a daughter, a member of one race or another, or someone young or old, one culturally defined position is impacted by its association with other culturally defined positions. And people—being people— consistently rank these positions from bottom to top. If you are young, for example, and live in a society that values respect for elders, then your value, power, and prestige in relation to your elders is low. If, on the other hand, you live in a society that values the "youth culture" over that of the elders, then you have more value, power, and prestige than your elders.

Once again, gender is fundamental to this process. Anthropologists have known for many years that in any given society, because men and women (and, in many cases, alternate genders) are assigned certain tasks and roles—a phenomenon called the **sexual division of labor**—these activities take on particular values that people use to rank the status of certain activities over other activities. Although notable exceptions have surfaced in the ethnographic literature (e.g., the case in Nazaré), in most societies past and present, the tasks and roles associated with the sexual division of labor generally place men's activities above the activities of women. Even among relatively egalitarian societies like the !Kung (foragers of southern Africa from the previous chapter), men's activities were valued above women's. Although !Kung women did the majority of work collecting food, the meat hunted by men was often more highly valued.[26] In our own "progressive" times, some things have not changed. Throughout our world, most women's work is largely undervalued—whether the woman is an executive, stay-at-home mom, factory worker, or computer engineer. In the workforce, men consistently get paid more than women for the same job performed. And women, regardless of whether they are employed in the external workforce, still do most of the world's housework—including care of children, a task that is devalued and generally unpaid no matter what country she lives in.[27]

Even in the most presumably "modern" and purportedly egalitarian societies, women—no matter what other jobs they might have—still for the most part maintain primary responsibility for housework and child care. Photo by Danny Gawlowski.

Thus, gender builds on biological sex and assigns diverse behaviors, roles, and meanings to "male," "female," and alternate identities. But gender is also much more; it is deeply intertwined with issues of power and inequality.

GENDER, INEQUALITY, AND FEMINIST ANTHROPOLOGY (1970s TO THE PRESENT)

Why do so many people the world over consistently devalue women's tasks and activities? Is it natural? Does it have to be this way? To address these questions, I'd like to return to my anthropological story. Fast-forward from anthropological elders like Boas, Malinowski, and Mead to the early 1970s. At the height of the women's movement, several women anthropologists took inspiration from Mead (and other scholars who had written about gender) and began to address questions like these.[28] With ethnography in mind (e.g., what can we learn about ourselves through the study of culture?), these researchers questioned how anthropological knowledge could be applied to problems faced by women in the United States. They knew that their own lives were characterized by inequality in the workplace; were women's lives everywhere characterized by this kind of inequality?

Several anthropological books and essays appeared on the scene. Among the most prominent was a work titled *Women, Culture, and Society*, edited by Michelle Rosaldo and Louise Lamphere.[29] This cross-cultural comparison was significant because it brought together solid ethnographic examples, key questions about gender-based inequality, and suggestions for thinking about and acting on the current civil rights struggles of women in the United States. As anthropologists, the authors of *Women, Culture, and Society* knew from the vast amount of ethnographic information collected about the world's people that the sexual division of labor was universal. In the mid-1970s, gender-based inequality also appeared to be universal, with women's work generally devalued in societies around the world. Although *matriarchies*, societies in which women ruled in totality over men, existed in mythology and legend, no ethnographers had ever discovered or described one. The authors thus began with a key assumption that although there were notable exceptions, male domination and female subordination were generally universal. Having established this (at the time), several of the authors sought to address *why* male dominance seemed to be so widespread. The

ethnographic evidence could not support an entirely biological explanation
for the sexual division of labor and thus the origin of gender-based inequality. Indeed, biological differences between men and women are minuscule
compared to the culturally based differences like those I described earlier.
Although factors like relative strength surely play a role in the sexual division of labor, culture and not biology creates the *learned* differences between
genders and, in turn, the values that people place on their roles and activities.
(Tradition, not genes, tells Americans that Thanksgiving means women in
the kitchen and men in front of the television.)

Instead of relative strength, several of the authors (most notably, Michelle Rosaldo and Sherry Ortner) argued that other biological trends—
chief among them, childbirth—are the broad base on which culture *builds*
and *maintains* a division of labor and thus gender-based inequality. While
childbirth is natural, the culturally defined positions relative to men, the
meanings, and the roles built around the act are not. The authors argued
that, by virtue of childbirth, women are associated with children, the home,
and the "hearth" over and over again, from foraging bands to agriculture
states: in a word, they are seen as *domestic*. Men, by virtue of not bearing
children, are usually free from the responsibilities of child care (in many
societies, they have absolutely nothing to do with it beyond conception).
Because they are "child free," they are more mobile, free to roam from the
home. Men are rarely associated with the domestic. Instead, they are associated with that which is *public*, like religion. Out of this biological base, then,
culture not only constructs gender but also constructs learned gender-based
inequalities. Men do not get the idea that their work may be more important
than women's from their genes or by virtue of their relative strength; rather,
they learn it through enculturation as they grow up.

Importantly, the authors of *Women, Culture, and Society*—having established that women's subordination seemed to be a universal and that culture,
not biology, was most responsible for gender-based inequality—engaged in a
cultural critique of their own society. Taking inspiration from Margaret Mead
(who, as you'll remember, argued in *Coming of Age in Samoa* that ethnography provides alternatives to our own cultural assumptions and convictions),
Rosaldo, Lamphere, and colleagues suggested that this knowledge (women's
subordination, its cultural construction, and its potential for cultural critique)

could work to *change* women's subordination in our own society—that is, *if gender-based inequality is learned, it can be changed.*

Coming at the height of the women's movement in the United States, this contention was an important component of *Women, Culture, and Society.* For example, one of the authors, Michelle Rosaldo, argued that nearly everywhere both men and women consistently valued that which was public and thus that which was the domain of men. In the United States, this meant the workplace, and Rosaldo argued that Americans value it more highly than the domestic, notably child care. (Consider the importance of money in our society and how salary is a measure of "success," and then compare the income of business executives [still mostly men] to the income of homemakers [still mostly women].) During the women's movement of the 1970s, many feminists sought to carve out an equal place for women in the workplace—an equal place that has yet to be fully achieved. While Rosaldo argued that this was indeed important to women's rights, she focused on the way our society consistently devalued the domestic (especially child care) and valued work outside the home:

> American society is in fact organized in a way that creates and exploits a radical distance between private and public, domestic and social, female and male. It speaks, on one level, of the conjugal family, while on another it defines women as domestic (an invisible army of unemployed) and sends its men into the public, working world. This conflict between ideal and reality creates illusions and disappointments for both men and women. . . . This conflict is at the core of the contemporary rethinking of sex roles: we are told that men and women should be equals and even companions, but we are also told to value men for their work. So far, women concerned to realize their equality have concentrated on the second half of this paradox, and have sought grounds for female solidarity and opportunities for women in the men's working world. . . . Yet as long as the domestic sphere remains female, women's societies, however powerful, will never be the political equivalents of men's; and, as in the past, sovereignty can be a metaphor for only a female elite. If the public world is to open its door to more than the elite among women, the nature of work itself will have to be altered, and the asymmetry between work and the home reduced. . . . [M]en who have in the past committed their lives to public achievement will recognize women as true equals only when men themselves help to raise new generations by taking on the responsibilities of the home.[30]

Cross-cultural, comparative studies like *Women, Culture, and Society* were important because of the questions they raised and the discussions they helped to initiate among anthropologists about gender, power, and inequality. But some of the assumptions underlying these questions and discussions have long since been called into question. Chief among the criticisms concerned assumptions about male dominance and women's subordination. Many anthropologists, beginning in the late 1970s and early 1980s, argued that this assumption was based on a narrow either/or proposition; it ignored the diversity and complexity of **gender roles** within societies around the world. For example, among the Onondaga and other Iroquois tribes (who live in the northeastern United States and Canada), men serve as public political leaders; yet they were (and still are) elected by clan mothers—women who head large extended families, or clans. From the outside, it *appears* that men have more power to make binding decisions for the tribal government and thus for the tribe as a whole, but their power is mediated by clan mothers who elect them and have the right to remove them if they wish.[31] This practice shares similarities with the Nazaré case mentioned earlier, doesn't it? And this was the point. Gender relations were and are much more complex than identifying one society or another as "male dominated." Clearly, women have little power relative to men in some societies; yet in many others, men may dominate some activities while women dominate others. Anthropologist Carol P. MacCormack, for example, writes that "[i]n field work I have talked with women chiefs, women heads of descent groups, heads of women's secret societies, and women household heads who . . . would say that women are inferior to men in some ways and men are inferior to women in some ways."[32] On the Ryūkyū Islands, which I mentioned near the beginning of this chapter, women dominate activities of religion in the home and community but not on the state level, which, incorporated into Japan in 1972, is male dominated.[33] Are the Ryūkyū Islands male or female dominated? It depends on where you stand and from which angle you approach. Issues concerning both religion and the state are highly valued, and, apparently, so are the activities of men and women alike in their respective roles.

Examples like these spawned a new debate about gender in 1980s anthropology. In another important cross-cultural, comparative study, *Female*

Power and Male Dominance, anthropologist Peggy Reeves Sanday rejected the argument of ubiquitous women's subordination and suggested instead that certain patterns of female power and male dominance were not solely built on biological differences (such as childbirth) but emerged most powerfully through historical processes in relation to other cultural systems, like politics, economics, and religion. Sanday argued that many tribal societies change their "sex-role plan"—the template for defining gender, power, and its relationships—as they encounter political or economic stress such as migration, food shortages, or colonialism. Many tribal societies were transformed from relatively egalitarian societies to hierarchical ones as states colonized them, for example. And gender-based inequality changed with the transition. Male dominance, then, was not necessarily universal. Gender-based inequality was least pronounced among foragers and small "shifting cultivation economies"; it increased markedly as societies became "associated with increasing technological complexity, an animal economy, sexual segregation in work, a symbolic orientation to the male creative principle, and stress."[34]

The negotiation of gender extends beyond that between men and women. Anthropologists have also called attention to how women and men negotiate gender among themselves. Photo by Danny Gawlowski.

Works such as Sanday's moved the explanation of gender-based inequalities further away from the realm of biology. But others argued that the study of gender must move even further from the assumptions of biological sex— namely, that all women are virtually the same and have virtually the same experiences because of their common biological sex. Black feminists, in particular, argued that an assumption of "sameness" undermined the larger feminist project to uncover the workings of gender and, in turn, to address inequality broadly. "The way the gender of the black woman is constructed," wrote black feminist Hazel Carby, "differs from constructions of white femininity because it is also subject to racism."[35] The study of gender, Carby and other black feminists argued, could not be separated from history, race, and class. Indeed, the category of "woman" was just as problematic and ethnocentric as the categories of "male dominance" or "women's subordination."[36]

For anthropologists, this heated discussion began to define a new era for understanding gender more fully within its cultural context, a cultural context within which genders were not diametrically opposed but were always in the process of being negotiated. A renewed emphasis on ethnography ensued so that anthropologists might more fully elaborate the negotiation of gender in local contexts.[37] In turn, these ethnographies opened a new window into the utilization of anthropological knowledge for understanding gender-based inequality in particular and larger systems of inequality in general. Importantly, this discussion began to shift the focus away from "women," as rooted in an assumption about common biology, and forcefully toward "gender," as grounded in a more broadly based knowledge, one that accounted for the diverse cross-cultural experiences found on the continuum from "male" to "female." Thus, Louise Lamphere, one of the original authors in *Women, Culture, and Society*, would write over a decade later that

> [a]ll this discussion and debate has led us to call for more attention to individual cases, more attention to historical data so that particular cultural configurations can be analyzed as changing and not static, and more effort to construct complicated models that see men and women, not as opposed, unitary categories but as occupying a number of different roles in each society, which in turn have a complex set of interrelationships.[38]

By the late 1980s and through the 1990s, **feminist anthropology** had solidly committed itself to understanding gender within more complex, culturally specific frameworks that included both women and men, alternate genders, race, and class. More than this, feminist anthropology had reconfigured the way all anthropologists thought about the very makeup and structure of culture. Indeed, it arguably produced a profound shift in the culture of anthropology as a whole. As Henrietta Moore notes, "Feminist anthropology is more than the study of women. It is the study of gender, of the interrelations between women and men, and the role of gender in structuring human societies, their histories, ideologies, economic systems and political structures. Gender can no more be marginalized in the study of human societies than can the concept of 'human action,' or the concept of 'society.' It would not be possible to pursue any sort of social science without a concept of gender."[39]

COMING FULL CIRCLE: LESSONS FROM GENDER, INEQUALITY, AND FEMINIST ANTHROPOLOGY

Given these developments in feminist anthropology, many of the assumptions explored in *Women, Culture, and Society* still hold today. From international prostitution rings to date rape and from unequal pay scales to unequal hiring practices, gender-based inequality is a very real phenomenon, and so is male dominance and the exploitation of women. While women's subordination may not be true everywhere and in all cases (Nazaré, the Ryūkyū Islands), women's subordination does have a pervasive pattern throughout the world in the past (especially since humans abandoned foraging) and in the present (especially as articulated by the economic divisions between the world's core and periphery). Moreover, discrimination against homosexuals, transsexuals, and other alternative genders is just as pronounced as discrimination against women in some parts of the world. To be sure, gender-based inequality is as real as it was ten or thirty or one hundred years ago.[40]

What do we learn from the deeper and more nuanced intricacies of gender, power, and inequality? The study of gender and feminist anthropology offers us two important lessons. First, understanding the complexities of gender can significantly broaden our holistic understanding of culture. Being aware of the cultural processes of gender gives us unique insight into one of the most basic human phenomena. While not all people everywhere and in all times (past and present) share the experience of class (see chapter 4) or race (see chapter 1), for example, all people in all places and at all times have shared the experience of being part of a society or culture in which we

ANTHROPOLOGY HERE AND NOW

You can learn more about the field of feminist anthropology, including publications, current research activities, and other topics, at the website of the Association for Feminist Anthropology, posted at www.aaanet.org/sections/afa. (See especially "Links and Resources.")

CHECK IT OUT!

build on biological sex and negotiate gender. Indeed, gender is one of the cornerstones of culture—from marriage to family to kinship, which are the subjects of the next chapter.

Second, feminist anthropology offers both a perspective for understanding gender-based inequality more deeply and a call to action.[41] Like Boas, feminist anthropologists were not content on *just* understanding, in this case, the relationships between gender, power, and inequality. A complex and hotly debated knowledge has necessitated a more complex redress of women's and gender issues on local and international stages alike. But this call to action is not limited to the study of women or the study of gender. While much of feminist scholarship continues to address the widespread domination and exploitation of women in our world, feminist anthropology (and feminist scholarship in general) has opened new ways to understanding and acting on the deeper complexities of all types of inequality in our world—a project to which anthropology has been deeply committed since its modern inception.

NOTES

1. Margaret Mead, *Sex and Temperament in Three Primitive Societies* (New York: Morrow, 1935), 279.

2. Ibid.

3. Ibid.

4. Ibid., 279–80.

5. Elsie Clews Parsons, *Pueblo Indian Religion* (Chicago: University of Chicago Press, 1939), 9ff.

6. See George Gallup Jr. and D. Michael Lindsay, *Surveying the Religious Landscape: Trends in U.S. Beliefs* (Harrisburg, PA: Morehouse Publishing, 1999).

7. Susan Starr Sered, *Priestess, Mother, Sacred Sister: Religions Dominated by Women* (Oxford: Oxford University Press, 1994), 13–14.

8. Serena Nanda, *Neither Man nor Woman: The Hijras of India*, 2nd ed. (Belmont, CA: Wadsworth, 1999), especially 24–37.

9. Cf., for example, Raymond C. Kelly, "Witchcraft and Sexual Relations: An Exploration in the Social and Semantic Implications of the Structure of Belief," in *Man and Woman in the New Guinea Highlands*, ed. Paula Brown, Georgeda Buchbinder, and David Maybury-Lewis (Washington, DC: American Anthropological Association, 1976), 36–53, and Robert F. Murphy, "Social Structure and Sex Antagonism," in *Peoples and Cultures of Native South America*, ed. Daniel R. Gross (Garden City, NY: Doubleday, 1973), 213–24.

10. Susannah M. Hoffman, Richard Cowan, and Paul Aratow, *Kypseli Women and Men Apart: A Divided Reality* (Berkeley: University of California Extension Media Center, 1973).

11. Jan Brøgger, *Nazaré: Women and Men in a Prebureaucratic Portuguese Fishing Village* (Forth Worth, TX: Harcourt Brace Jovanovich, 1992).

12. Ibid., 16.

13. Carol P. MacCormack, "Nature, Culture, and Gender: A Critique," in *Nature, Culture, and Gender*, ed. Carol P. MacCormack and Marilyn Strathern (Cambridge: Cambridge University Press, 1980), 18.

14. Will Roscoe, *Changing Ones: Third and Fourth Genders in Native North America* (New York: St. Martin's Press, 1998), 7, 223–47.

15. See Charles Callender and Lee M. Kochems, "The North American Berdache," *Current Anthropology* 24, no. 4 (1983): 443–70.

16. Alfred W. Bowers, *Hidatsa Social and Ceremonial Organization* (Washington, DC: Bureau of American Ethnology, 1965), 167.

17. Ibid., 166–67; Callender and Kochems, "The North American Berdache," 451.

18. See Callender and Kochems, "The North American Berdache," 451–53.

19. Ibid.

20. George Devereux, "Institutionalized Homosexuality of the Mohave Indians," *Human Biology* 9: 498–527. For a concise description, see also Serena Nanda, *Gender Diversity: Crosscultural Variations* (Prospect Heights, IL: Waveland Press, 2000), 21–23. My placement of the Mohave in the Greater Southwest follows Alice B. Kehoe, *North American Indians: A Comprehensive Account*, 2nd ed. (Englewood Cliffs, NJ: Prentice Hall, 1992), 103–59.

21. In addition to Devereux, "Institutionalized Homosexuality of the Mohave Indians," see George Bird Grinnell, *The Cheyenne Indians: Their History and Ways of Life*, 2 vols. (New Haven, CT: Yale University Press, 1923), 39–47, and Wesley Thomas, "Navajo Cultural Constructions of Gender and Sexuality," in *Two-Spirit People: Native American Gender Identity, Sexuality, and Spirituality*, ed. Sue-Ellen Jacobs, Wesley Thomas, and Sabine Lang (Urbana: University of Illinois Press, 1997), 156–73. Cf. Roscoe, *Changing Ones*, 213–47.

22. See Beatrice Medicine, "'Warrior Women': Sex Role Alternatives for Plains Indian Women," in *The Hidden Half: Studies of Plains Indian Women* (Lanham, MD: University Press of America, 1983), 267–80.

23. Ibid., 276.

24. See, for example, Brian Joseph Gilley, *Becoming Two-Spirit: Gay Identity and Social Acceptance in Indian Country* (Lincoln: University of Nebraska Press, 2006).

25. Nanda, *Neither Man Nor Woman: The Hijras of India*, 130–37. See also Unni Wikan, "Man Becomes Woman: Transsexualism in Oman as a Key to Gender Roles," *Man* 12 (1977): 304–19; Niko Besnier, "Polynesian Gender Liminality through Time and Space," in *Third Sex, Third Gender: Beyond Sexual Dimorphism in Culture and History*, ed. Gilbert Herdt (New York: Zone, 1996), 285–328; and Antonia Young, *Women Who Become Men: Albanian Sworn Virgins* (Oxford: Berg, 2000).

26. See Marjorie Shostak, *Nisa: The Life and Words of a !Kung Woman* (New York: Vintage Books, 1981), 243.

27. See Martha Ward, *A World Full of Women* (Boston: Allyn & Bacon, 1996), 218–22.

28. In addition to Mead's *Sex and Temperament*, see also Simone de Beauvoir, *The Second Sex*, trans. H. M. Pashley (New York: Knopf, 1953), and Margaret Mead, *Male and Female* (New York: Morrow, 1949).

29. Michelle Zimbalist Rosaldo and Louise Lamphere, eds., *Women, Culture, and Society* (Stanford, CA: Stanford University Press, 1974). Other important books included Ernestine Freidl, *Women and Men: An Anthropologist's View* (New York: Holt, Rinehart and Winston, 1975), and Rayna Reiter, *Toward an Anthropology of Women* (New York: Monthly Review Press, 1975). The following discussion is drawn from several sources, including Micaela Di Leonardo, *Gender at the Crossroads of Knowledge: Feminist Anthropology in the Postmodern Era* (Berkeley: University of California Press, 1991); Louise Lamphere, "Feminism and Anthropology: The Struggle to Reshape Our Thinking about Gender," in *The Impact of Feminist Research in the Academy*, ed. Christie Farnham (Bloomington: University of Indiana Press, 1987), 11–33; Henrietta Moore, *Feminism and Anthropology* (Minneapolis: University of Minnesota Press, 1988); Sandra Morgen, "Gender and Anthropology: Introductory Essay," in *Gender and Anthropology: Critical Reviews for Research and Teaching*, ed. Sandra Morgen (Washington, DC: American Anthropological Association, 1989), 1–20; and Michelle Rosaldo, "The Use and Abuse of Anthropology: Reflections on Feminism and Cross-Cultural Understanding," *Signs* 5, no. 3 (1980): 389–417.

30. Rosaldo and Lamphere, "Women, Culture, and Society: A Theoretical Overview," in *Women, Culture, and Society*, 42.

31. Cara E. Richards, personal communication. See also Peggy Reeves Sanday, *Female Power and Male Dominance: On the Origins of Sexual Inequality* (Cambridge: Cambridge University Press, 1981), 24–28.

32. MacCormack, "Nature, Culture, and Gender," 17.

33. Sered, *Priestess, Mother, Sacred Sister*, 14.

34. Sanday, *Female Power and Male Dominance*, 171.

35. Hazel Carby, "White Women Listen! Black Feminism and the Boundaries of Sisterhood," in *The Empire Strikes Back: Race and Racism in 70's Britain*, ed. Birmingham University Centre for Contemporary Cultural Studies (London: Hutchinson, 1982), 214.

36. In addition to Carby, see, for example, Patricia Hill Collins, *Black Feminist Thought: Knowledge, Consciousness, and the Politics of Empowerment*, 2nd ed. (New York: Routledge, 2000); Gloria Hull, Patricia Bell Scott, and Barbara Smith, eds., *All the Women Are White, All the Blacks Are Men, But Some of Us Are Brave* (Old Westbury, NY: Feminist Press, 1982); and bell hooks, *Yearning: Race, Gender, and Cultural Politics* (Boston: South End Press, 1990). Also important to this critique—

and not discussed here—was the issue of feminist anthropologists choosing to speak for other women through ethnography and other modes of representation. Ethnographers, in particular, began to grapple with the very real differences in agendas between themselves and the women they studied. For a particularly intriguing discussion of this ethnographic problem, see Elaine Lawless, "'I Was Afraid Someone Like You . . . an Outsider . . . Would Misunderstand': Negotiating Interpretive Differences between Ethnographers and Subjects," *Journal of American Folklore* 105 (1992): 301–14. Cf. Elaine Lawless, *Holy Women, Wholly Women: Sharing Ministries through Life Stories and Reciprocal Ethnography* (Philadelphia: University of Pennsylvania Press, 1993), especially 1–7.

37. See, for example, Joan Newlon Radner, ed., *Feminist Messages: Coding in Women's Folk Culture* (Urbana: University of Illinois Press, 1993).

38. Louise Lamphere, "Feminism and Anthropology: The Struggle to Reshape Our Thinking about Gender," in *The Impact of Feminist Research in the Academy*, ed. Christie Farnham (Bloomington: Indiana University Press, 1987), 24.

39. Henrietta Moore, *Feminism and Anthropology* (Minneapolis: University of Minnesota Press, 1988), 6. For a host of other developments both in feminist anthropology and in the anthropological study of gender not discussed here, see Lila Abu-Lughod, *Writing Women's Worlds* (Berkeley: University of California Press, 1993); Sherry Ortner, *Making Gender: The Politics and Erotics of Culture* (Boston: Beacon Press, 1996); and Peggy Reeves Sanday and Ruth Gallagher Goodenough, eds., *Beyond the Second Sex: New Directions in the Anthropology of Gender* (Philadelphia: University of Pennsylvania Press, 1990).

40. See United Nations Population Fund, *The State of World Population 2000* (New York: United Nations Population Fund), especially chap. 3, "Violence against Women and Girls: A Human Rights and Health Priority."

41. See, for example, Moore, *Feminism and Anthropology*.

Work, Success, and Kids

On Marriage, Family, and Kinship

So many of us in today's world find our lives revolving around the same problem: we need money in order to survive, and we must have a job in order to make money. This imperative is reflected in the way we think about ourselves and others—increasingly we define ourselves by the jobs we do. In the United States, one of our first questions on meeting another is "What do you do?" which, of course, means "What's your job?" This conversational move is fast spreading through our contemporary world.

We follow jobs from city to city, or country to country, bringing our families along—our small, *portable* families. Two parents often work full time to rear one, two, or more children, or, often, a single parent (almost always the mother) works one, two, or more jobs and is responsible at home for rearing children. For most of human history, this was very unusual—that is, one or two people, off by themselves, rearing children alone—but, increasingly, it is now par for the course.

At first glance, our small, portable families may seem similar to small foraging bands that also followed "the job" of gathering and hunting. But in function, purpose, and consequences, our families—as arranged around the search for work within an international capitalist economy—are relatively new in the human scheme of things. Indeed, when we compare people from around the world, past and present, this kind of family is extremely unusual. Today, mainstream America's family ideal hinges on the union or marriage of two people who establish their household separate from other family households and who rear children within this separate space. These children are expected to grow up, leave their parents' home, and establish independent households, where they will repeat the process.

For mobile Americans, then, the abandonment of the extended family is the norm. We view those who remain ensconced within their families as aberrations, deviates, or losers. It is within this base of experience that we view talk shows regularly featuring sensationalist topics like "Grown Men and Women Who Haven't Left Home." A forty-year-old man who still lives with his mother. Positively shocking. "My God, get out of the house, man!" an audience member yells when she finally gets the microphone. "You can't depend on your mom forever. You should be ashamed of yourself!"

If the rest of the world were watching (and many of them are), they would (and sometimes do) view such displays with bewilderment. Why would anyone want to leave their family to establish their own household and remake a brand new family? What was wrong with the old family? Why would Americans condone such wholesale abandonment of their families? And this is a place that claims to have "family values"? What is wrong with these people?

I remember addressing these questions with one of my Kiowa consultants, Billy Evans Horse. We were talking about the meaning of success in America. I grew up defining success through the well-known American equation of "get a job + make money + get out of the house + start your own family = success," but Billy Evans Horse defined success as raising his children so that they would stay in the house, take care of their parents, and raise the next generation of Horses in that *same* house. Indeed, three-plus generations had raised their families in the Horse household. For traditional Kiowa people like Billy Evans Horse, choosing to live with your family—instead of leaving home to establish your own—constituted true family values. How could most Americans claim to have family values, he asked, when they consistently choose jobs and money and independence (and getting out of the house) over their families?[1]

When we do cross-cultural comparisons of both past and present human concepts of family, we find that most of the world would agree with Billy Evans Horse. He is expressing value not just for a Kiowa tradition but also for a human tradition in which family is the primary social commitment and the basis of personal identity. The desire to leave your old family behind and make a new one is relatively novel in the human scheme of things.

Billy Evans Horse.
Photo by author.

INTRODUCING FAMILY: ON KINSHIP

For most of human history (and presently for many of the world's people), "family" has conventionally consisted of large networks of relatives, or kin—networks that anthropologists call **kinship**. Cross-culturally, kinship is based on the relationships created by marriage (or **affinity**) and birth (or **consanguinity**). Both of these human phenomena, we will find, are—like everything else human—constructed by culture. While we may find many societies that assign relatedness of children to both parents and their families equally, for example, we find others that assign relatedness of children more to the mother and her family than to the father and his family and vice versa. Humans build on marriage and birth to construct "family" in amazingly diverse ways.²

Take an example close at hand: the Kiowa. Like most Americans, Kiowa people reckon kinship through each side of the family, assigning relatedness more or less equally through both males and females (any given individual is more or less equally related to both mother's and father's brothers and sisters). Unlike most Americans, though, many Kiowa people put into practice a way of reckoning family that is more specific to their own Kiowa tradition.[3] For instance, many of those whom most Americans would call "cousins" are often called (in English) "brothers" and "sisters" in the Kiowa community. Many of the relatives whom most Americans would call "uncles" and "aunts" Kiowas would also call, in English, their "fathers" and "mothers." Your mother's sisters are called "mother," and your father's brothers are called "father." And *their* spouses also can be, and sometimes are, called "mother" or "father."[4] (There are separate Kiowa-specific terms for mother's brothers and father's sisters in the Kiowa language, but today these individuals are often called, in English, "aunts" and "uncles." Bernadine Herwona Toyebo Rhoades puts the contemporary practice succinctly: "Your mother's sisters are called 'mother' and her brothers are your uncles. Your father's brothers are addressed as 'father' and his sisters are your aunts."[5])

ANTHROPOLOGY HERE AND NOW

You can learn more about the Kiowa Tribe of Oklahoma—including various cultural organizations (many of which are descent organizations)—on their official tribal office website at www.kiowatribe.org.

CHECK IT OUT!

Kiowa people today may embrace several different variations on this theme—especially because the Kiowa way of reckoning kin, particularly in its older form, can be incredibly involved and complex, with numerous specific terms for different relatives. Kiowa people currently build on this older system and often combine it to varying degrees with the way of reckoning kin in mainstream American families (using, for example, English terms like "aunt," "uncle," "sister," "brother," "mother," and "father").[6] The point here is that, even today, any individual in the Kiowa community can conceivably have several dozen brothers, sisters, mothers, and fathers (and aunts and uncles).

The Kiowa kinship system gets more interesting when we add more "vertical" relatives. Among the Kiowa, you don't have just two sets of grandparents: your grandparents' brothers and sisters can also be your grandparents. Of course, it works the other way, too. Just as an elder can conceivably have dozens of grandchildren, grandchildren can have as many grandparents.

I'll get to what this means shortly. But let's add another generation. (This is where it gets really interesting to me.) Your great-grandparents may be addressed in the same way as your siblings, as "brothers" and "sisters." In fact, you may call your great-grandmother "big sister," and she may call you "little brother" or "little sister," depending on your gender.

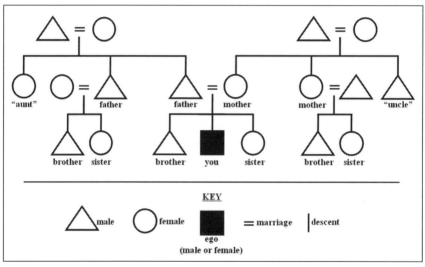

Relatives most Americans would call "cousins" are often called (in English) "brothers" and "sisters" in the Kiowa community. Many of the relatives whom most Americans would call "uncles" and "aunts" Kiowas would also call, in English, their "fathers" and "mothers." Your mother's sisters are called "mother," and your father's brothers are called "father."

Taking all this into account, imagine having dozens of brothers and sisters, fathers and mothers, grandparents, and "big brothers" and "big sisters." It works in the other direction, too. Even if you are not married, you can conceivably have a good many sons and daughters (who are your brothers' or sisters' children), grandchildren, and even perhaps "little brothers" and "little sisters." Can you even imagine keeping up with a system like this from day to day? Well, many Kiowas do, even today. "That Kiowas put a lot of stock in how they are related to other Kiowas is pretty well known in southwestern Oklahoma," writes Kiowa and anthropologist Gus Palmer Jr. "As it turns out, Kiowas are actually one big family in ways that puzzle most non-Indians. They can't believe you have so many grandpas and uncles and brothers."[7]

Significantly, the terms that Kiowa relatives call one another are not merely labels. They also imply certain kinds of relationships with and responsibilities to others. As an individual in the Kiowa world, your many parents may have responsibilities for you just like your biological parents: they may discipline you, they may take care of you if your parents die or divorce, and they may help out, if they are able, with your education just like your biological parents. The relationship between grandparents and grandchildren is a bit different: you are meant to spoil one another. In the same way that grandparents spoil their grandchildren, grandchildren, as they grow up, may reciprocate by indulging their grandparents; grandchildren take their grandparents to powwows, take them to the movies, and may even care for them if they become ill. Your dozens of brothers and sisters can be the most important relationships you have. Historically, the Kiowa brother-sister bond was the most important of all: it was often more important than your relationship to your fathers or mothers or even to your spouse. "A woman can always get another husband," it was said, "but she cannot get another brother."[8] Even today, a sister may ask anything of her brother and he will respond, and vice versa. And your relationship with your "big sister" or "big brother" can be much like your relationship with your brothers and sisters: you take care of one another, whatever the cost. In the Kiowa world, no one is left unrelated; hence, no one is left uncared for. "Almost every Kiowa is related to another Kiowa in one way or another," writes Palmer.[9]

This particular way of reckoning kinship is also found in other parts of the world (other indigenous groups have similar ways of reckoning kin). But even within this system there can be an amazing amount of diversity. Indeed, anthropologists make a number of distinctions concerning how kin are labeled like this from society to society. But in general, anthropologists refer to kin systems that reckon each side of the family as being similarly related through both male and female links (like the usual American family—"cousins" are "cousins" on each side) as **bilateral kinship**. While both mainstream Americans and Kiowa Americans may have very different ways of labeling and referring to their kin, they do generally share a system of bilateral kinship with many other groups around the world.

Even still, anthropologists have identified a great variety of kinship systems along these lines, many of which are also based on **descent**—that is, the assignment of relatedness traced through common ancestry. Some bilateral groups may reckon descent more or less informally through both male and female links—what anthropologists often call **cognatic descent**. (For example, the Kiowa community has several family descendant organizations whose members trace their relatedness to each other back to prominent Kiowa leaders.[10]) Other groups, however, may trace descent much more formally through either male or female links exclusively, a way of reckoning kinship relations that can be very different from that found among bilateral groups— a kind of kinship that anthropologists often call **unilineal descent**. These two ways of reckoning descent, through either the father's or the mother's family, are referred to as **patrilineal descent** and **matrilineal descent**, respectively.

Let's consider matrilineal descent. In societies that practice matrilineal descent, all people—male and female—trace their kinship relations through their mother's side of the family. As a member of a matrilineal society, regardless of your gender, you are (of course) related to your mother and your father. Although you may recognize your father and his kin as related through marriage, by birth you are considered more directly related to (and are a member of) your mother's family. This means that your relatedness to the unilineal kin on your father's side stops, in a way, with your father. Although, again, you may (depending on what society you reside in) recognize his kin as distant relatives through marriage, you are not directly related to his parents, his brothers and sisters, or their children. Simply put, they are outside the membership of your mother's kin, which consists of your mother's relatives.

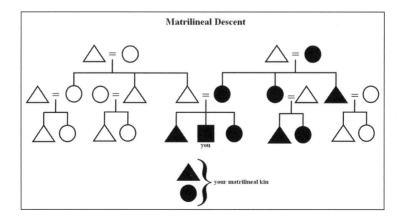

Matrilineal Descent

you

your matrilineal kin

In this system, then, you are closely related to your mother, her parents, her brothers and sisters, and the children of your mother's *female* relatives. Because in the matrilineal system descent does not pass through male relatives, you are not closely related to any children (cousins) of your mother's *male* relatives.

Patrilineal descent is the exact opposite of matrilineal descent: all people, both male and female, reckon their unilineal kin through their father's side of the family. Kinship is not traced through female relatives—which means, of course, that you are *not* closely related to any children (cousins) of your father's *female* relatives. Of the two unilineal descent systems, matrilineal descent is more rare, but ethnographers have described both in various forms all over the world—from Africa to Europe, Asia, the South Pacific, and North and South America.

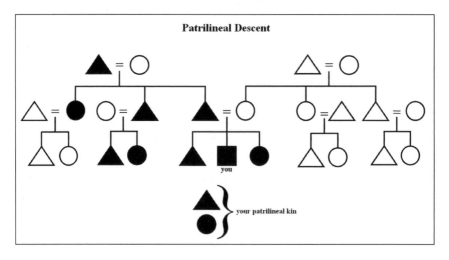

Unilineal descent can get very complicated. In the bilateral system—like most Americans, including the Kiowas—the boundaries of families (where they begin and leave off) can be ambiguous. Yet in many unilineal societies (patrilineal or matrilineal), families in space (who is alive and a member of the family right now) and time (who was a member of the family in the past or who will be a member of the family in the future) are often much more formally organized as **lineages**—larger descent groups made of several patrilineal or matrilineal families who often have power above and beyond any particular family within the lineage. This larger family lineage, then, can extend back in time and will continue into the future—that is, everyone will be born into a lineage, not just a family. The lineage can be important for organizing several villages within a tribal political structure, for example. Or the lineage can be important for passing property or land from fathers to sons or from mothers to daughters.

Lineages can be organized (and often are) into much larger collective units called **clans**, which are composed of several lineages. When we start talking about clans, we're no longer talking about hundreds of people; we're talking about thousands of people. Indeed, among those people who practice clan descent rules, the clan may stretch back to the beginning of time and may continue, presumably, well into the future.

In the clan system, people remember and keep up with what clan you are from and to which clan you belong from the time you are born. In these societies, it is among the first things you learn. In many unilineal Native American groups, for example, among the first things that people ask one another is to which clan they belong. Such questions are significant for a number of reasons, among the most important being to determine whom you can and cannot marry.

THE INCEST TABOO, EXOGAMY, AND ENDOGAMY

Generally, all people past and present have made a distinction between whom they may and may not marry. While people define and practice **marriage** in a diversity of ways (which I'll address in the next section), prohibitions are universally based on three things: the **incest taboo** (which regulates sex and/ or marriage between people considered kin), **exogamy** (marriage outside a certain group), and **endogamy** (marriage within a certain group).[11]

The incest taboo is perhaps the most important of these. Like everything else cultural, the incest taboo is constructed differently from society to society, from culture to culture. In America today, for example, incest is commonly defined as having sexual relations with someone closely related—for example, a sibling, parent, grandparent, aunt, uncle, or cousin. As bilateral people, we tend to see everyone as generally equally related to everyone else on both our mother's and our father's side of the family. In this context, it makes sense that we would not want to have sexual relations with them.

Among many other people of the world, the incest taboo isn't this simple. In many unilineal descent systems, the incest taboo can be defined quite differently from the way it is among those who practice bilateral kinship. In these systems of descent, certain so-called cousins (from our bilateral point of view) are outside the incest taboo: they are not directly related to you because descent cannot be passed through males (in matrilineal descent systems) or females (in patrilineal descent systems). Thus, in matrilineal societies the incest taboo does not apply to cousins on your father's side of the family or cousins who are your mother's brother's children. They are considered *exogamous* (outside your own lineage). In some matrilineal societies, these cousins can be considered ideal marriage partners (a marriage practice that anthropologists call **cross-cousin marriage**)—ideal because such an arrangement helps to continue already established relationships between and among families.

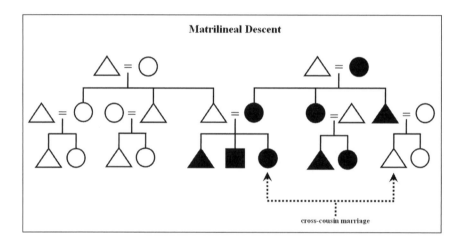

The same pattern of cross-cousin marriage can occur in patrilineal societies. Here, cousins on the mother's side of the family and the father's sister's children are not directly related; thus, they are outside the incest taboo. But in a few patrilineal societies (e.g., among some Arab groups), there is a rare exception to the rule. In these societies, because property is passed through the male line, a marriage to the father's brother's children is ideal because it maintains and strengthens the passage of property within the lineage (anthropologists call this marriage practice **parallel-cousin marriage**). Although parallel cousins are endogamous (inside the lineage), they are still considered marriageable partners. Marrying "within" family happens elsewhere as well.

Extreme cases include brother-sister marriage, such as that among royalty in ancient states (remember Cleopatra?). Nevertheless, when we examine the practices of marriage around the world, cousin marriage is not as unusual as it sounds to us. But this brings me back to an important point: the incest taboo, and thus exogamy and endogamy, are incredibly variable when viewed through an ethnological lens; what seems strange to us is so because we view the world through a bilateral system. But even among those of us who share a bilateral system, considerations of "family" and "marriage" can be highly variable, as the Kiowa example illustrates. How much more important it is, then, that we recognize that those who live within a patrilineal or a matrilineal system view the world through their kinship systems as strongly as we do.

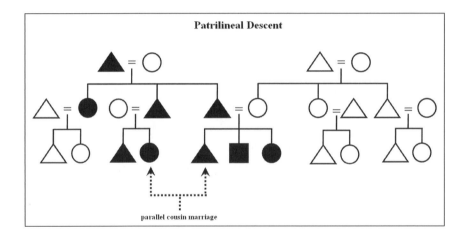

Patrilineal Descent

parallel cousin marriage

DEFINING MARRIAGE CROSS-CULTURALLY

Obviously, part of the purpose of the incest taboo, exogamy, endogamy—and, ultimately, marriage—is to regulate sex and to produce offspring, but cross-culturally, past and present, marriage has a range of purposes that far exceed the regulation of sex or the production of offspring. Marriage is critical to kinship for a number of reasons; perhaps most important, it is through marriage that kin groups build and maintain family through time. Anthropologists have long struggled to define marriage because its practice is so diverse, it takes on so many different forms, and it serves so many purposes.[12]

Many modern Americans tend to think about marriage as the union of a man and woman who may or may not produce offspring. Simple enough. But in addition to being ethnocentric, this idea of marriage does not easily account for all the forms of marriage that we find in the ethnographic record, past and present. Take, for example, the widespread occurrence of "female husbands" or **woman marriage** in many African societies.[13] Among the Nuer, patrilineal pastoralists of Sudan, a woman unable to have children may take a "wife" who enters into sexual relations with a man to bear children. The children, in turn, refer to the first woman (the one who has taken a wife) as "father" and inherit property (e.g., cattle) through her father's patrilineal lineage (because children cannot inherit property through women). Among the Nandi, patrilineal pastoralists of Kenya, a woman who does not bear sons for her husband—which is critical for passing property from father to son—may enter into a nonsexual marriage with another woman, who, as in the Nuer case, enters into sexual relations with a man to bear children. Again, as in the Nuer case, the children can now inherit property through their female "father." In parts of West Africa, a wealthy married woman who works outside the home may marry another woman who will take care of the home and children. Among some Bantu peoples of southern Africa, "woman marriage" takes several different forms: among the Zulu, when a father dies and has no male heirs, his eldest daughter may take his place and marry another woman who will bear male heirs on his behalf.[14]

This certainly does not match the definition of marriage we have in mind when we think about marriage in the United States, does it? While the "female husband" or "woman marriage" may seem bizarre to most Americans, this kind of flexibility shows up rather often in the ethnographic record, past and present. (So, too, does inflexibility—for instance, in some patrilineal societies,

ANTHROPOLOGY HERE AND NOW

BBC recently ran a story about the traditional practice of same-sex marriages between women in Kenya, and how the passing of property via these traditional marriage arrangements has been recently bolstered by a high-court ruling. The story, "Kenya's Legal Same-Sex Marriages," can be accessed at www.bbc.co.uk/news/world-africa-16871435.

CHECK IT OUT!

a woman could face death for not producing male heirs.) With these kinds of examples in mind, we might think about marriage cross-culturally as a union between a *socially acknowledged* (if not biological) "male" and "female." But the human practice of marriage is much more diverse than what this might imply. Many modern nation-states recognize same-sex unions, which do not always involve the social or legal acknowledgment of one person as "husband" and the other as "wife." Or consider the much more common practice of **polygamy**, which is marriage of one person to two or more spouses.

Polygamy has been described all over the world. Generally, it takes on two forms: **polygyny** (one man married to more than one woman) and **polyandry** (one woman married to more than one man). Polyandry is the rarer of the two, and anthropologists have described it in cultures primarily in south Asia. In the Himalayas, for example, several brothers may marry one wife to keep from splitting up their property (especially land, which can be limited) among their children. Additionally, the wife always has a husband at home if the brothers must travel for long periods of time.[15] The more common form of polygamy is polygyny. Unlike polyandry, it has surfaced all over the world from Asia to Africa to the Americas. Take, for example, the Rashaayda

Many Americans think that same-sex unions, like the public ceremony pictured here, are a modern phenomenon. But in some parts of the world, same-sex marriages— such as the widespread occurrence of "female husbands" or "woman marriage"— actually represent a very old practice. Photo by Danny Gawlowski.

Bedouin, Arab pastoralists of eastern Sudan. Here, a man may enter into a marriage with several cowives, each of whom may have her own household where she and her children live. Tensions do arise between cowives, but the husband is bound by tradition to provide for each wife equally. Ethnographer William C. Young reports that "if a polygynously married woman finds any sign of unequal treatment, she will complain to her brothers, who will also resent the slight of their family and will, consequently, back her in a quarrel with her husband and support her if she leaves him and asks for a divorce."[16]

When we consider that the husband must treat each wife equally—which includes providing for each of them and their children—you might reason that all Bedouin men would neither want nor be able to enter into a polygynous marriage. Well, you would be reasoning correctly. While polygyny may be the Bedouin ideal, in actuality very few men and their families can afford it. This raises an important point about polygyny in general: among the world's people for whom polygyny is the ideal, few men and their families actually enter into the practice because they do not have the resources to do so.[17] As Americans, we tend to view such polygamous unions (both polyandrous and polygynous ones) through our own concepts of marriage, which found the institution on the sexual relations between two people. But polygamy is about much more than different sexual partners. Among some Plains Indian tribes, for example, men often took the unmarried sisters of a first wife as cowives. These sisters might otherwise have been left uncared for in a warrior-based society in which shortages of men were common.[18] And among the Rashaayda Bedouin, men often engage in polygyny to enlarge the size of their families, which can further their political careers.[19]

Like everything else cultural, people all over the world today debate and negotiate these marriage customs. Indeed, an international debate rages about the purposes and meanings of polygamy, especially concerning polygyny and its relationship to women's subordination.[20] While this might seem to be a "no-brainer," it is actually a complex issue. Consider, for example, what U.S. journalist, attorney, and polygynist Elizabeth Joseph says about what she calls her "ultimate feminist lifestyle":

> I've often said that if polygamy didn't exist, the modern American career woman would have invented it. Because, despite its reputation, polygamy is the one lifestyle that offers an independent woman a real chance to "have it all." . . .

As a journalist, I work many unpredictable hours in a fast-paced environment. The news determines my schedule. But am I calling home, asking my husband to please pick up the kids and pop something in the microwave and get them to bed on time just in case I'm really late? Because of my plural marriage arrangement, I don't have to worry. I know that when I have to work late my daughter will be at home surrounded by loving adults with whom she is comfortable and who know her schedule without my telling them. My eight-year-old has never seen the inside of a day-care center, and my husband has never eaten a TV dinner. And I know that when I get home from work, if I'm dog-tired and stressed-out, I can be alone and guilt-free. It's a rare day when all eight of my husband's wives are tired and stressed at the same time. . . . Polygamy is an empowering lifestyle for women.[21]

Regardless of where you stand on this issue, marriage seems a little more complex when we attempt to put aside our own ethnocentrisms and seek to understand (not necessarily agree with) "the native point of view."

This brings me back to a point about the purposes of ethnography (from chapter 3): while a study of culture allows us to appreciate others' way of life, it also should teach us something about ourselves. When we work to comprehend the cross-cultural role of marriage in a larger world context, we begin to understand that marriage can be much more than two people "bound in a sacred union" who produce *their* children, who, in turn, are *their parents'* sole responsibility. When we consider the complexity of the ethnographic record, marriage has been most often conceived among most humans within much larger networks of kin. Simply put, in the larger human scheme of things, marriage is not about sex or love in the way that most Americans think about it; *cross-culturally, marriage is about creating and maintaining social rather than sexual relations.* It is more often social (i.e., again, conceived within much larger networks of kin) because it involves more than the husband-wife-children triad through which many Americans judge our own and others' experiences with marriage and family.

WHAT MARRIAGE CREATES AND MAINTAINS: MORE ON MARRIAGE AS A SOCIAL UNION

Just as family can be extremely important in defining social commitment and personal identity, the people with whom a family enters into marriage can also be significant. In actuality, they do not exist entirely outside of family ("not related to us") just because they are not marriageable. Chief among the things to consider about marriage are its consequences and ramifications, especially the responsibilities to other families that these unions engender.

Take, for example, the !Kung San—who, you'll remember, live in southern Africa and who, up until very recently, were hunter-gatherers. After a !Kung marriage, a new couple may, ideally, live with or near the bride's family for a time (in general terms, anthropologists call this **matrilocal** or **uxorilocal residence**). In the meantime, a !Kung man must hunt for his wife's family, a service that anthropologists call **bride service**. As you might imagine, it is in the family's best interest to have daughters marry because their husbands will help to provide for the larger family. The wife's family reciprocates by providing the couple with a place to live and raise children in the first years of the marriage. Through this system, all married people are essentially tied to a large network of people to whom they are immediately responsible.[22]

The practice of bride service is not found only among the !Kung; indeed, it's widespread. Compare the !Kung case with the Kiowa, who practiced a kind of bride service in certain cases. Recall that the brother-sister relationship was key to Kiowa kinship. Marriage was sometimes constructed around this most important relationship. Elite and high-status warriors, for example, could beseech their sisters to marry in order to oblige their sisters' new husbands to aid them in battle. Simply put, an elite warrior could put less prestigious warriors in his service through marriage; essentially, he could put the new brothers-in-law to work for him and his family. In a raid for horses, for example, the less prestigious warrior was bound to give a good number of his captured horses to his wife's brother. For less prestigious warriors trying to increase their status, it was in their best interest to be associated with a wife's brother who was a prestigious warrior.[23]

Bride service is widespread, but it is not the only kind of marriage/family responsibility. Many unilineal societies (and some bilateral folks, too) practice what anthropologists often call **bridewealth**, a practice in which the husband's kin gives gifts to the wife's kin at marriage. For many societies, the importance of bridewealth is that it sets up a reciprocal relationship that can last for the lifetime of the marriage. In some matrilineal societies, for example, the wife's matrilineage is obligated to reciprocate the original bridewealth by helping out the husband's matrilineage when there is a death or birth in the family. The husband's matrilineage is also obligated to help the wife's matrilineage in times of need. This back-and-forth reciprocation continues throughout the life of the marriage; each family has a responsibility to help the other in child care, to help pay for family ceremonies, or anything else that the matrilineage may face or enter into.

Imagine living in a society in which you have responsibilities both to your own family and to the families with whom you are connected through marriage. In many societies past and present, this responsibility is inescapable. You live your entire life through a network of kin relations, a network composed of relatives in your immediate family and relatives through marriage. Indeed, everyone lives and dies within the collective charter of multiple responsibilities and commitments generated and maintained by marriage.

This pattern is also pervasive in patrilineal societies. Take, for example, many traditional European and Asian societies, in which the wife's family is expected to give the woman's inheritance to the husband's family, a practice that anthropologists often call **dowry**. You might imagine that it would be in the best interest of the husband's family to marry. But it is also in the best interest of the husband's family to *maintain* the marriage because the wife's family can ask for the dowry back if there is a divorce. Indeed, these families—especially the men, who often run the show—have a great deal invested in this marriage.

Take another example from traditional China, in which marriage and the production of sons is seen as absolutely crucial to the longevity of the patrilineage. After a marriage, the wife resides with the husband's family (in general terms, **virilocal** or **patrilocal residence**), and her primary role is to produce children (especially males) to continue the patrilineage. Here, unlike the ideal brother-sister relationship among the Kiowa, the key relationship is between a father and son. Daughters will always leave the home to produce children for another patrilineage.[24]

The practice of producing children for the patrilineage is widespread among patrilineal societies, but it takes on a number of forms. The African "female husband" practice is one example, although, as you'll remember, the insistence that property or children pass through males is not as strict as it is (or was) in traditional China. Today, of course, these practices are increasingly being negotiated on an international scale. Within the past several decades, Chinese legislators, for example, have passed laws to deemphasize the role of the male in the traditional patrilineal system, and the dowry has been

Marriage doesn't just unify individuals; it can also strengthen relationships between and among groups. Building on traditions both old and new, a bride and groom exchange rings during a Coast Salish wedding at Lummi Nation in Washington State (top). Members of the bride's family prepare a canoe, filled with groceries and other gifts, to give to the groom's family (bottom). Photos by Josie Liming.

outlawed in some nation-states.[25] Changing something as basic as the ways people structure family does not come easily. Imagine if the U.S. Congress passed a law decreeing that we would reckon kinship matrilineally from here forward. We'd go crazy. "What, men taking the surnames of their wives?" There would be rioting in the streets.

Nevertheless, regardless of how we view these practices, these examples illustrate, once again, that marriage cross-culturally is not as much about the sexual union of two people as it is about generating and maintaining larger social networks. The larger social exchanges that pass through marriage cannot be underestimated, especially when the exchanges are being negotiated between large and powerful families.

With this in mind, it is easy to understand why many of these larger family groups have an interest in maintaining marriage; it is because maintaining marriage means maintaining larger social networks. In some societies, when the wife dies, the widower may marry a sister or another woman from his wife's family (a widespread practice that anthropologists call **sororate**), in this way maintaining his relationship with the family. For example, among the Kiowa, if a wife died, it was not unheard of for an unmarried sister to take over where her sister had left off. After all, the children were as much hers as her sister's. (Remember, because she was the deceased woman's sister, the children already called her "mother.")

This marriage practice can go the other way, too. When a husband dies, the widow may marry a brother or another man from her husband's family (another widespread practice that anthropologists call **levirate**). For example, when my wife's paternal grandfather died, two of his brothers came to the United States from Ireland to help rear and provide for his children. They stayed until the children left the home. For all intents and purposes, they acted as surrogate husbands and fathers during this time.

These practices (*levirate, sororate*) are found all over the world and are an indication of how seriously people take marriage, family, and kinship. To reiterate, marriage is especially important for *what it means to larger groups*; its significance extends way beyond our own ethnocentric assumptions of marriage being based on two people alone, who, once married, establish independent households (a practice that, in general terms, anthropologists call **neolocal residence**). Even with a divorce (which is also common in the ethnographic record), in many societies a break in the marriage does not always mean a break in family responsibilities. In societies like the !Kung or the Kiowa, a divorce does not mean that one parent is left to rear children alone. Because the children belong to a much larger kinship group, they are taken care of by both sides of the family, even after the divorce. It is an obligation set into motion by the original marriage. The kinship connections created by the marriage don't just disappear. Indeed, children belong to larger groups and hence are the responsibility of those larger groups, not just of two isolated individuals.

Marriage, then, is universal because of the larger groups it creates, re-creates, and maintains. Founded in the incest taboo, it forces people to build groups outside the narrow confines of their own family. Because humans depend on culture for survival and culture exists within a society (a system of interacting people), there is vastly more to marriage, ethnologically speaking. The practice of marriage forces people to transcend narrow notions of "us" and "them" and to create connections and alliances between and among larger groups. It's the cultural correlative of kinship; it requires that people think outside themselves and their immediate relatives. Consequently, it is at the very heart of the workings of traditional society the world over.[26]

Many anthropologists (although certainly not all) thus argue that the incest taboo and what it creates, marriage, is all about building what we know to be human society. The incest taboo, marriage, and the group alliances they created have engendered societies in which everyone was obligated to everyone else, in which everyone not only felt a responsibility to all those around them but also knew it as their family duty on a profound level—a level that is hard for most of us to fully appreciate and understand today.[27]

MARRIAGE, FAMILY, AND KINSHIP: LESSONS FOR CONTEMPORARY FAMILIES

Today, families continue to change at a rapid pace. More and more of us live in small, portable, relatively confined, nuclear families—not necessarily because we want to but because we must. As members of a global market system, we are obliged to work within this system to survive. And one thing this system values highly is mobility; simply put, if we want to work, we must follow the jobs. Only modest nuclear families are small enough to move from job to job. As a result, we regularly make and remake our families from generation to generation as we move and split up and move again.

My parents, for instance, left their respective family farms in the mid-twentieth century because small-family farming was no longer viable in a world increasingly dominated by larger and larger corporate-run farms. Both of my parents' families parted with the communities in which they had lived for generations to pursue jobs other than farming. The second and third generations of these families have since left the communities in which *they* had been raised and are now scattered all over the United States. My family scattered not because we wanted to live apart but because we had to follow the jobs in our respective fields. Like most Americans, we have come to define ourselves and our success primarily through the jobs we have, not by our connections to our families.

Over the past one hundred years or so, such experience with family and work has become commonplace. American families are becoming more and more alike: the small nuclear family is the ideal type for the larger market system. Nuclear families are the production grounds for future consumers and future workers who will consistently choose work, production, and consumption over family because they have to.

Photos from my mother's family farm. Photos by author.

Of course, depending on where you stand, you could point out lots of positive things about this new "family": we can *choose* not to have children (as my wife and I have chosen) and not be ostracized for it, we are not bound to family control or censure (my wife's brothers did not force her to marry me), and we are not obliged to live with or provide for our in-laws ("Thank God!" my wife's relatives would say).

From many points of view (mine included), this is an ideal situation. But—and there's always a *but*—a price must be paid. From an ethnological point of view, we no longer live in the kinds of families that conceptualize responsibility to others in a broad way. For example, where once dozens of parents (e.g., the mom and dad and their brothers and sisters) reared children and saw them as their shared responsibility, today one or two people raise children alone. Ethnologically speaking, this is brand new; never have so many people the world over reared their children like this. We have yet to understand fully the consequences of these changes: we often blame parents exclusively for the problems with children in our society without even considering the larger economic system that breaks up our communities, scatters our families, and dictates our lives.

So what do we do? What can we take from this anthropologically based discussion of marriage, family, and kinship and apply to our own families and our own lives? Several things come to mind. Importantly, we must recognize that as long as we live and work in a world capitalist economy, the structure of our lives has changed, and thus the very idea of family has changed; indeed, families will most likely never be as they once were. When we compare the modern nuclear family with other families past and present, our sense of familial responsibility to others has narrowed considerably. Consequently, our overall outlook about responsibility to others—especially when compared to other societies more connected to larger ideals about family—has deteriorated remarkably.

This does not mean that people today have no conception of responsibility to others, for they clearly do. In large societies, people have always made social, political, and economic alliances outside the range of kinship (see chapter 4). They have adapted to changing circumstances in amazingly flexible ways. With this and our new understanding of family in mind, perhaps we should more consciously and explicitly recognize the importance and significance of making connections and crafting responsibilities to others outside

ANTHROPOLOGY HERE AND NOW

Anthropologists have closely studied the diverse changes experienced by families over the past several decades. Anthropologist Brian Hoey studies how many middle-class families have actively chosen to renegotiate their work lives (some at great expense) and relocate to places where they can have more control over their relationships with family and community. In his forthcoming book *Opting for Elsewhere*, he suggests that the stories of these families are part of a public debate about what constitutes the good life in a time of economic uncertainty coupled with shifting social categories and cultural meanings. Hoey's work documents how sweeping changes born of postindustrial economic restructuring impact both people and the places in which they live and work. You can learn more about his research on his website at brianhoey.com/research/research-lifestyle-migration.

CHECK IT OUT!

the narrow frameworks of the human families we have left. To be sure, it is harder to do today, but it's not impossible. In America, for example, we are quick to point out that "My neighbor's kids are my neighbor's responsibility, not mine." In a world where family truly matters, my neighbor's kids will be my responsibility. And so will those of everyone else.

NOTES

1. Billy Evans Horse, conversation with author, July 1992.

2. I collapse kinship and family here for ease of reference. Admittedly, many anthropologists make a clear distinction between family and kinship. At the same time, there is little consensus on "family," and anthropologists continue to argue about how to define it as an analytical category. See George P. Murdock, *Social Structure* (New York: Macmillan, 1949); David Schneider, *American Kinship: A Cultural Account* (Englewood Cliffs, NJ: Prentice Hall, 1968); Barrie Thorne, ed., *Rethinking the Family*, 2nd ed. (Boston: Northeastern University Press, 1992); and Sylvia Yanagisako, "Family and Household: The Analysis of Domestic Groups," *Annual Review of Anthropology* 8 (1979): 161–205.

3. The following description is based on my ongoing fieldwork in the Kiowa community from the early 1990s to the present (see, for example, Luke E. Lassiter, *The Power of Kiowa Song: A Collaborative Ethnography* [Tucson: University of Arizona Press, 1998]). As I note below, Kiowa kinship is today reckoned in a diversity of ways among various families, and the historical patterns are much more complicated than those briefly (and only partially) presented here. When using Kiowa terminology exclusively, many more specific terms are also used; indeed, Kiowa linguist and historian Parker McKenzie once noted that at one time Kiowas used over thirty different relationship categories ("Kiowa Relationship Terms," Parker McKenzie Collection, Oklahoma Historical Society Research Center, Oklahoma City). For a historical description of Kiowa kinship, see, for example, Robert H. Lowie, "A Note on Kiowa Kinship Terms and Usages," *American Anthropologist* 25 (1923): 279–81.

4. Ralph Kotay, personal communication, March 2002. See also "Kiowa Relationship Terms," Parker McKenzie Collection.

5. Bernadine Herwona Toyebo Rhoades, "Keintaddle," in *Gifts of Pride and Love: Kiowa and Comanche Cradles*, ed. Barbara A. Hail (Bristol, RI: Haffenreffer Museum of Anthropology, Brown University, 2000), 89.

6. In earlier editions, to avoid confusion I did not qualify my presentation of Kiowa kinship thusly in the main text (though I did so briefly in the notes). After reviewing this chapter with Billy Evans Horse in June 2007, however, Horse felt strongly that I should clarify up front that the current practice of reckoning kin in the Kiowa community is a contemporary (and, at times, highly variable) expression of the older and more involved Kiowa way of reckoning kinship. See note 3.

7. Gus Palmer Jr., *Telling Stories the Kiowa Way* (Tucson: University of Arizona Press, 2003), xvi.

8. Adapted from Jane Richardson, *Law and Status among the Kiowa Indians* (Seattle: University of Washington Press, 1940), 65.

9. Palmer, *Telling Stories the Kiowa Way*, xv.

10. See, for example, Lassiter, *The Power of Kiowa Song*, 86–88, 167–69.

11. I limit my discussion here primarily to the incest taboo and its relation to cross-cousin and parallel-cousin marriage. Anthropologists usually engage a much larger discussion about incest, exogamy, and endogamy. See, for example, William Arens, *The Original Sin: Incest and Its Meanings* (Oxford: Oxford University Press, 1986);

Linda Stone, ed., *New Directions in Anthropological Kinship* (Lanham, MD: Rowman & Littlefield, 2001); and Claude Lévi-Strauss, *The Elementary Structures of Kinship* (Boston: Beacon Press, 1969).

12. See, for example, Edmund Leach, "Polyandry, Inheritance and the Definition of Marriage," *Man* 55 (1955): 182–86, and *Rethinking Anthropology* (London: Athlone Press, 1961); Rodney Needham, ed., *Rethinking Kinship and Marriage* (London: Tavistock, 1971), and *Remarks and Inventions: Skeptical Essays about Kinship* (London: Tavistock, 1974); W. H. R. Rivers, *Kinship and Social Organization* (New York: Humanities Press, 1968); Judith R. Shapiro, "Marriage Rules, Marriage Exchange, and the Definition of Marriage in Lowland South American Societies," in *Marriage Practices in Lowland South America*, ed. Kenneth M. Kensinger (Urbana: University of Illinois Press, 1984), 1–30; and Linda Stone, ed., *New Directions in Anthropological Kinship* (Lanham, MD: Rowman & Littlefield, 2001).

13. See Eileen Jensen Krige, "Woman-Marriage, with Special Reference to the Lovedu—Its Significance for the Definition of Marriage," *Africa* 44 (1974): 11–36, who writes that "marriage of a woman to a woman [is] found in many African societies" (11). See also Denise O'Brien, "Female Husbands in Southern Bantu Societies," in *Sexual Stratification: A Cross-Cultural View*, ed. Alice Schlegel (New York: Columbia University Press, 1977), 109–26, who writes that "the female husband may belong to any one of over 30 African populations, and she may have lived at any time from at least the eighteenth century to the present" (109).

14. See E. E. Evans-Pritchard, *Kinship and Marriage among the Nuer* (London: Oxford University Press, 1951); Regina Smith Oboler, "Is the Female Husband a Man? Woman/Woman Marriage among the Nandi of Kenya," *Ethnology* 19 (1980): 69–88; Ifi Amadiume, *Male Daughters, Female Husbands* (London: Zed Books, 1987); and M. Gluckman, "Kinship and Marriage among the Lozi of Northern Rhodesia and the Zulu of Natal," in *African Systems of Kinship and Marriage*, ed. A. R. Radcliffe-Brown and D. Forde (London: Oxford University Press, 1950), 166–206, respectively. See also Krige, "Woman-Marriage, with Special Reference to the Lovedu," and O'Brien, "Female Husbands in Southern Bantu Societies."

15. See Nancy Levine, *The Dynamics of Polyandry: Kinship, Domesticity, and Population in the Tibetan Border* (Chicago: University of Chicago Press, 1988).

16. William C. Young, *The Rashaayda Bedouin: Arab Pastoralists of Eastern Sudan* (Fort Worth, TX: Harcourt Brace, 1996), 65.

17. Ibid., 64–65.

18. Robert Lowie, *Indians of the Plains* (Washington, DC: American Museum of Natural History, 1954), 79–80.

19. Young, *The Rashaayda Bedouin*, 64.

20. See, for example, United Nations Population Fund, *The State of World Population 2000* (New York: United Nations Population Fund), especially chap. 6, "Women's Rights Are Human Rights."

21. Excerpted from Elizabeth Joseph, "Creating a Dialogue: Women Talking to Women" (paper presented to the Utah chapter of the National Organization of Women, May 1997).

22. Richard Lee, *The Dobe Ju/'hoansi*, 2nd ed. (Fort Worth, TX: Harcourt Brace, 1993), 80–82.

23. Cf. Jane Fishburne Collier, "Rank and Marriage: Or Why High-Ranking Brides Cost More," in *Gender and Kinship: Essays toward a Unified Analysis*, ed. Jane Fishburne Collier, Sylvia Junko Yanagisako, and Maurice Bloch (Stanford, CA: Stanford University Press, 1987), 197–220.

24. See Margery Wolf, *Women and the Family in Rural Taiwan* (Stanford, CA: Stanford University Press, 1972).

25. Cf. Margery Wolf, "Chinese Women: Old Skills in a New Context," in *Women, Culture, and Society*, ed. Michelle Zimbalist Rosaldo and Louise Lamphere (Stanford, CA: Stanford University Press, 1974), 157–72.

26. See Lévi-Strauss, *The Elementary Structures of Kinship*. But also see Arens, *The Original Sin*.

27. Ibid.

7

Knowledge, Belief, and Disbelief

On Religion

The belief in and engagement with the supernatural—in a word, **religion**—is universal among human beings, but, just like everything else that is cultural, it varies greatly. Take, for example, the Spiritist (not to be confused with "Spiritualist") religious tradition of Brazil. The history of Spiritism, or "Kardecism," is complicated, but suffice it to say that since its importation from Europe to Brazil in the late nineteenth century, it has come to combine Christian beliefs with a belief in the efficacy of spirits to affect the material world (a combination of religious beliefs that anthropologists call **syncretism**). Specifically, Spiritism centers on the belief that dead human spirits inhabit the spirit world apart from the living. These spirits may return to this, the material world, several times through various incarnations, which allows them to advance morally, which is in turn required to live in the spirit world indefinitely. If spirits have led a morally degenerate life, for example, they may have to pass through numerous incarnations to learn the moral lessons necessary for immortality. Spiritists who live in the material world can aid these incarnations by allowing spirits to possess them and perform healings, which allows the spirits to advance morally through helping others who are in need. One well-known spirit is Dr. Adolf Fritz, who, since around the mid-twentieth century, has returned from the spirit world and performed such healings. According to Spiritists, Dr. Fritz was a surgeon during World War I who returns for moral advancement because of bad deeds he enacted in his last life. With the aid of other spirits, Dr. Fritz is most famous for possessing Spiritists and performing surgeries on those in need of medical help—without anesthetics or antiseptics.[1]

Some Pentecostal Holiness believers handle live rattlesnakes in their services, as this gentleman is doing in a church in southeastern Kentucky. Photo by Keith Tidball.

Compare this to the many Christian traditions that take seriously the incarnation of the Holy Spirit. Many Holiness and Pentecostal believers, for example, believe that "being filled" with the Holy Spirit is central to their experience and faith as Christians. Some Pentecostal congregations, however, take the incarnation of the Holy Spirit one step further: they explain that being filled with the Holy Spirit compels them to speak in tongues, take up serpents, and heal the sick in accordance with Mark 16:17–18, which reads,

Faith will bring with it these miracles: believers will cast out devils in my name and speak in strange tongues; if they handle snakes or drink any deadly poison, they will come to no harm; and the sick on whom they lay their hands will recover.[2]

Hence a very few Pentecostal church services thus include the handling of snakes and the drinking of strychnine as the Holy Spirit moves the service.[3] Compare this, further, with spirit possession in Malaysia. As in many societies, many Malaysians believe that angry spirits can inhabit and possess the body, causing harm. These spirits can sometimes be calmed or dispersed by religious practitioners, however. In modern Malaysian factories, spirit possession is a problem, especially among women who are pressured to work long hours, are underpaid, and are poorly treated. Easily susceptible to spirit possession, many women factory workers are possessed and enter into near madness. They, in turn, seek help from local religious practitioners to dispel the spirit, which may or may not be effective.[4]

ANTHROPOLOGY HERE AND NOW

The anthropology of religion is a broad and complex field, and anthropologists study and describe religion in diverse ways. A variety of resources can be found on the Internet, but a good brief description of the current state of the field (which also includes several references to helpful resources) can be found at hirr .hartsem.edu/ency/anthropology.htm.

CHECK IT OUT!

Although these beliefs might sound bizarre to us at first, these three examples share several elements; indeed, they reflect the basic tenets of all belief systems and all religions. Generally speaking, people everywhere, both past and present, identify powers that define, articulate, and engage the "supernatural," that which lies beyond what is "natural" and "everyday." These powers may take an impersonal form (such as among the !Kung, who describe a substance or force called *n/um* that can be used to influence desired outcomes, such as in healing an illness)—which is called **animatism**—or they may take a very personal form (such as, in very general terms, the Spiritists' Dr. Fritz, the snake handlers' Holy Spirit, or the Malaysians' angry spirits)—which is called **animism**. And people everywhere, both past and present, tell stories about how they and their world came to be, how their gods or beliefs came into being, and how they should conduct their lives. Here, in the context of these stories, a people's **mythology**—the larger "truths" of a particular belief tradition—is expressed, shaped, and reshaped from generation to generation, often via **ritual**—patterned group practice meant to engage the supernatural (church service, healing ceremony, group prayer).

Anthropologists make much more involved and complex distinctions when it comes to religion—such as the kinds of religion, the various ways in which religion is organized, and the broad range of meanings that religion can have in practice. Importantly, the **functions of religion** can include things like articulating the standards of right and wrong, addressing the unexplainable, easing the psychological stress brought on by misfortune, displacing decision making, or promoting community cohesion and solidarity.

As religions practiced in the modern world, Spiritism healing, Pentecostal snake handling, and Malaysian spirit possession have something else in common, though. Far from the mainstream of institutionalized religion, they share the experience of judgment from the outside, an ethnocentric assumption that presumes that such belief systems are backward, unenlightened, and irrational.

KNOWLEDGE AND BELIEF

In the natural and social sciences, we make a clear distinction between knowledge and belief—that is, between what we "know" (defined as true and factual) and what we "believe" (accepted on faith as true and real). We further rank knowledge *over* belief, asserting that knowledge, which is based on clear reasoning and experience, is *more substantiated* than belief, which may not be based on "clear evidence" or "proof." Indeed, to say "I believe that X is true" just isn't as strong as saying "I *know* X to be true."[5]

This opposition between knowledge and belief is based in part on the assumptions of **empiricism** (the position that experience serves as the source of knowledge), **positivism** (the position that knowledge is only useful if it can be "proved"), and **reason** (the position that knowledge is logical, factual, and sound). Following this logic, we might argue that belief (being based on faith and not knowledge) is unempirical, unprovable, and unreasonable. But if beliefs in Dr. Fritz, the Holy Spirit, or Malaysian spirit possession are not based on empiricism, positivism, or reason in the strictest sense, just how do they arise in culture in the first place?

We might answer that the ontological belief in spirits, for example, is based on hallucination, illusion, or the simple misinterpretation of reality.[6] Indeed, many social scientists, philosophers, and laypeople have long followed this rationale. Take Thomas Hobbes, who in 1651 wrote that

> [f]rom [an] ignorance of how to distinguish dreams from other strong Fancies, from Visions and Sense, [there arose] the greatest part of the Religion, of the Gentiles in time past, that worshipped Satyrs, Fauns, Nymphs and the like.[7]

Hobbes is saying that religious belief is rooted in ignorance and irrational thought and that, in times before the "progress" of civilization, religious belief developed from mistaking things like dreams or fantasies with reality. Writing at the dawn of the Enlightenment, Hobbes implied that in order for us to break free of ignorance, we must shake belief and embrace "truth" as evidenced by facts—that is, in today's terms, empiricism, positivism, and reason. The inverse assumption is that belief is not based on truth as evidenced by facts; it is based merely on *assuming* something to be true.[8]

Generally speaking, empiricism, positivism, and reason are very good things. These concepts force us to think about the links between facts and evidence, between theory and practice, or between motive and action. For example, I am using reason right now: I am navigating through a problem and following a tradition of logical thought that I have in part inherited from the likes of Hobbes, the scientific revolution, and the Enlightenment. But *reason* also forces us to *question* the links between facts and evidence, between theory and practice, or between motive and action. And then we are forced to ask: Is Hobbes's statement correct? Is religious belief irrational? Does it really lack evidence? Does it lack the rigors of logic rooted in experience and observation? Are "Satyrs, Fauns, Nymphs and the like" truly figments of people's imaginations?[9]

Following Hobbes, the scientific revolution, and the Enlightenment, social scientists have continued to assume that we should answer all these questions in the affirmative. Social evolutionists, for example, argued that because religion evolved in stages—presumably progressing from a "primitive" belief in multiple spirits, beings, or gods (called **polytheism**) to a more advanced belief in a single god (called **monotheism**)—supernatural belief would eventually give way to science, the final and most advanced expression of civilization. James Frazer, among the most prominent proponents of this view, suggested that early primitive peoples sought to control their world through **magic**, invoking or manipulating the supernatural to bear on a desired outcome. But for Frazer, magic represented a savage state wherein people failed to recognize their own limitations, that their invocation of the supernatural to affect a certain outcome was mistaken. In Frazer's scheme, magic was a precursor (and was separate from) religion, which—with its more formalized rituals, distinctive specialists, and all-powerful gods—evolved as people began to recognize that their individual power to affect the natural world, compared to that of their gods, was actually much more limited. "The savage," wrote Frazer,

> whether European or otherwise, fails to recognize those limitations to his power over nature which seems so obvious to us. In a society where every man is supposed to be endowed more or less with powers which we should call supernatural, it is plain that the distinction between gods and men is somewhat blurred, or rather has scarcely emerged. The conception of gods as supernatural beings entirely distinct from and superior to man, and wielding powers to which he possesses nothing comparable in degree and hardly even in kind, has been slowly evolved in the course of history.[10]

Simply put, religion was more "realistic" than magic and placed the supernatural beyond the reach of everyday believers. But by the same token, science, argued Frazer, was much more "realistic" than religion. Unlike magic and religion, science "worked" and was based on a clearer understanding of *causation* (i.e., that one action causes another). As such, science would eventually replace religion as people developed a clearer understanding of their world—just as religion had replaced magic in the larger evolutionary story.

Most contemporary anthropologists and other social scientists reject this view, that magic and religion are clearly distinct from one another, and that magic, religion, and science represent points along a continuum in the presumed progress of civilization. (Indeed, science has not replaced religion in the modern world, and many contemporary people believe and find meaning in both magic/religion *and* science.) Importantly, however, as social evolutionists' evolutionary scheme was discredited, anthropologists and other social scientists became less interested in the actual truth or verity of religion and focused instead on the *function* and *meaning* of religion. (Remember this; it's important.) In many ways, this approach helped to sidestep the deeper assumptions about the nonexistence and efficacy of the supernatural. Folklorist and medical anthropologist David J. Hufford writes that this assumption is deeply rooted in a Euro-American **worldview** and "has traditionally been the starting point for most academic work on the subject." Hufford goes on to write that

> [t]he research design begins with the question "Why and how do some people manage to believe things which are so patently false?" This question, of course, is usually implicit in modern writing, and attention is typically deflected from it by an obligatory statement to the effect that "We are not concerned here with the truth of these beliefs or the ontological status [whether they are systematically true] of the agents they posit." Nonetheless, the interpretations that follow often obtain most or all of their explanatory force from the assumption that the beliefs under study are objectively incorrect.[11]

In fact, a good deal of what we in the social sciences know about religion becomes expressed in ways described by Hufford. Introductory discussions to religion (in textbooks like this one) often describe the functions of religion, for example, in very predictable ways. Religion, you'll remember, may articulate standards of right and wrong, address the unexplainable, ease the psychological stress brought on by misfortune, displace decision making, or promote community cohesion and solidarity.[12] Simple enough. Any religious person— no matter what her tradition—might agree that her deeply held beliefs help to explain why her son, for instance, would die so suddenly ("addressing the unexplainable"), help her cope with his death ("easing the psychological stress brought on by misfortune"), or help bring her family together during this very difficult time ("promoting community cohesion and solidarity"). But what happens when this same person remarks that a spirit healed her son and prevented his death? Because it enters into the realm of truth or verity of belief, here is where many social scientific studies of religion diverge.

Take the Spiritist tradition in Brazil, which several medical and social scientists have studied since the 1960s and 1970s. They describe Dr. Fritz

surgeries that are conducted by incarnates (Spiritists who have been possessed by Dr. Fritz) who have absolutely no medical training. Interestingly,
in one study almost 70 percent of surveyed patients reported a cure or an
improvement in their condition as a result of Dr. Fritz surgeries. While
Spiritists say that Dr. Fritz is directly responsible for the healings, many
researchers have a different explanation. They argue that the "power of the
mind" (or the placebo effect) to relieve the stress of illness is among the keys
to understanding why Dr. Fritz surgeries and healings are so successful (and
so popular).[13] Or take the predominant explanations of snake handling, to
which researchers have directed a lot of scholarly attention. These researchers argue that (among other things) the snake-handling ritual is symbolic of
the capitalist domination of Appalachia or other rural regions where snake-
handling congregations are found. As poor and uneducated Americans,
the argument goes, Pentecostal congregations take up serpents as a kind of
"cultural critique" of the capitalist-based class system that dominates them
(despite the fact that some serpent handlers today include middle-class and
college-educated congregants).[14] This scholarly explanation is similar to explanations of spirit possession in Malaysia. While the women are adamant
about being possessed by angry spirits, the scholarly explanation emphasizes
that this is an unconscious resistance to exploitative work conditions.[15]

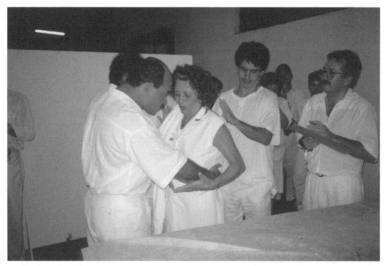

Dr. Fritz and Spiritists prepare a patient for surgery. Photo by Darrell Lynch.

In such cases, because social science has conventionally avoided the verity or truth of belief and instead focused on function and meaning, it has often avoided engaging or addressing Dr. Fritz, the Holy Spirit, or Malaysian spirit possession on their own terms: Dr. Fritz or the Holy Spirit or Malaysian spirit possession, the argument goes, are *real* only inasmuch as people *believe* they are real.[16] Belief is a product of culture, and because culture is very real, so, too, is belief in Dr. Fritz: "Dr. Fritz did not heal your son; your son's *belief* in Dr. Fritz healed him."

Don't get me wrong here. I am not saying that these kinds of scholarly explanations have no value, for they clearly do. Malaysian spirit possession as a form of resistance, for example, has a lot of explanatory power. Yet all these explanations are based on a pivotal assumption, an assumption derived from what David Hufford calls a *tradition of disbelief*—a tradition that is firmly situated in ways the social sciences have traditionally taken up the study of religion. Hufford argues that perspectives that elaborate the functions of religion clearly have their "usefulness but also . . . [their] limitations, limitations arising primarily from the fact that it is necessarily ethnocentric in the most fundamental sense." Hufford goes on to say,

> [This tradition of disbelief] takes a body of knowledge and considers it to be simply "the way things are" rather than a product of culture. It says over and over again: "What I know I *know*, what you know you only *believe*—to the extent that it conflicts with my knowledge."[17]

What Hufford means by this, of course, is that most of us—whether students of religion or not—proceed in our examinations, evaluations, or studies with an assumption about belief and its separation from knowledge. This assumption is not based on empiricism, positivism, or reason. It is, itself, based on belief and tradition, in the strictest sense (again, in Hufford's terms) our "tradition of disbelief." That is, we decide on faith that the Holy Spirit or Dr. Fritz or Malaysian spirit possession cannot be real; therefore, we posit, belief and its outgrowths (such as Dr. Fritz's healings) must be explained by other factors, such as "the power of the mind," "the power of suggestion," or "the power of belief to shape experience."

Because we may approach spirit healing or snake handling or spirit possession through the lens of our own tradition of disbelief, we look for other ways to explain why these folks would "believe things which are so patently false."[18] There *has* to be something else because we *believe* these things could not possibly be real. We draw these conclusions, of course, because down deep we "know" that Dr. Fritz, the Holy Spirit, or spirit possession are ultimately unempirical, unprovable, and unreasonable. But are they?

Malinowski (and a host of ethnographers since) illustrated how belief in powers or spirits or gods like Dr. Fritz, the Holy Spirit, or Malaysian spirit possession are universally experienced and universally logical. It turns out that supernatural belief is based not just on faith but also—when examined on its own terms—on experience, proof, and reason. Ethnographer Darrell Lynch, for example, reports that Spiritists are extremely critical of Dr. Fritz surgeries:

> Many Spiritists openly question whether such and such a medium of Dr. Fritz is truly authentic, or is really faking it. . . . Little if anything of the communications from spirits is taken at face value. Each is generally weighed for its authenticity and logic within the belief system by each individual. And many communications are rejected as false or non-authentic. Belief among Spiritists is often a very critical process; more so, I would venture to say, than perhaps many of our mainstream beliefs, religious or academic.[19]

Lynch's description reminds me of an example from my own fieldwork in the Kiowa community. I once had a conversation about spirits with an elderly Kiowa man, a man who was often called on to drive spirits out of homes where they were not welcome. He told me about several cases he had solved, but two are of particular interest here. In the first, he was summoned to a home where the family asked him to examine a room from which strange noises had sporadically been heard. As he always did, he planned to stay with the family—for several days, if need be—to ascertain the nature of the problem. During the first night of his visit, he heard the noise but was not convinced that it was a ghost of any sort. Having been a carpenter in his younger days, he had a good idea what it might be. The next morning he wriggled under the house and retrieved a loose piece of PVC pipe. Case solved. In the second story, he told how he had been summoned to a home where a young boy had recently died. His ghost, the family said, had been visiting the house; they had seen him several times walking the halls. The elderly Kiowa man stayed with the family for several days, until one evening he saw the ghost of the boy walk down the hallway and into the bathroom. He followed. There, before him, the boy stood in front of two towels on which his initials were embroidered. "You can't have these," the Kiowa elder said. "You need to leave them here with your parents." The boy's ghost disappeared, and after the family had destroyed the towels, the spirit was never seen again. Case solved.

What's the point here? "Very few believers," writes Hufford, "ever categorically exclude material explanations from consideration, because their worldview includes both kinds of possibility."[20] Interestingly, disbelievers (engendered by a "tradition of disbelief") are not so quick to include both kinds of possibilities because they assume that there is a clear hierarchical division between knowledge and belief.

CRITICALLY EXAMINING BELIEF AND DISBELIEF: LESSONS FOR BELIEVERS AND DISBELIEVERS

Pointing out that all people have "logical systems of belief," elaborating only the "functions of religion," or disallowing "both kinds of possibility," it turns out, may actually evade the deeper issues of supernatural experience and religious belief. And here I come to the point of this chapter. Two things have traditionally kept all of us (scientists, scholars, and lay alike) from more deeply understanding the diversity of religion we find in this world: first, our tradition of disbelief, and, second, our own deeply held religious (or other belief) traditions. Indeed, the idea that Dr. Fritz or the Holy Spirit or Malaysian spirit possession might be real not only challenges our tradition of disbelief but also can fundamentally undermine our own deeply held beliefs, whatever they might be. Thus, what often prevents a researcher from understanding more deeply the religious beliefs of others is a tradition of disbelief, and what may prevent a deeply dogmatic Christian and an equally dogmatic Muslim from understanding each other's religious beliefs is a tradition of belief that refuses to allow room for other beliefs, for other gods, or for other supernatural experiences (and this is especially true today, as **fundamentalism** of all stripes has increasingly engendered an antagonistic worldview, sometimes extreme, regarding the broad range of diverse beliefs and practices found in our modern world). Because of these two obstacles to understanding religion and belief more deeply, we really know very little about supernatural encounter and experience beyond the way religion functions in society.[21] We hold our respective beliefs and disbeliefs much too strongly.

In the end, we can all choose to be more conscious of our own assumptions and how they ultimately blind us to understanding others and their beliefs. Does this mean that we get to believe anything we want, with no consequences? Or that all belief (scientific, religious, or otherwise) essentially exists on an equal par? Not exactly. In our modern world certain beliefs may not be very functional, may even be dysfunctional, depending on the context in which you live and what your ultimate goals are. A belief, for example, that disavows the reality of evolutionary change won't get you very far if you're trying to, say, develop a vaccine for the influenza virus (which heavily depends on a deep and dynamic understanding of how evolutionary processes work). But if our goal is to understand the deeper experiential complexities of religious belief as it exists in our world today, then we must prepare ourselves to be more critical of our own ethnocentrisms, recognizing what is science, what is religion, what is knowledge, what is belief, what is disbelief. We can, for example, prove beyond a shadow of a doubt that the world is round, that the earth revolves around the sun, and that change is a biological constant— regardless of whether others believe it (and most people didn't until relatively recently). But we cannot always prove in the same way that another's belief in and encounter with, for example, Dr. Fritz is not real. With this in mind, what if we made a conscious decision to put aside our own disbelief in Dr. Fritz for a moment, embraced how Spiritists saw their world from the Spiritist point of view, and assumed, just for a moment, that Dr. Fritz is real? I am not suggesting that we wholeheartedly embrace the Spiritist belief in Dr. Fritz—only that we allow for the *possibility* that he just might be empirically real. What if the belief in Dr. Fritz is produced not by prior belief but by encounter and experience? If we took this point of view, we would find Spiritists to be very much like us. We would find that they have deeply held beliefs about the universe, about others, and about themselves. We would find that Dr. Fritz has a deeply significant impact on the lives of Spiritists, that he works to heal them most of the time. We would find many Spiritists who uncritically accept Dr. Fritz as a reality. We would also find many Spiritists who, though skeptical at first, came to believe in Dr. Fritz after having been healed by him. We would find that Spiritist belief is based on encounter and experience and not just on faith. Here, in the space of understanding another belief system from an ethnographic "native point of view," we would see the hierarchical divisions between "knowledge" and "belief " begin to dissipate.[22]

Anthropologist James Peacock relates a story in which he asked one of his Indonesian consultants if he believed in spirits. The consultant was puzzled, Peacock writes. "Are you asking," the man replied, "do I believe what spirits tell me when they talk to me?" "For him," says Peacock, "spirits were not a belief but an unquestionable relationship, part of the unity of his life."[23]

If our goal is to understand the complexities of religious experience, we must first and foremost be more critical of our own assumptions—whether rooted in traditions of belief or disbelief—and how we impose our ethnocentrism on others. Photo by Danny Gawlowski.

When the hierarchical divisions between knowledge and belief dissipate, we discover where the real fabric of human religious experience begins and ends. Because everywhere, it turns out, people encounter the supernatural, take it into their lives, and forge it as their own. Encounter and experience with the supernatural is as fundamental to humanity as life and death. Life and death, of course, are fundamental to humanity because they are real and tangible experiences we all share. What I am daring to say here is that when we approach belief from a truly ethnographic point of view—a truly "native point of view"—we might reason that belief is also shaped by real and tangible supernatural encounters that people everywhere seem to share.[24]

I make this proposition with extreme trepidation and caution because I am not sure I believe it, but I believe/know through cross-cultural comparison and my own ethnographic research that the stuff of belief (and experience) is enormously powerful.[25] And because religious belief engenders perhaps *the* most basic of ethnocentrisms, few human beings are actually able to transcend it. But even if we are not willing to go that far, there are some basic lessons for us all: before we can even claim to understand the seemingly bizarre beliefs of others, we must critically evaluate how we—whether students of science or art or religion—recurrently and so confidently discount others' beliefs without any regard for how our own blinders prevent us from grasping more deeply, as Bronislaw Malinowski put it in 1922, "tolerance and generosity, based on the understanding of other men's point of view."[26]

ANTHROPOLOGY HERE AND NOW

Trying to understand another belief system can be difficult, especially because it can extend far beyond just learning about beliefs and practices. And it can also take time—lots of time. Anthropologist Paul Stoller (West Chester University) began studying the religion of the Songhay people in West Africa over thirty years ago. Studying as an apprentice to a Songhay sorcerer, Stoller learned to appreciate the deeper complexities of things like magic and spirit possession and how these processes worked in the lives of Songhay people. But when he was diagnosed with cancer in 2001, he began to see all that he had learned in a new light. In his book, *Stranger in the Village of the Sick: A Memoir of Cancer, Sorcery, and Healing* (2004), he recounts how Songhay teachings transformed his own dread and fear of living with cancer and at the same time deepened his understanding of Songhay belief and practice. You can read the introduction to the book on the publisher's website at www.beacon.org/client/pdfs/7260_ch1.pdf.

CHECK IT OUT!

NOTES

1. For a much more detailed discussion of Spiritism and the Dr. Fritz phenomenon, see Sidney M. Greenfield, "The Return of Dr. Fritz: Spiritist Healing and Patronage Networks in Urban, Industrial Brazil," *Social Science and Medicine* 24, no. 12 (1987): 1095–107; David Hess, *Samba in the Night: Spiritism in Brazil* (New York: Columbia University Press, 1994) and *Spirits and Scientists: Ideology, Spiritism, and Brazilian Culture* (University Park: Pennsylvania State University Press, 1991); and Darrell William Lynch, "Patient Satisfaction with Spiritist Healing in Brazil," MA thesis, University of Tennessee, Knoxville, 1996.

2. *The New English Bible*, 1st ed. (New York: Oxford University Press, 1961).

3. As I discuss in the text, many anthropologists and other scholars have taken up the study of snake handling. See, for example, Thomas Burton, *Serpent-Handling Believers* (Knoxville: University of Tennessee Press, 1993); David Kimbrough, *Taking Up Serpents* (Chapel Hill: University of North Carolina Press, 1994); and Weston LaBarre, *They Shall Take Up Serpents* (Minneapolis: University of Minnesota Press, 1962).

4. Aihwa Ong, *Spirits of Resistance and Capitalist Discipline: Factory Women in Malaysia* (Albany: State University of New York Press, 1987).

5. Much of this discussion finds inspiration with my graduate professor, Glenn D. Hinson of the University of North Carolina at Chapel Hill. In addition to Hinson, the following discussion relies heavily on David Hufford, "Traditions of Disbelief," *New York Folklore Quarterly* 8 (1982): 47–55. For other ethnographically based discussions that take up this issue as an epistemological problem, see, for example, Karen McCarthy Brown, *Mama Lola: A Vodou Priestess in Brooklyn* (Berkeley: University of California Press, 1991); Bruce T. Grindal, "Into the Heart of Sisala Experience: Witnessing Death Divination," *Journal of Anthropological Research* 39 (1983): 60–80; Glenn D. Hinson, *Fire in My Bones: Transcendence and the Holy Spirit in African American Gospel* (Philadelphia: University of Pennsylvania Press, 2000), especially the appendix; Luke E. Lassiter, *The Power of Kiowa Song: A Collaborative Ethnography* (Tucson: University of Arizona Press, 1998), especially chaps. 12 and 13, and "From 'Reading Over the Shoulders of Natives' to 'Reading Alongside Natives,' Literally: Toward a Collaborative and Reciprocal Ethnography," *Journal of Anthropological Research* 57, no. 2 (2001): 137–49, especially 140–41; Bonnie Blair O'Connor, *Healing Traditions: Alternative Medicine and the Health Professions* (Philadelphia: University of Pennsylvania Press, 1995); and Edith Turner, "A Visible Spirit Form in Zambia," in *Being Changed by Cross-Cultural*

Encounters: The Anthropology of Extraordinary Experience, ed. David E. Young and Jean-Guy Goulet (Peterborough, ON: Broadview Press, 1994).

6. Hufford, "Traditions of Disbelief," 49–53.

7. Excerpted from Hufford, "Traditions of Disbelief," 47.

8. Hufford, "Traditions of Disbelief."

9. Ibid.

10. James G. Frazer, *The Golden Bough: The Roots of Religion and Folklore* (New York: Gramercy Books, 1981 [1890]), 30.

11. Hufford, "Traditions of Disbelief," 47.

12. See, for example, introductory discussions of religion in anthropological textbooks. Compare Daniel G. Bates, *Cultural Anthropology* (Boston: Allyn & Bacon, 1996), chap. 12; Carol R. Ember and Melvin Ember, *Cultural Anthropology*, 9th ed. (Upper Saddle River, NJ: Prentice Hall, 1999), chap. 14; Marvin Harris, *Cultural Anthropology*, 4th ed. (New York: HarperCollins, 1995), chap. 17; William A. Haviland, *Cultural Anthropology*, 9th ed. (Fort Worth, TX: Harcourt Brace, 1999), chap. 13; Michael C. Howard, *Contemporary Cultural Anthropology*, 5th ed. (New York: HarperCollins, 1996), chap. 13; Conrad Phillip Kottak, *Anthropology: The Exploration of Diversity*, 8th ed. (Boston: McGraw-Hill, 2000), chap. 17; Barbara D. Miller, *Cultural Anthropology* (Boston: Allyn & Bacon, 1999), chap. 13; Serena Nanda and Richard L. Warms, *Cultural Anthropology*, 6th ed. (Belmont, CA: Wadsworth, 1998), chap. 13; Michael Alan Park, *Introducing Anthropology: An Integrated Approach* (Mountain View, CA: Mayfield Publishing, 2000), chap. 12; James Peoples and Garrick Bailey, *Humanity: An Introduction to Cultural Anthropology*, 5th ed. (Belmont, CA: Wadsworth, 2000), chap. 13; Richard H. Robbins, *Cultural Anthropology: A Problem-Based Approach*, 3rd ed. (Itasca, IL: Peacock, 2001), chap. 4; Emily A. Schultz and Robert H. Lavenda, *Cultural Anthropology: A Perspective on the Human Condition*, 5th ed. (Mountain View, CA: Mayfield Publishing, 2001), chap. 8; and Mari Womack, *Being Human: An Introduction to Cultural Anthropology* (Upper Saddle River, NJ: Prentice Hall, 1998), chap. 9.

13. See Greenfield, "The Return of Dr. Fritz"; Hess, *Samba in the Night* and *Spirits and Scientists*; and Lynch, "Patient Satisfaction with Spiritist Healing in Brazil."

14. See, for example, Billings, "Religion as Opposition"; Kimbrough, *Taking Up Serpents*; and Schwartz, "Ordeal by Serpents, Fire, and Strychnine." A thorough survey of this and other themes in the literature on snake handling can be found

in Keith G. Tidball and Chris Toumey, "Serpent Handling in Appalachia and Ritual Theory in Anthropology," in *Signifying Serpents and Mardi Gras Runners: Representation and Identity in Selected Souths*, ed. Celeste Ray and Luke Eric Lassiter (Athens: University of Georgia Press, 2003).

15. See Ong, *Spirits of Resistance and Capitalist Discipline*.

16. Hufford, "Traditions of Disbelief."

17. Ibid., 47–48.

18. Ibid., 47.

19. Adapted from Darrell Lynch, personal communication, March 13, 2002.

20. Hufford, "Traditions of Disbelief," 53.

21. The ethnographic literature is replete with descriptions of religious belief and behavior and their meanings as a function of particular cultural systems. To be sure, ethnography comes closest to describing the deeper meanings of supernatural encounter and experience. Yet, as Edith Turner writes, "[R]eports of experiences with spirits . . . are regarded as appropriate anthropological material, not the experiences themselves. It is the same in religious studies. Scholars of religion tend to explain accounts of spirit encounters in terms of metaphor. The issue of whether or not spirits actually exist has not been faced" ("A Visible Spirit Form in Zambia," 71).

22. See Greenfield, "The Return of Dr. Fritz"; Hess, *Samba in the Night* and *Spirits and Scientists*; and Lynch, "Patient Satisfaction with Spiritist Healing in Brazil."

23. James L. Peacock, *The Anthropological Lens: Harsh Light, Soft Focus* (Cambridge: Cambridge University Press, 1986), 18.

24. See Hufford, "Traditions of Disbelief," who does not go this far explicitly but implicitly argues as much.

25. See, for example, Lassiter, *The Power of Kiowa Song*, and Luke E. Lassiter, Clyde Ellis, and Ralph Kotay, *The Jesus Road: Kiowas, Christianity, and Indian Hymns* (Lincoln: University of Nebraska Press, 2002).

26. Bronislaw Malinowski, *Argonauts of the Western Pacific* (New York: Dutton, 1922), 518.

Afterword

Every once in a while, Kiowa singers sing this song:

> I will sing until I die.
> The religions, they live.
> But they too will die.

For many, this song is especially meaningful. It implies that we are here only for a short time, but song lasts forever. Song lingers on, waiting to be "caught" by those who can listen closely. In the Kiowa world, this is significant because song enacts a powerful relationship: the word for Kiowa song is *daw-gyah*, which means "to catch power." Without song, nothing has power. From powwows to church services, from birthday celebrations to funerals, song gives life to Kiowa memory, heritage, and culture. The act of singing, then, is a deeply significant service in the Kiowa community; singers see themselves as servants for their people. Indeed, for some Kiowa singers, the words "I will sing until I die" can also imply that "I will serve until I die."

I was twenty years old when I first began to take this perspective to heart. At least, I thought I was taking it to heart. I remember distinctly the summer I told the Williamses (the Kiowa and Cheyenne-Arapaho family with whom I lived at the time) that I had thought long and hard about what singing meant. I had begun to recognize its central place in Native American life. And so I had decided to quit college and come live full time in "Indian country." Here, I could "sing until I die."

I also remember distinctly the Williamses' reaction. I especially remember Billy Gene's reaction. A singer himself, Billy Gene understood my growing love of song. But he chided me for my decision. How could I throw away an education? he asked. With an education, I had an opportunity to do something for myself and others—especially others. How could I pass up the rare opportunity of college? So many Indian kids my age never even got the chance, and here I was ready to throw it away. He would hear none of it. I had a responsibility to myself, to my family, and to him to finish.

Billy Gene made me think long and hard about the privilege of higher education, about what it means, and about the responsibilities that the "knowledge" gained by education engenders. It was the first time I had ever really thought about education as privileged opportunity. I returned and finished college, then went to graduate school. When I eventually graduated from the University of North Carolina with a PhD in anthropology, Billy Gene and his wife, Shirley, drove all the way from Oklahoma for the graduation. My education was that important to him.

Billy Gene died a few years later. But, like song, Billy Gene's words have lingered way past his death. In my own education, and in the education I now impart to others, I have tried to live up to Billy Gene's challenge, to use knowledge in a way that serves others. Most of the time I am far from realizing this goal. But Billy Gene's words have become a driving metaphor for how I see anthropology. Indeed, from that conversation until this very day, I have never separated anthropology from Billy Gene's challenge.

Billy Gene's challenge is much like anthropology's call to use the knowledge of culture in the service of humanity. From Franz Boas to Bronislaw Malinowski, from Margaret Mead to Michelle Rosaldo, anthropology has *always* been about serving others. Anthropology's uniquely produced knowledge has an activist slant today, and it has had that activist slant since its modern inception. While some transgressions have surfaced, most anthropologists remain committed to putting knowledge to work for others. From human rights to women's rights, from racism to the human abuses of the environment, anthropologists have taken steps to translate the wisdom of culture into relevant and applicable frameworks.

Anthropology recognizes the connection between knowledge and action. Anthropology understands that culture has potent lessons to offer—*complex* lessons that provoke us to take up complex action both within our society and with each other. Anthropology challenges us to think about how powerful culture is, how culture constructs the contours of our lives, and how culture engenders an ethnocentrism that often prevents us from seeing others more clearly.

In the end, anthropology is like song and the words of Billy Gene: putting anthropology's lessons into action in the service of humanity can last forever. We have only to "catch it" and give the song life.

Glossary

affinity: kin relations engendered by marriage.

agriculture: the cultivation of crops for food, which, as it grows in intensity and scale, often becomes associated with several other subsidiary farming practices, including continuous land use, the use of fertilizers, irrigation, and/or livestock production.

alternate genders: the varied meanings and practices associated with differences in sexuality not easily ascribed to the conventional cultural definitions of "male" and "female" in any particular society, such as that expressed by homosexuals, transsexuals, or third/fourth genders.

ancient states: clearly defined states that emerged five to six thousand years ago but were not modern nation-states. See also states.

animatism: the belief in nebulous and impersonal powers or forces.

animism: belief in spirits.

anthropology: the study of human beings in all of their biological and cultural complexities, both past and present. The field is conventionally split into four subfields: biological anthropology, archaeology, linguistic anthropology, and cultural anthropology.

applied anthropology: the application of anthropology to human problems.

archaeology: the subfield of anthropology that deals with the study of material culture.

artifact: an object created by humans.

band: a type of social, political, and economic organization common among foragers who live in small, unsettled mobile groups that is characterized by strong kinship ties, loosely defined leadership roles, and a dependence on reciprocity.

bilateral kinship: a kind of kinship that reckons kin similarly through both male and female links, in which the children produced by a marriage assign relatedness to both parents' families.

biological anthropology: the subfield of anthropology that deals with the biological experience of humans.

biological sex: differences in male and female biology, especially as it relates to biological reproduction.

bride service: the service (such as hunting) of a man to his wife's family after marriage.

bridewealth: a practice in which the husband's kin gives gifts to the wife's kin at marriage.

capitalism: an economic system having its roots in seventeenth- and eighteenth-century Europe and characterized by the production and distribution of goods and services for profit, the means for which are privately owned.

catastrophism: an idea that change is set into motion by catastrophic events; before the emergence of uniformitarianism, this doctrine posited that the earth had changed only through major catastrophes set into motion by the Judeo-Christian God, like the Great Flood detailed in the Bible.

clans: the organization of several lineages into one collective unit.

class: the division of people into groups with differing access to resources.

cognatic descent: the reckoning of descent more or less informally through both male and female links.

collaborative ethnography: a kind of ethnography that systematically engages consultants in the process of both practicing fieldwork *and* writing ethnography.

communication: in simple terms, the sending and receiving of information through sounds, gestures, and/or other indicators; in anthropological terms, the use of arbitrary symbols (including those nonverbal, such as those written) to impart meaning. See also language.

comparativism: the search for or study of similarities and differences between and among human beings in all of their biological and cultural complexities. See also holism.

consanguinity: kin relations engendered by birth.

consultant: in ethnography, someone who informs and regularly consults on the ethnographer's understanding of a particular community's culture.

core: the so-called First World, the world's wealthiest and most powerful nation-states. See also periphery and semiperiphery.

cross-cousin marriage: the marriage of a woman or man to her or his "cross-cousin" (i.e., mother's brother's son/daughter or father's sister's son/daughter).

cultural anthropology: the subfield of anthropology that deals specifically with the study of culture in its many different forms, expressions, and practices.

cultural critique: the use of anthropological understandings gained through ethnography to critique the practices of one society or culture. Associated with Margaret Mead.

cultural evolution: the social, political, and economic changes that accompany the shift in human adaptive strategies, such as that illustrated in the shift from foraging to domestication.

cultural relativity: the idea that each society or culture must be understood on its own terms, not those of outsiders. Associated with Franz Boas.

cultural reproduction: the replication of cultural traits that enhance survival.

cultural selection: the influence of culture on biology—in particular, on biological reproduction.

culture: a shared and negotiated system of meaning informed by knowledge that people learn and put into practice by interpreting experience and generating behavior. Interdependent with society.

culture shock: the meeting of two or more systems of meaning in the body and in the psyche, expressed as anxiety, inappropriate behavior, or physical illness.

descent: the assignment of relatedness traced through common ancestry.

descent groups: groups that claim a common ancestor or ancestors and like lineages can extend in time (past, present, and future) and space (across social, political, or geographical boundaries) and hold power above and beyond any one individual.

domestication: the modification and adaptation of wild plants and animals for use as food, which may take the form of horticulture, pastoralism, or agriculture.

dowry: a practice in which the wife's kin is expected to give the woman's inheritance to the husband's kin at marriage.

empiricism: the position that experience (broadly defined, such as that implied by direct observation) serves as the source of knowledge.

enculturation: the process of learning culture.

endogamy: marriage within a certain group.

ethnocentrism: the tendency to view the world, sometimes exclusively, from the basis of one's own experience.

ethnographer: someone who undertakes ethnography as an approach to studying culture.

ethnography: the study and description of culture, which specifically refers to both (1) a field method of studying culture in its social context and (2) the approach to writing about culture.

ethnology: the expression of comparativism in the study of culture that concentrates on comparing varied cultural descriptions from around the world to make generalizations about human beings and the role of culture in human life. Often synonymous with cultural anthropology.

ethnomusicology: the cross-cultural study of music.

ethnoscience: a kind of ethnography that focuses on recording the knowledge of culture as articulated through language.

eugenics: a popular movement that gained momentum in the late nineteenth and early twentieth centuries that, putting social Darwinism into practice, focused on the selective breeding, and elimination, of human populations. The movement climaxed with the end of World War II—although eugenics still has adherents today.

evolution: the process of biological change over time. See also natural selection.

evolutionism. See social evolution.

exogamy: marriage outside a certain group.

experimental ethnography: an extension of Clifford Geertz's interpretive anthropology, which emphasized experimentation in translating the complexities of culture through ethnography.

feminist anthropology: the branch of anthropology that first dealt with male bias in anthropology and questions concerning women's subordination, but expanded to include the much larger study of gender and its relationship to culture and power.

foraging: a kind of human subsistence strategy characterized by the gathering of plants and/or hunting of animals for food.

functions of religion: model often used for explaining the existence of religion, the purposes for which include but are not limited to articulating the standards of right and wrong, addressing the unexplainable, easing the psychological stress brought on by misfortune, displacing decision making, or promoting community cohesion and solidarity.

fundamentalism: in the study of religion, belief in and adherence to absolute religious tenets and principles, such as the literal interpretation of religious texts.

gender: the wide range of meanings assigned to biological sexed individuals.

gender roles: the attitudes, identities, practices, and meanings deemed appropriate to one's specific gender. See also sexual division of labor.

genocide: the extermination of one group of people by another.

globalization: a worldwide process of socioeconomic interdependence.

Great Chain of Being: a belief about the order of the natural world as created by the Judeo-Christian God having currency into the eighteenth and nineteenth centuries that posited that the earth was only a few thousand years old, that its fundamental and hierarchical design had always existed as God had created it, and that it had changed little since creation.

historical particularism: an approach to understanding cultural diversity that postulates that each society or culture is the outgrowth of its past. Associated with Franz Boas.

holism: a perspective emphasizing the whole rather than just the parts. See also comparativism.

horticulture: a kind of human subsistence strategy characterized by the small-scale, nonindustrial cultivation of plants for food.

incest taboo: a rule or rules regulating sex and/or marriage between people considered to be kin.

industrialism: the intensive and large-scale production of manufactured goods having its roots in the industrial revolution, which first emerged in Europe in the eighteenth century with the shift from handcrafted to factory-produced goods.

interpretive anthropology: ushered in primarily by Clifford Geertz, this form of symbolic anthropology focused on understanding and studying culture as a form of text, dialogue, and interpretation. See also experimental ethnography.

kinship: networks of relatives based on affinity and consanguinity.

Kula: an extensive network consisting of trading partners scattered throughout several western Pacific islands. Associated with Bronislaw Malinowski, who described the Trobriand trade of arm shells and shell necklaces, each of which moved on this larger trading network in opposite directions.

language: a system of communication, verbal and/or nonverbal, that among humans depends on the cultural assignment of meaning to symbols, the arrangement of which depends on grammatical rules.

levirate: a practice in which a widow marries the brother or another man from the family of her deceased husband.

lineages: large descent groups that extend in time (past, present, and future) and space (across social, political, or geographical boundaries) and that hold power above and beyond any one individual.

linguistic anthropology: the subfield of anthropology that deals specifically with the study of language and its relationship to culture.

linguistics. See linguistic anthropology.

Linnaean hierarchy: the classification of the natural world into kingdoms, phyla, classes, orders, families, genera, and species. Associated with Carolus Linnaeus.

magic: the invocation or manipulation of the supernatural to bear on a desired outcome.

market exchange: the exchange of goods and services through the use of money.

marriage: in the study of kinship, the broadly diverse, socially sanctioned union of two or more individuals, which, being based largely on the incest taboo, exogamy, and endogamy, widens any given network of kin.

material culture: materials that human beings purposefully create either as tools to adapt to their environment or as meaningful expressions of their experience.

matrilineal descent: a kind of kinship that reckons descent through female links, in which the children produced by a marriage trace their descent through the mother's side of the family.

matrilocal residence: a marriage practice that establishes residence with the wife's family after marriage (though at times associated with matrilineal societies exclusively, it is often used synonymously with uxorilocal residence).

monotheism: belief in a single deity.

mythology: stories that express the larger "truths" of a particular belief tradition.

nation-states: modern states characterized by a centralized political authority that consolidates power, minimizes dissension through force and other means, maintains rigid geographical and territorial boundaries, and governs a population who embrace expressed socially, politically, and/or economically based principles via a "national identity." (The prestate Cahokia, for example, was not a nation-state: its boundaries, for instance, were fluid. The United States, however, is a nation-state: its boundaries, for instance, are clearly and rigidly defined.)

natural selection: the complex process of adaptation to change in the physical environment, which depends, on its most basic level, on reproduction and variability. Associated with Charles Darwin and his original theory of how biological change, or evolution, worked.

neolocal residence: a marriage practice that establishes a separate household from that of a married couple's parents and/or parents' kin.

parallel-cousin marriage: the marriage of a woman or man to her or his "parallel-cousin" (i.e., mother's sister's son/daughter or father's brother's son/daughter).

participant observation: an approach to doing fieldwork involving long-term participation and systematic documentation (such as taking field notes and conducting interviews) within a particular society, community, or group. Often it engages four stages: making entrée, culture shock, establishing rapport, and "understanding the culture."

pastoralism: a kind of human subsistence strategy characterized by the domestication, control, and breeding of a specific herd of animals.

patrilineal descent: a kind of kinship that reckons descent through male links, in which the children produced by a marriage trace their descent through the father's side of the family.

patrilocal residence: a marriage practice that establishes residence with the husband's family after marriage (though at times associated with patrilineal societies exclusively, it is often used synonymously with virilocal residence).

periphery: the world's poorest nation-states. See also core and semiperiphery.

physical anthropology. See biological anthropology.

political economy: the large-scale integration and interdependence of political and economic systems, especially as it relates to industrialism, capitalism, and the development of modern nation-states.

polyandry: the marriage of one woman to more than one man.

polygamy: the marriage of one person to two or more spouses at the same time, it takes the form of either polygyny or polyandry.

polygyny: the marriage of one man to more than one woman.

polytheism: belief in multiple spirits, beings, or gods.

population: in biology, an interbreeding group.

positivism: the position that knowledge is only useful if it can be "proved."

power: the far-reaching process of influence that can be expressed directly or indirectly, implicitly or explicitly.

prestates: a type of social, political, and economic organization characterized by mounting social integration (which is often kinship based), centralized political leadership, and market exchange. Also called chiefdoms and kingdoms. See also states.

race: a powerful social and cultural category that, while having no actual counterpart in human biology, differentiates groups of people based on observable physical characteristics and their presumed relationships to behavioral differences.

reason: the position that knowledge is, or should be, logical, factual, and sound.

reciprocity: the exchange of goods and services between two or more people without the use of money.

redistribution: the flow of resources into a centralized locale and/or political authority, which is in turn reallocated to support the wealth, power, prestige, and/or logistics of that political authority.

relativity. See cultural relativity.

religion: the belief in and engagement with the supernatural.

ritual: in the study of religion, patterned group practice meant to engage the supernatural.

semiperiphery: nation-states that mediate the flow of economic resources between the world's core and its periphery.

sexual division of labor: the division of labor and assignment of specific tasks based on gender. See also gender roles.

social Darwinism: a form of social evolution popular in the late nineteenth and early twentieth centuries, surmised from Charles Darwin's theory of natural selection, which posited that, first, "inferior" groups of people remained inferior because of their biological differences or, more simply, because of their race and, second, that "favored races" would inevitably supplant the unfavorable ones through the process of "survival of the fittest." Associated with Herbert Spencer. See also eugenics.

social evolution: a theory of cultural change popular in nineteenth-century anthropology that posited that all human societies passed through a progressive sequence of development from savages to barbarians and, finally, to civilization. Also called evolutionism or unilineal evolution.

society: a group of interacting individuals, which, among humans, is interdependent with culture.

sociocultural anthropology. See cultural anthropology.

sororate: a practice in which a widower marries the sister or another woman from the family of his deceased wife.

states: a type of social, political, and economic organization characterized by large-scale social integration (which may or may not be kinship based); centralized, hierarchical, and bureaucratized political systems; and market exchange.

symbolic anthropology: the ethnographic study of symbolic forms and their negotiation within and between human groups.

syncretism: a combination of different cultural traits, such as that expressed in many religious beliefs and practices.

taxonomy: in biology, the classification of the natural world. See Linnaean hierarchy.

tribe: a type of social, political, and economic organization whereby different settled or nomadic communities are united through descent groups or common organizations (like warrior or religious societies).

uniformitarianism: a geological theory positing that the earth's physical features result from steady, gradual processes. Associated with Charles Lyell and his popularization of the theory in *Principles of Geology*.

unilineal descent: a kind of kinship that reckons descent through either male or female links, in which the children produced by a marriage trace their descent through either the father's or the mother's side of the family. See also matrilineal descent and patrilineal descent.

unilineal evolution. See social evolution.

uxorilocal residence: a marriage practice that establishes residence with the wife's family after marriage (often used synonymously with matrilocal residence).

virilocal residence: a marriage practice that establishes residence with the husband's family after marriage (often used synonymously with patrilocal residence).

woman marriage: the practice in many historic and some contemporary African societies in which women entered into nonsexual marriages with other women, whereby one woman was socially recognized as male (i.e., as a "female husband") and thus could, for example, pass property from "father" to son.

world system: the global integration of the world's people into a single economic system based on capitalism. Associated with Immanuel Wallerstein, who argued that the world's political economy is split into a core, periphery, and semiperiphery.

worldview: a way of looking at the world through which reality is constructed specific to a particular society or culture.

Suggested Readings

1. EVOLUTION AND THE CRITIQUE OF RACE: A SHORT STORY

Baker, Lee D. *From Savage to Negro: Anthropology and the Construction of Race, 1896–1954*. Berkeley: University of California Press, 1998.

———, ed. *Life in America: Identity and Everyday Experience*. Oxford: Blackwell, 2004.

———. *Anthropology and the Racial Politics of Culture*. Durham, NC: Duke University Press, 2010.

Boas, Franz. *The Central Eskimo*. Washington, DC: Smithsonian Institution, 1888.

———. "The Limitations of the Comparative Method in Anthropology," *Science* 4 (1896): 901–8.

———. *Anthropology and Modern Life*. New York: Norton, 1928.

———. *Race, Language, and Culture*. New York: Free Press, 1940.

Bowler, Peter J. *Evolution: The History of an Idea*. 3rd ed. Berkeley: University of California Press, 2003.

Bush, Melanie E. L. *Breaking the Code of Good Intentions: Everyday Forms of Whiteness*. Lanham, MD: Rowman & Littlefield, 2004.

Cole, Douglas. *Franz Boas: The Early Years, 1858–1906*. Seattle: University of Washington Press, 1999.

Feagin, Joe R., and Karyn D. McKinney. *The Many Costs of Racism*. Lanham, MD: Rowman & Littlefield, 2003.

Grant, Peter R. *Ecology and Evolution of Darwin's Finches*. Princeton, NJ: Princeton University Press, 1986.

Madison, James H. *A Lynching in the Heartland: Race and Memory in America*. New York: Palgrave, 2001.

Marks, Jonathan. *Human Biodiversity: Genes, Race, and History*. New York: Aldine de Gruyter, 1995.

———. *What It Means to Be 98% Chimpanzee: Apes, People, and Their Genes*. Berkeley: University of California Press, 2002.

Montagu, Ashley. *Man's Most Dangerous Myth: The Fallacy of Race*. New York: Columbia University Press, 1942.

Nesse, Randolph M., and George C. Williams. *Why We Get Sick: The New Science of Darwinian Medicine*. New York: Times Books, 1994.

Scupin, Raymond, ed. *Race and Ethnicity: An Anthropological Focus on the United States and the World*. Upper Saddle River, NJ: Prentice Hall, 2003.

Smedley, Audrey. *Race in North America: Origin and Evolution of a Worldview*. 3rd ed. Boulder, CO: Westview Press, 2007.

Stocking, George W. *Race, Culture, and Evolution: Essays in the History of Anthropology*. New York: Free Press, 1968.

Weiner, Jonathan. *The Beak of the Finch*. New York: Vintage Books, 1995.

Wills, Christopher. *Children of Prometheus: The Accelerating Pace of Human Evolution*. New York: Perseus Books, 1998.

Wray, Matt. *Not Quite White: White Trash and the Boundaries of Whiteness*. Durham, NC: Duke University Press, 2006.

2. ANTHROPOLOGY AND CULTURE

Bourdieu, Pierre. *Outline of a Theory of Practice*. Translated by R. Nice. Cambridge: Cambridge University Press, 1977.

Boyd, Colleen E., and Luke Eric Lassiter, eds. *Explorations of Cultural Anthropology*. Lanham, MD: AltaMira Press, 2011.

Clifford, James. *The Predicament of Culture*. Cambridge, MA: Harvard University Press, 1988.

Delaney, Carol. *Investigating Culture: An Experiential Introduction to Anthropology.* Oxford: Blackwell, 2004.

DeVita, Philip R., ed. *Stumbling toward Truth: Anthropologists at Work.* Prospect Heights, IL: Waveland Press, 2000.

Field, Les, and Richard G. Fox. *Anthropology Put to Work.* Oxford: Berg, 2007.

Geertz, Clifford. *The Interpretation of Cultures.* New York: Basic Books, 1973.

———. *Local Knowledge: Further Essays in Interpretive Anthropology.* New York: Basic Books, 1983.

Goodenough, Ward. *Culture, Language, and Society.* Menlo Park, CA: Benjamin/ Cummings, 1981.

Hirschberg, Stuart, and Terry Hirschberg. *One World: Many Cultures.* 7th ed. New York: Pearson, 2008.

Jackson, Michael, ed. *Things As They Are: New Directions in Phenomenological Anthropology.* Bloomington: Indiana University Press, 1996.

Langness, L. L. *The Study of Culture.* Novato, CA: Chandler & Sharp, 2005.

MacClancy, Jeremy, ed. *Exotic No More: Anthropology on the Front Lines.* Chicago: University of Chicago Press, 2002.

Moore, Jerry D. *Visions of Culture: An Introduction to Anthropological Theories and Theorists.* 3rd ed. Walnut Creek, CA: AltaMira Press, 2008.

Ortner, Sherry B. *Anthropology and Social Theory: Culture, Power, and the Acting Subject.* Durham, NC: Duke University Press, 2006.

Peacock, James L. *The Anthropological Lens: Harsh Light, Soft Focus.* 2nd ed. Cambridge: Cambridge University Press, 2002.

Perry, Richard J. *Five Concepts in Anthropological Thinking.* Upper Saddle River, NJ: Prentice Hall, 2003.

Rosaldo, Renato. *Culture and Truth: The Remaking of Social Analysis.* Boston: Beacon Press, 1993.

Salzman, Philip Carl. *Understanding Culture: An Introduction to Anthropological Theory.* Prospect Heights, IL: Waveland Press, 2001.

Selig, Ruth Osterweis, Marilyn R. London, and P. Ann Kaupp, eds. *Anthropology Explored: The Best of Smithsonian AnthroNotes.* 2nd ed. Washington, DC: Smithsonian Books, 2004.

Spradley, James P., ed. *Culture and Cognition: Rules, Maps, and Plans.* San Francisco: Chandler, 1972.

Tedlock, Dennis, and Bruce Mannheim, eds. *The Dialogic Emergence of Culture.* Urbana: University of Illinois Press, 1995.

Turner, Victor W., and Edward M. Bruner. *The Anthropology of Experience.* Chicago: University of Illinois Press, 1986.

Van der Elst, Dirk, with Paul Bohannan. *Culture as Given, Culture as Choice.* 2nd ed. Prospect Heights, IL: Waveland Press, 2003.

3. ETHNOGRAPHY

Angrosino, Michael V. *Projects in Ethnographic Research.* Prospect Heights, IL: Waveland Press, 2005.

Bourgois, Philippe. *In Search of Respect: Selling Crack in El Barrio.* 2nd ed. Cambridge: Cambridge University Press, 2003.

Clifford, James, and George E. Marcus, eds. *Writing Culture: The Poetics and Politics of Ethnography.* Berkeley: University of California Press, 1986.

Counts, Dorothy Ayers, and David R. Counts. *Over the Next Hill: An Ethnography of RVing Seniors in North America.* 2nd ed. Peterborough, Ontario: Broadview Press, 2001.

DeWalt, Kathleen M., and Billie R. DeWalt. *Participant Observation: A Guide for Fieldworkers.* Walnut Creek, CA: AltaMira Press, 2002.

Emerson, Robert M. *Contemporary Field Research: Perspectives and Formulations.* 2nd ed. Prospect Heights, IL: Waveland Press, 2001.

Emerson, Robert M., Rachel I. Fretz, and Linda L. Shaw. *Writing Ethnographic Fieldnotes.* Chicago: University of Chicago Press, 1995.

Faubion, James D., and George E. Marcus, eds. *Fieldwork Is Not What It Used to Be: Learning Anthropology's Method in a Time of Transition.* Ithaca, NY: Cornell University Press, 2009.

Kemper, Robert V., and Anya Peterson Royce. *Chronicling Cultures: Long-Term Field Research in Anthropology.* Walnut Creek, CA: AltaMira Press, 2002.

Lassiter, Luke E. *The Chicago Guide to Collaborative Ethnography*. Chicago: University of Chicago Press, 2005.

Lassiter, Luke Eric, Hurley Goodall, Elizabeth Campbell, and Michelle Natasya Johnson, eds. *The Other Side of Middletown: Exploring Muncie's African American Community*. Walnut Creek, CA: AltaMira Press, 2004.

Malinowski, Bronislaw. *Argonauts of the Western Pacific*. New York: Dutton, 1922.

Marcus, George E. *Ethnography through Thick and Thin*. Princeton, NJ: Princeton University Press, 1998.

Marcus, George E., and Michael M. J. Fischer. *Anthropology as Cultural Critique: An Experimental Moment in the Human Sciences*. 2nd ed. Chicago: University of Chicago Press, 1999.

Mead, Margaret. *Coming of Age in Samoa*. New York: Morrow, 1928.

Schensul, Jean J., and Margaret D. LeCompte, eds. *Ethnographer's Toolkit*. 7 vols. Walnut Creek, CA: AltaMira Press, 1999.

Spradley, James P. *The Ethnographic Interview*. New York: Holt, Rinehart and Winston, 1979.

Stocking, George W. *The Ethnographer's Magic and Other Essays in the History of Anthropology*. Madison: University of Wisconsin Press, 1992.

Sunstein, Bonnie Stone, and Elizabeth Chiseri-Strater. *Fieldworking: Reading and Writing Research*. 3rd ed. Boston: Bedford/St. Martin's, 2007.

Tedlock, Barbara. *The Beautiful and Dangerous: Dialogues with the Zuni Indians*. New York: Viking, 1992.

Van Maanen, John. *Tales of the Field: On Writing Ethnography*. Chicago: University of Chicago Press, 1988.

Wagner, Melinda Bollar. *God's Schools: Choice and Compromise in American Society*. New Brunswick, NJ: Rutgers University Press, 1990.

4. HISTORY, CHANGE, AND ADAPTATION: ON THE ROOTS OF OUR WORLD SYSTEM

Bodley, John H. *Anthropology and Contemporary Human Problems*. 5th ed. Walnut Creek, CA: AltaMira Press, 2007.

Cohen, Mark Nathan. *The Food Crisis in Prehistory: Overpopulation and the Origins of Agriculture*. New Haven, CT: Yale University Press, 1977.

——. *Health and the Rise of Civilization*. New Haven, CT: Yale University Press, 1989.

Cohen, Mark Nathan, and George J. Armelagos, eds. *Paleopathology at the Origins of Agriculture*. Orlando, FL: Academic Press, 1984.

Cook, Samuel R. *Monacans and Miners: Native American and Coal Mining Communities in Appalachia*. Lincoln: University of Nebraska Press, 2000.

Dahlberg, Frances, ed. *Woman the Gatherer*. New Haven, CT: Yale University Press, 1981.

Diamond, Jared. *The Third Chimpanzee: The Evolution and Future of the Human Animal*. New York: HarperCollins, 1992.

——. *Guns, Germs, and Steel: The Fates of Human Societies*. New York: Norton, 1997.

——. *Collapse: How Societies Choose to Fail or Succeed*. New York: Viking, 2005.

Earl, Timothy, ed. *Chiefdoms: Power, Economy, and Ideology*. Cambridge: Cambridge University Press, 1991.

Fagan, Brian. *Floods, Famines and Emperors: El Niño and the Fate of Civilizations*. New York: Basic Books, 1999.

Haas, Jonathan. *The Evolution of the Prehistoric State*. New York: Columbia University Press, 1982.

Johnson, Allen, and Timothy Earle. *The Evolution of Human Societies: From Foraging Group to Agrarian State*. Stanford, CA: Stanford University Press, 1987.

Jones, Grant, and Robert Kautz. *The Transformation to Statehood in the New World*. Cambridge: Cambridge University Press, 1981.

Kehoe, Alice. *The Land of Prehistory: A Critical History of American Archaeology*. New York: Routledge, 1998.

Inda, Jonathan Xavier, and Renato Rosaldo, eds. *The Anthropology of Globalization*. 2nd ed. Oxford: Blackwell, 2008.

Lee, Richard. *The Dobe Ju/'hoansi*. 3rd ed. Belmont, CA: Wadsworth Thomson Learning, 2003.

Lee, Richard, and Irven DeVore, eds. *Man the Hunter*. Chicago: Aldine, 1968.

Menzie, Charles. *Red Flags and Lace Coiffes: Identity and Survival in a Breton Village.* Toronto, ON: University of Toronto Press, 2011.

Pauketat, Timothy R., and Thomas E. Emerson, eds. *Cahokia: Domination and Ideology in the Mississippian World.* Lincoln: University of Nebraska Press, 1997.

Peacock, James L. *Grounded Globalism: How the U.S. South Embraces the World.* Athens: University of Georgia Press, 2007.

Pieterse, Jan Nederveen. *Globalization and Culture: Global Mélange.* Lanham, MD: Rowman & Littlefield, 2004.

Price, T. Douglas, and Anne Birgitte Gebauer. *Last Hunters, First Farmers: New Perspectives on the Prehistoric Transition to Agriculture.* Santa Fe, NM: School of American Research Press, 1995.

Robbins, Richard H. *Global Problems and the Culture of Capitalism.* 4th ed. Boston: Allyn and Bacon, 2007.

Sahlins, Marshall. *Tribesmen.* Englewood Cliffs, NJ: Prentice Hall, 1968.

———. *Stone Age Economies.* Chicago: Aldine-Atherton, 1972.

Schweitzer, Peter P., Megan Biesele, and Robert K. Hitchcock, eds. *Hunters and Gatherers in the Modern World: Conflict, Resistance, and Self-Determination.* New York: Berghahn Books, 2000.

Service, Elman. *Origins of the State and Civilization: The Process of Cultural Evolution.* New York: Norton, 1975.

Smith, Bruce D. *The Emergence of Agriculture.* New York: W. H. Freeman, 1995.

Steward, Julian. *Theory of Culture Change: The Methodology of Multilinear Evolution.* Urbana: University of Illinois Press, 1955.

Tainter, Joseph A. *The Collapse of Complex Societies.* New York: Cambridge University Press, 1990.

Wallerstein, Immanuel. *The Modern World System: Capitalist Agriculture and the Origins of European World-Economy in the Sixteenth Century.* New York: Academic Press, 1974.

———. *Geopolitics and Geoculture: Essays on the Changing World-System.* Cambridge: Cambridge University Press, 1991.

———. *World-Systems Analysis: An Introduction*. Durham, NC: Duke University Press, 2004.

Wenke, Robert J., and Deborah I. Olszewski. *Patterns in Prehistory: Mankind's First Three Million Years*. 5th ed. Oxford: Oxford University Press, 2006.

5. SEX, POWER, AND INEQUALITY: ON GENDER

Abu-Lughod, Lila. *Writing Women's Worlds: Bedouin Stories*. 2nd ed. Berkeley: University of California Press, 2008.

Bonvillain, Nancy. *Women and Men: Cultural Constructs of Gender*. 4th ed. Upper Saddle River, NJ: Prentice Hall, 2006.

Brettell, Caroline B., and Carolyn F. Sargent, eds. *Gender in Cross-Cultural Perspective*. 5th ed. Upper Saddle River, NJ: Prentice Hall, 2008.

Brøgger, Jan. *Nazaré: Women and Men in a Prebureaucratic Portuguese Fishing Village*. Fort Worth, TX: Harcourt Brace Jovanovich, 1992.

Carby, Hazel. "White Women Listen! Black Feminism and the Boundaries of Sisterhood." In *The Empire Strikes Back: Race and Racism in 70's Britain*, edited by Birmingham University Centre for Contemporary Cultural Studies. London: Hutchinson, 1982.

Collins, Patricia Hill. *Black Feminist Thought: Knowledge, Consciousness, and the Politics of Empowerment*. 2nd ed. New York: Routledge, 2000.

De Beauvoir, Simone. *The Second Sex*. Translated by H. M. Pashley. New York: Knopf, 1953.

Di Leonardo, Micaela. *Gender at the Crossroads of Knowledge: Feminist Anthropology in the Postmodern Era*. Berkeley: University of California Press, 1991.

Farnham, Christie, ed. *The Impact of Feminist Research in the Academy*. Bloomington: Indiana University Press, 1987.

Fisher, Melissa S. *Wall Street Women*. Durham, NC: Duke University Press, 2012.

Freidl, Ernestine. *Women and Men: An Anthropologist's View*. New York: Holt, Rinehart and Winston, 1975.

Gilley, Brian Joseph. *Becoming Two-Spirit: Gay Identity and Social Acceptance in Indian Country*. Lincoln: University of Nebraska Press, 2006.

Herdt, Gilbert, ed. *Third Sex, Third Gender: Beyond Sexual Dimorphism in Culture and History*. New York: Zone, 1996.

hooks, bell. *Yearning: Race, Gender, and Cultural Politics*. Boston: South End Press, 1990.

Hull, Gloria, Patricia Bell Scott, and Barbara Smith, eds. *All the Women Are White, All the Blacks Are Men, But Some of Us Are Brave*. Old Westbury, NY: Feminist Press, 1982.

Jacobs, Sue-Ellen, Wesley Thomas, and Sabine Lang. *Two-Spirit People: Native American Gender Identity, Sexuality, and Spirituality*. Urbana: University of Illinois Press, 1997.

MacCormack, Carol P., and Marilyn Strathern, eds. *Nature, Culture, and Gender*. Cambridge: Cambridge University Press, 1980.

Mead, Margaret. *Sex and Temperament in Three Primitive Societies*. New York: Morrow, 1935.

———. *Male and Female*. New York: Morrow, 1949.

Moore, Henrietta. *Feminism and Anthropology*. Minneapolis: University of Minnesota Press, 1988.

Morgen, Sandra, ed. *Gender and Anthropology: Critical Reviews for Research and Teaching*. Washington, DC: American Anthropological Association, 1989.

Nanda, Serena. *Neither Man nor Woman: The Hijras of India*. 2nd ed. Belmont, CA: Wadsworth, 1999.

———. *Gender Diversity: Crosscultural Variations*. Prospect Heights, IL: Waveland Press, 2000.

Ortner, Sherry. *Making Gender: The Politics and Erotics of Culture*. Boston: Beacon Press, 1996.

Radner, Joan Newlon, ed. *Feminist Messages: Coding in Women's Folk Culture*. Urbana: University of Illinois Press, 1993.

Reiter, Rayna. *Toward an Anthropology of Women*. New York: Monthly Review Press, 1975.

Robertson, Jennifer. *Same-Sex Cultures and Sexualities*. Oxford: Blackwell, 2005.

Rosaldo, Michelle Zimbalist, and Louise Lamphere, eds. *Women, Culture, and Society*. Stanford, CA: Stanford University Press, 1974.

Roscoe, Will. *Changing Ones: Third and Fourth Genders in Native North America.* New York: St. Martin's Press, 1998.

Sanday, Peggy Reeves. *Female Power and Male Dominance: On the Origins of Sexual Inequality.* Cambridge: Cambridge University Press, 1981.

Sanday, Peggy Reeves, and Ruth Gallagher Goodenough, eds. *Beyond the Second Sex: New Directions in the Anthropology of Gender.* Philadelphia: University of Pennsylvania Press, 1990.

Sered, Susan Starr. *Priestess, Mother, Sacred Sister: Religions Dominated by Women.* Oxford: Oxford University Press, 1994.

Shostak, Marjorie. *Nisa: The Life and Words of a !Kung Woman.* New York: Vintage Books, 1981.

Ward, Martha C. *A World Full of Women.* 5th ed. Boston: Allyn and Bacon, 2008.

Young, Antonia. *Women Who Become Men: Albanian Sworn Virgins.* Oxford: Berg, 2000.

6. WORK, SUCCESS, AND KIDS: ON MARRIAGE, FAMILY, AND KINSHIP

Boswell, John. *Same-Sex Unions in Premodern Europe.* New York: Vintage Books, 1995.

Carsten, Janet. *After Kinship.* Cambridge: Cambridge University Press, 2004.

Fox, Robin. *Kinship and Marriage: An Anthropological Perspective.* Cambridge: Cambridge University Press, 1984.

Franklin, Sarah, and Susan McKinnon. *Relative Values: Reconfiguring Kinship Studies.* Durham, NC: Duke University Press, 2001.

Hoey, Brian. *Opting for Elsewhere.* Nashville, TN: Vanderbilt University Press, forthcoming.

Leach, Edmund. *Rethinking Anthropology.* London: Athlone Press, 1961.

Levine, Nancy. *The Dynamics of Polyandry: Kinship, Domesticity, and Population in the Tibetan Border.* Chicago: University of Chicago Press, 1988.

Lévi-Strauss, Claude. *The Elementary Structures of Kinship.* Boston: Beacon Press, 1969.

Murdock, George P. *Social Structure.* New York: Macmillan, 1949.

Needham, Rodney, ed. *Rethinking Kinship and Marriage*. London: Tavistock, 1971.

———. *Remarks and Inventions: Skeptical Essays about Kinship*. London: Tavistock, 1974.

Parkin, Robert, and Linda Stone, eds. *Kinship and Family: An Anthropological Reader*. Oxford: Wiley-Blackwell, 2004.

Rivers, W. H. R. *Kinship and Social Organization*. New York: Humanities Press, 1968.

Schneider, David. *American Kinship: A Cultural Account*. Englewood Cliffs, NJ: Prentice Hall, 1968.

Stone, Linda, ed. *New Directions in Anthropological Kinship*. Lanham, MD: Rowman & Littlefield, 2001.

Thorne, Barrie, ed. *Rethinking the Family: Some Feminist Questions*. 2nd ed. Boston: Northeastern University Press, 1992.

7. KNOWLEDGE, BELIEF, AND DISBELIEF: ON RELIGION

Bowen, John R. *Religions in Practice: An Approach to the Anthropology of Religion*. 3rd ed. Boston: Pearson Education, 2005.

Bowie, Fiona. *The Anthropology of Religion*. 2nd ed. Oxford: Wiley-Blackwell, 2006.

Brown, Karen McCarthy. *Mama Lola: A Vodou Priestess in Brooklyn*. Berkeley: University of California Press, 1991.

Burton, Thomas. *Serpent-Handling Believers*. Knoxville: University of Tennessee Press, 1993.

Crapo, Richley H. *Anthropology of Religion: The Unity and Diversity of Religions*. Boston: McGraw-Hill, 2002.

Grindal, Bruce T. "Into the Heart of Sisala Experience: Witnessing Death Divination." *Journal of Anthropological Research* 39 (1983): 60–80.

Hess, David. *Spirits and Scientists: Ideology, Spiritism, and Brazilian Culture*. University Park: Pennsylvania State University Press, 1991.

———. *Samba in the Night: Spiritism in Brazil*. New York: Columbia University Press, 1994.

Hinson, Glenn D. *Fire in My Bones: Transcendence and the Holy Spirit in African American Gospel*. Philadelphia: University of Pennsylvania Press, 2000.

Hufford, David. "Traditions of Disbelief." *New York Folklore Quarterly* 8 (1982): 47–55.

Kimbrough, David. *Taking Up Serpents*. Chapel Hill: University of North Carolina Press, 1994.

Lassiter, Luke Eric, Clyde Ellis, and Ralph Kotay. *The Jesus Road: Kiowas, Christianity, and Indian Hymns*. Lincoln: University of Nebraska Press, 2002.

Moro, Pamela, James Myers, and Arthur Lehmann. *Magic, Witchcraft, and Religion: An Anthropological Study of the Supernatural*. 7th ed. Boston: McGraw-Hill, 2006.

O'Connor, Bonnie Blair. *Healing Traditions: Alternative Medicine and the Health Professions*. Philadelphia: University of Pennsylvania Press, 1995.

Ong, Aihwa. *Spirits of Resistance and Capitalist Discipline: Factory Women in Malaysia*. Albany: State University of New York Press, 1987.

Stein, Rebecca L., and Philip L. Stein. *The Anthropology of Religion, Magic, and Witchcraft*. 2nd ed. Boston: Pearson Education, 2007.

Stoller, Paul. *Stranger in the Village of the Sick: A Memoir of Cancer, Sorcery and Healing*. Boston: Beacon Press, 2004.

Tidball, Keith G., and Christopher P. Toumey. "Serpent Handling in Appalachia and Ritual Theory in Anthropology." In *Signifying Serpents and Mardi Gras Runners: Representation and Identity in Selected Souths*, edited by Celeste Ray and Luke Eric Lassiter. Athens: University of Georgia Press, 2003.

Turner, Edith. "A Visible Spirit Form in Zambia." In *Being Changed by Cross-Cultural Encounters: The Anthropology of Extraordinary Experience*, edited by David E. Young and Jean-Guy Goulet. Peterborough, Ontario: Broadview Press, 1994.

Winzeler, Robert L. *Anthropology and Religion: What We Know, Think, and Question*. Walnut Creek, CA: AltaMira Press, 2007.

Index

AAA. *See* American Anthropological Association
adaptation, biological. *See* evolution
adaptation, human. *See* cultural adaptation
affinity, 163
agriculture, 119–22, *123*, *181*; emergence of, 115; population influence on, 124–25; trends of, 122–28
alternate genders, 143–46. *See also* gender
alyha, 144
Amazon, 137–38, 141
American Anthropological Association (AAA), 29
American culture, 43–46; adolescence and, 99–100; family and, 161–62, 180–83; gender and, 150, 151–52; kinship and, 163–64, 166; marriage and, 161, 171; Mead and, 99; movies and, 94; study of, 55; "success" and, 150, 163, 180; work and, 161
Appalachia, *112*, 194
ancient states, 121–22, 125
animatism, 189

animism, 190
anthropology, 35–66; subfields of, 35–39, 40, 41. *See also* applied anthropology; archaeology; biological anthropology; cultural anthropology; feminist anthropology; linguistic anthropology; symbolic anthropology
applied anthropology, 39
Arapesh, 135–36
Aratow, Paul, 138
archaeology, 36–37, 39
Argonauts of the Western Pacific (Malinowski), 72
artifact, 36–37
Association for Feminist Anthropology, 155

Baker, Lee D., 29
band, 115–17
Bangladesh, 63
Bantu, 172
Baptists, 42, 50
The Beautiful and the Dangerous: Dialogues with the Zuni Indians (Tedlock), 96

beauty, notion of, 59–60, *60*
Bedouin, 42, 174
belief: disbelief and, 91, 195–98;
    knowledge and, 190–97. *See also*
    religion
Bell, Alexander Graham, 46
berdache. See two-spirits
bilateral kinship, 166–67
biological anthropology, 36
biological sex, 141–42, *143. See also*
    gender
Boas, Franz, 17–23, 25, 26–27, 28, 29,
    35, 40, 41, 71, 72, 79, 80, 91, 95, 99,
    206; American anthropology and,
    17–19; historical particularism,
    19; Inuit (Eskimo) research with,
    18–19; on race, 19–23, 27. *See also*
    anthropology; cultural relativity
Bodley, John H., 124
Booth, Jessica, *90*
Botswana, 114
Bourgois, Philippe, 57–58, 62, 80, 83,
    84, *85*
Bowers, Alfred, 144
bride service, 176
bridewealth, 176–77
British social anthropology, 71–79
Brøgger, Jan, 140
Burundi, 63

Cahokia, 120–21, *121*, 122, 125
Cambodia, 63
capitalism, 81, 110
Carby, Hazel, 153
catastrophism, 6, 7
Cheyenne, 144
Cheyenne-Arapaho, 61, 205
chiefdoms. *See* prestates

children. *See* family
China, 64, *110*, *118*, 177
Christian schools, 80–81
clans, 169
class, 124
cognatic descent, 167
collaborative ethnography, 89–90, 96–98
colonialism, 19–20, 152
Coming of Age in Samoa (Mead), 99, 100
communication, 38. *See also* language
comparativism, 40, 41, 58, 66
consanguinity, 163
consultants, 81, 83, 86
core (economic), 125, 126
Counts, David, 86
Counts, Dorothy, 86
Cowan, Richard, 138
cross-cousin marriage, 170, *170*
Crow, *146*
cultural adaptation, 111–12
cultural anthropology, 36, 38–39
cultural critique, 99–100, *101*, 149–50,
    194
cultural evolution, 123
cultural relativity, 17–18, 59, 61–64, *65*,
    66, 95
cultural reproduction, 111
cultural selection, 25
culture, 17–20, 25, 26, 28, 36,
    37; adaptation and, 110–12;
    arbitrariness of, 51–52; artifacts
    of, 42; behavior, 51–52; common
    elements of, 58–59; complexities
    of, 64–65, 100, 102; conscious and
    unconscious, 47; defining of, 41–54;
    knowledge and, 46–47; as learned,
    47–49; maladaptive practices and,
    112; power and, 53; as practice,

49–53; as shared and negotiated, 43–46; similarities and differences of, 58; study of, 54–66; as a system of meaning, 38
culture shock, 80, 83–85, 87. *See also* participant observation

Darwin, Charles, 7–8, 9–10, 11, 12
Deloria, Ella, 28
demolition derby, 45, *45*, 46, 50, 51
descent, 167. *See also* lineages
descent groups, 119
Diamond, Jared, 125–26
disbelief, 195–96, 197–99
domestication, 117–19, 122, 123
dowry, 177, 179
DuBois, W. E. B., 14, 20, 28, 29

East Harlem, 57–58, 80, *85*
eating, culture of, 48
economics, and culture, 76, 115–17
Edison, Thomas, 46
empiricism, 190
enculturation, 48–49
endogamy, 169, 170–71
Enlightenment, 191
environment: living organisms and, 111; relationship with, 126–27, 128
Eskimo. *See* Inuit
ethics, research, 83
ethnocentrism, 59–61, 88; cultural relativity and, 64, 66; culture shock and, 85; ethnography and, 90; gender and, 135; marriage and, 175; religion and, 198
ethnocide. *See* genocide
ethnographer, 73, 74, 80–81; behavioral mistakes of, 83–84; culture shock

and, 83–85; establishing rapport, 86–87; ethical standards/laws for, 83
Ethnographic Film Unit, University of British Columbia, 128
ethnography, 71–102; as cultural critique, 99–100; ethnology and, 79; experimentation with, 96–99; field method of, 79–90; field notes for, 72–73, 78, 88, 89; interview in, 88–89, 90; participant observation and, 79–90; purposes of, 97–102; written, 90–100
ethnology, 58, 59, 71, *78*, 79
ethnomusicology, 55–56
ethnoscience, 92–93
eugenics, 15–16, 17
evolution, 7–12; biological change and, 4, 7, 11; biological populations and, 8–9; as change, 4–11; human, 4, 110–11; misinterpretation of, 11, 17; natural selection in, 8, 8–9, 11–12, 24, 111; variability in, 8, 9–10. *See also* Darwin, Charles
evolutionism, 12. *See also* social evolution
exogamy, 169, 170, 171
experimental ethnography, 96–99

family: American culture and, 161–62, 180–82; change and, 180–83; child care and, 149, 150, 177; extended, 162; nuclear, 180–82; work and, 161, 180–81. *See also* kinship; marriage
"female husbands," 172. *See also* marriage
Female Power and Male Dominance (Sanday), 151–52
feminism, black, 153
feminist anthropology, 148–50, 153–54

fieldwork, 73, 79–90
Firmin, Anténor, 29
Fisher, Melissa, 76
Fluehr-Lobban, Carolyn, 64
foraging, 112–17; diet of, 113;
    domestication and, 117–18;
    reciprocity and, 116–17
forensic anthropology, 39
Frazer, James George, 73, 192
Fritz, Adolf, 187, 190, 191, 193–94, 194,
    195, 196
functions of religion, 74–75, 77, 190,
    193, 195, 197, 198
fundamentalism, 55, 80, 83, 197

gathering and hunting. See foraging
Geertz, Clifford, 94–96
gender, 135–55; class and, 153, 154;
    colonialism and, 152; complexities of,
    151, 154–55; ethnography and, 148;
    feminist anthropology and, 148–50,
    153–54; inequality and, 146–55;
    negotiation of, 151–52, 152, 153;
    power and, 146–48; race and, 153; sex
    v., 141–46; status and, 143–44, 147. See
    also alternate genders; men; women
gender-based inequality, 146–55
gender roles, 151
genocide, 63–64
globalization, 109, 127
God's Schools: Choice and Compromise
    in American Society (Wagner), 80
Great Chain of Being, 5–6
Great Zimbabwe, 13
Greece, 42, 138–39

herding. See pastoralism
Hidatsa, 144

Himalayas, 173
Hindu, 52, 137
hijras, 137, 138, 143, 145
historical particularism, 19
Hitler, Adolf, 16
Hobbes, Thomas, 191
Hoey, Brian, 183
Hoffman, Susannah M., 138
holism, 40–41, 56–57
holy wells, Irish, 57
Horse, Billy Evans, 162, 163
horticulture, 118–19
Hufford, David J., 193, 195
human behavior, 52
human biology, 22–28
hunting and gathering. See foraging
Hurston, Zora Neale, 28
Hutus, 63
hwame, 144

immigration, 125
imperialism. See colonialism
incest taboo, 169–70, 171. See also
    family; marriage
India, 137, 143
Indians, American. See Native
    Americans
industrialism, 9, 110, 124
inequality. See gender-based inequality;
    social inequality
informants. See consultants
interpretive anthropology, 96
Inuit, 18–19
Iroquois, 151

Japan, 24, 137, 151
Joseph, Elizabeth, 174–75
Ju/'hoansi. See !Kung San

Kalahari Peoples Fund, 114
Kenya, 172
Khmer Rouge, 63
kingdoms. *See* prestates
kinship, 116, 161–83. *See also* clans;
    descent; family; lineages; marriage
Kiowa, 86–87, 100, *101*, 162, 163–67,
    176, 177, 179, 180, 196–97
kiva, 137
Kula, 76–77
!Kung San, 89, 113–15, 116, 117, 119,
    123, 147, 176, 180, 189
Kypseli, Greece, 138–39, 140

Lamphere, Louise, 148, 153
language, *37*, 37–38, 92, 93. *See
    also* ethnoscience; linguistic
    anthropology; Sapir-Whorf
    hypothesis
Lee, Richard, 113, 114–15
levirate, 179
lineages, 119, 168–69
linguistic anthropology, 37–38
Linnaeus, Carolus, 25; hierarchy of,
    25–26
Lyell, Sir Charles, 6–7, 11, 17
Lynch, Darrell, 196
lynchings, 14–15, *15*

MacCormack, Carol P., 142, 151
magic, 74–75, 76, 77, 91–92, 192–93
mahu, 145
Malaysia, 189, 190
Malinowski, Bronislaw, 72–79, 80, 88,
    91–92, 95, 99, 196, 200
Mandela, Nelson, *65*
"manly hearted" women, 144
market exchange, 122, 180

Marks, Jonathan, 24
marriage, 58, 116, 138, 169–83; in
    American culture, 161, 171; cross-
    cousin, 170, *170*; cross-cultural
    definition of, 171–75; divorce and,
    174, 177, 179–80; parallel-cousin,
    170, *171*; purposes of, 171–80; same-
    sex union and, 172, 173, *173*; as
    social union, 175–80
Martinez, Fred, 145
material culture, 36
matrilineal descent, *167*, 167–68, 170,
    170
matrilocal residence, 140, 176
Maya, 122
McCurdy, David, 51–52, 85
Mead, Margaret, 28, 99–100, 135–36,
    148, 149
medical anthropology, 39
Medicine, Beatrice, 145
men: religion and, 136–37; roles of,
    138–40, 148–50. *See also* gender
men's houses, 138
Menzies, Charles, 128
miati, 144
"Middletown USA," 96–97
Mohave, 144
monotheism, 192
Mooney, James, 29
Moore, Henrietta, 154
morality, 48, 64, 187
Morgan, Lewis Henry, 12, 29
Mundugumor, 135–36
mythology, 190

Namibia, 114
Nandi, 172
Narcotics Anonymous, 84, 86, 93

National Association for Stock Car Auto
Racing (NASCAR), 81, *82*, 83
National Association for the
Advancement of Colored People
(NAACP), 28
nation-states, 55, 77, 113, 119, 173;
ancient states and, 124–25; core,
periphery, and semiperiphery, 125;
interdependence of, 126. *See also*
states
Native Americans, 119, 143–45, *146*,
199. *See also individual groups*
"native's point of view," 18, 19, 72,
73–74, 79, 87, 88, 91, 95, 100, 175,
198, 199, 200
natural selection, 8, *8*–9, 11–12, 24, 111
Navajo, 144, 145
Nazaré, 140, 141
Nazi Germany, 16, 63
Neighborhood Story Project, 89
Nelson, Willie, *23*
neolocal residence, 179
Nepal, 42
New Guinea, 52, 135, 137–38, *139*, 141
*Nisa: The Life and Words of a !Kung
Woman* (Shostak), 89
nuclear family, 180–82
Nuer, 172

Onondaga, 151
The Origin of Species (Darwin), 7, 11,
17
Opting for Elsewhere (Hoey), 183
Ortner, Sherry, 149
The Other Side of Middletown (Lassiter
et al.), *90*, *97*, 97–98
overpopulation. *See* population

*Over the Next Hill: An Ethnography
of RVing Seniors in North America*
(Counts and Counts), 86

Pahari, 42
Palmer, Gus, Jr., 166
parallel-cousin marriage, 170, *171*
parenting. *See* family
Parsees, 42
participant observation, 79–90
pastoralism, 118–19
patrilineal descent, 167, 168, *168*, 170,
171, 172, 177
patrilocal residence, 177
Peacock, James L., 54, 56, 57, 199
Pentecostalism, *188*, 188–89, 190, 194
peppered moths, 8–9, 11
periphery (economic), 125, 126, 154
physical anthropology, 36
political economy, 119, 123, 125
polyandry, 173
polygamy, 173–75
polygyny, 173–74
polytheism, 192
population, 8–9, 22, 23–25, 115, 117–18,
119, 123, 124–26
Portugal, 140
positivism, 190
poverty, 19, 78, 110
power, 53, 146–48
The Power of Kiowa Song (Lassiter), 100
prestates, 120
Principles of Geology (Lyell), 6, 17
Pueblo, 137

race, 17–30; critique of, 20–28;
eugenics and, 15–16; cultural

selection and, 25; inequality and, 27–28; in Linnaean hierarchy, 25–26; presumed similarities and differences of, 20–23; sickle-cell anemia and, 24; skin pigmentation (and other) variations, 21–23

"Race: Are We So Different?" (exhibit), 29

rapport, establishing, 86–87

Ray, Celeste, 57

reason, 190

reciprocity, 116–17, 119, 122

redistribution, 121, 122

regionalism, 81

relativity. *See* cultural relativity

religion, *75*, 187–200; anthropology of, 189; ethnocentrism and, 198–200; experience and, 188–89, 190, 199; functions of, 74–75, 77, 190, 193, 195, 197, 198; fundamentalism and, 55, 80, 83, 197; gender and, 136–37; kinds of, 192; magic and, 192–93; science and, 192–93; study of, 187–90. *See also* belief; *individual religions*

Rhoades, Bernadine Herwona Toyebo, 164

ritual, 190

Rosaldo, Michelle, 148, 149, 150

Rwanda, 63

Ryūkyū Islands, 137, 151

same-sex marriage/union. *See* marriage

Samoa, 99–100

Sanday, Peggy Reeves, 152

Sapir-Whorf hypothesis, 38

Schopenhauer, Arthur, 59

scientific revolution, 191

semiperiphery (economic), 125

sex. *See* biological sex

Sex and Temperament in Three Primitive Societies (Mead), 135

sex-role plan, 152

sexual division of labor, 146–47, 148, 149

sexuality. *See* gender

Shostak, Marjorie, 89

slavery, 27–28, 63, 64

Smedley, Audrey, 27

snake handling, Pentecostal, *188*, 188–89, 190, 194

social Darwinism, 12–16, 17, 20, 27, 30

social evolution, 12, *13*, 17, 19–20

social inequality, 123

society, 17, 19

sociocultural anthropology. *See* cultural anthropology

sororate, 179

Soviet Union, 63

Spencer, Herbert, 12

Spiritism, 187, 193–94, *194*, 195

spirits, 187–90, 191, 192; possession of, 187, 189, 194, 195–96

Spradley, James P., 51–52, 85, 92–93

states: complexity of, 123–24; dependence on trade in, 122, 123; emergence of, 119–22; exhaustion of resources in, 125; fragility of, 125–26; health and nutrition in, 123–24; interdependence and, 125–26; market exchange and, 122, 180; political centralization in, 121–22; population density and, 123; self-sufficient, 122; social class, 124. *See also* ancient states; nation-states; prestates

Stoller, Paul, 200

Stranger in the Village of the Sick
  (Stoller), 200
Sudan, 63, 64
"Sworn Virgins," 145
symbolic anthropology, 94
syncretism, 187
System of Nature (Linnaeus), 25

taxonomy, 25–26
Tchambuli, 135, 136
Tedlock, Barbara, 96
third/fourth genders. *See* alternate
  genders
Todd, James, 81, *82*, 83
trade, 76–77, 117, 122, 123, 124–25
tribe, 73, 119, 122
Trobriand Islanders, 72, 74–75, 76–77,
  91–92, 99
two-spirits, 143–44, 145, *146*
Tutsis, 63
Tylor, Edward Burnett, 41–42, 52

uniformitarianism, 6
unilineal descent, 167
unilineal evolution, 12. *See also* social
  evolution
Universal Declaration of Human Rights
  (UN), 64
uxorilocal residence, 176

violence, 58, 62–64, 83
virilocal residence, 177

Wall Street Women (Fisher), 76
Wagner, Melinda Bollar, 80–81, 83–84,
  85, 86, 87, 88, 102
Wallace, Mike, *82*
Wesch, Michael, 50
West, Cornell, 30
Williams, Billy Gene, 206
Winburn, Martel, Sr., *90*
"Woman Jim," *146*
woman marriage, 172
women: childbirth and, 149; exploitation
  of, 154, 155; inequality and, 135–41,
  148–55; power and, 146–48; religion
  and, 136–37; roles of, 138–40, 149–
  50, 151. *See also* alternate genders;
  gender; men; sexual division of labor
Women, Culture, and Society (Rosaldo/
  Lamphere), 148, 149–50, 151, 153,
  154
women's houses, 137–38, *139*
women's movement, 148, 150
work, 161, 162, 180–81, 182, 183
world system, 109–28
worldview, 193, 197

xanith, 145

YouTube, 50
Young, William C., 174

Zulu, 172
Zuni, 96

About the Author

Luke Eric Lassiter is professor of humanities and anthropology and director of the Graduate Humanities Program at Marshall University. He has authored and edited many books, including *The Other Side of Middletown* (coauthored with Hurley Goodall, Elizabeth Campbell, and Michelle Natasya Johnson, 2004), *The Chicago Guide to Collaborative Ethnography* (2005), and *Explorations in Cultural Anthropology* (coedited with Colleen Boyd, 2011). Lassiter also founded the journal *Collaborative Anthropologies* in 2007 and served as its editor/coeditor until 2013.